How to Control Your

Anxiety

Before It Controls You

Albert Ellis has authored or edited 70 books. Some of his most important books for the public and the psychology professional include:

How to Live With a Neurotic
Sex Without Guilt
The Art and Science of Love
A Guide to Rational Living (with Robert A. Harper)
The Encyclopedia of Sexual Behavior
Reason and Emotion in Psychotherapy
Executive Leadership
How to Master Your Fear of Flying
Humanistic Psychotherapy: The Rational–Emotive Approach
A Guide to Personal Happiness (with Irving Becker)
Clinical Applications of Rational–Emotive Approach (with Michael Bernard)
Overcoming Resistance
How to Stubbornly Refuse to Make Yourself Miserable About Anything— Yes, Anything!
Rational–Emotive Couples Therapy (with Joyce Sichel, Raymond Yeager, Dominic Di Mattia, and Raymond Di Giuseppe)
How to Keep People From Pushing Your Buttons (with Arthur Lange)
What to Do When AA Doesn't Work (with Emmett Velten)
Better, Deeper, and More Enduring Brief Therapy
Stress Couseling: A Rational Emotive Behavior Approach (with Jack Gordon, Michael Neenan, and Stephen Palmer
How to Control Your Anger Before It Controls You (with R.C. Tafrate)
Optimal Aging (with Emmett Veltan)
The Albert Ellis Reader (with Shawn Blau)

How to Control Your
Anxiety
Before It Controls You

Albert Ellis, Ph.D.

Citadel Press
Kensington Publishing Corp.
www.kensingtonbooks.com

CITADEL PRESS books are published by

Kensington Publishing Corp.
850 Third Avenue
New York, NY 10022

All Kensington titles, imprints, and distributed lines are available at special quantity discounts for bulk purchases for sales promotions, premiums, fund raising, educational, or institutional use. Special book excerpts or customized printings can also be created to fit specific needs. For details, write or phone the office of the Kensington special sales manager: Kensington Publishing Corp., 850 Third Avenue, New York, NY 10022, attn: Special Sales Department, phone 1-800-221-2647.

Kensington and the K logo Reg. U.S. Pat. & TM Office
Citadel Press is a trademark of Kensington Publishing Corp.

First printing 2000

10 9 8

Printed in the United States of America

Library of Congress Cataloging-in-Publication Data

Ellis, Albert
How to control your anxiety—before it controls you / Albert Ellis.
p. cm.
"A Citadel Press book."
Includes bibliographical references.
ISBN 0-8065-2136-8 (pbk.)
1. Anxiety. 2. Interpersonal relations. I. Title.
BF575.A6E45 1998
152.4'6—dc21 98—24928
CIP

For Janet L. Wolfe

A true helpmate for over three decades

Contents

Acknowledgments

I would like to thank Jim Runyon, who did some beautiful word-processing for me. Jim Ellison suggested this book and worked with me on it from the start. Steve Palme did a fine copyediting job. Ginamarie Zampano, the administrative director of the Albert Ellis Institute facilitated the gathering of material and the working out of innumerable administrative functions in her usual inimitable manner.

How to Control Your

Anxiety

Before It Controls You

1

Why I Am Convinced That You Can Control Your Anxiety Before It Controls You

Until the age of nineteen, I was an extremely anxious individual. In fact, I think that I was probably born with a tendency toward making myself anxious. My mother was like that: She was a generally happy person but she also made herself quite anxious about little things—money, for example. During my childhood and youth, she never really wanted for money. At one time, my father, who was a promoter and a great salesman, literally had a million dollars—and that was a great deal of money back in the 1920s. But she always worried about expenses, and whenever he left a fifty-dollar tip for a waiter, she would secretly take it back and substitute a much smaller tip. She saved her money in a separate account and had thousands of dollars in it. But she always worried about not having enough.

After my father lost his first million in the stock market, was on his way to making his second one, and the family really was doing well financially, my mother still worried about money—and several other relatively unimportant things—and kept saving and saving. She wasn't entirely wrong about this, for in 1929, my father lost his second million and couldn't pay her the regular alimony he was supposed to pay. But we got through the Great Depression all right because my brother, sister, and I started working and supporting the family. Still, my mother worried incessantly—till she died, with savings, at the age of ninety-three.

You could say that I probably learned how to worry from her, but that would hardly be accurate. My brother, who was nineteen months younger than I, also was raised in the same environment, and he was almost a pathological nonworrier. He took risks and did all kinds of "dangerous" things, and he never seemed to worry about the outcome. If these turned out all right, fine; and if they turned out badly, he was never thrown for a loop. He just went on to risk the next venture, whether it was social or business. In fact, he did very well for himself—just because he rarely worried about anything.

Not so I! I was afraid of all kinds of unseen eventualities. I was a definitely shy, conforming, and hesitant child and adolescent, and I rarely took any great risks—or, if I did take them, I worried about them. I especially had a great fear, and a real phobia, about public speaking. I was bright and talented enough and was often asked to make a little speech, be it in a class play or speaking out in class and giving answers to questions that the teacher felt sure I could answer. But, I voluntarily held myself in much of the time; and I particularly avoided public presentations.

Let me give you a typical example. I was a good speller, often the best in the class, but I avoided participating in spelling bees because I might make a mistake (which I practically never did) and thereby "make a fool" of myself. When forced by the teacher to participate, I would almost always outspell all the other kids and become the winner; but I was exceptionally anxious while doing so, and I didn't enjoy the spelling bees at all. I only enjoyed winning. Briefly.

Another example: Once in a while, we had to memorize a short poem and repeat it in front of the class the next day. I was terribly anxious that I would splutter and stutter while presenting, even though I was excellent at memorizing. Reciting the poem publicly was terrorizing for me. So the morning of the day I was supposed to recite the poem to the class, I would make myself get a splitting headache, and put the thermometer next to the radiator to show that I had a fever. This induced my mother to let me stay home from school that day. What, me recite badly and show the teacher and the other kids how anxious I was? Never!

One time, when I was about eleven years old, I won a medal in Sunday school and had to go up to the platform, at assembly time, to receive it and merely thank the president of the school as I received it. I went up and got the medal and thanked the president, but when I sat down again, a friend of mine said, "Why are you crying?" I was so anxious about appearing in public that my eyes were grandly watering and it looked like I was crying.

I also had extreme social anxiety—when meeting new kids, when talking to people in authority, and especially when meeting new females. I was most interested in girls ever since the age of five and a half, when I was madly in love with a neighborhood charmer. After she disappeared from my life, I kept falling passionately in love, practically every year, with the most attractive girl in my school class. Yes, passionately in love: a real obsessive–compulsive attachment. But no matter how much I adored these girls, and how constantly I thought about getting intimate with them—which I did practically all the time, for hours on end—I never spoke to them or actually tried to get close to them. I shyly, fearfully stayed away from them, shut my big mouth, and only looked lustfully at them without any verbal contact. I was scared to death that if I did approach them and try to become friendly, they would see my failings, rightly reject me, and make me feel impossibly small. I didn't exactly see myself falling through the floor if I actually got rejected, but very nearly!

Even into my teens, up to the age of nineteen, I never really approached any of the women to whom I was attracted. About two hundred days a year, I went to the Bronx Botanical Gardens, a lovely place near my home, and sat on a bench or on the grass in order to read one of my many books, and to look at the attractive women (of all ages) and flirt with them. But I never approached them or said a single thing to them. Typically, I would sit on one stone bench near the Bronx River Parkway, and a girl or a woman would sit on another bench, about ten feet away from me. I would immediately look at her (I was, at that age, interested in all females, yes, about a hundred times out of a hundred), and sometimes she would look back at me. I would keep sneaking looks at her, obviously flirting with her, and often she would flirt back at me. Some of them were definitely interested, and presumably would have been receptive had I approached them and started to talk to them.

Not me! I always copped out. I made up a million excuses to myself—she was too tall or too short, too old or too young, too smart or too stupid. I had all kinds of excuses and rationalizations. So I never talked to a single one of them—no matter how interested in me they appeared to be and how presumably receptive. Then, when the object of my passion finally got up and walked away or I had to get up and leave myself, I cursed my foolishness in not approaching, not taking a risk, put myself down severely for copping out, and resolved to try—really try—to approach the next suitable prospect. But I never did.

HOW I OVERCAME MY PUBLIC SPEAKING ANXIETY

Then, at the age of nineteen, I decided to get over my anxieties. First, I decided to rid myself of my fear of public speaking. At that time, I was actively immersed in a political organization, a liberal group of which I was actually the youth leader. It was only a small organization, and nearly all the young members were friends of mine, so I didn't have too much trouble speaking to eight or ten of them at a time. I didn't consider that a public kind of performance. On the other hand, I was supposed to speak to other organizations and groups, to tell them about my particular society and to try to get them to join it. I was supposed to be, especially as their youth leader, a public propagandist for my organization. But I was too afraid to try to fill that role, so I refused many invitations to do so— invitations that came mainly from the adult section of our group, New America, which ran the youth section, Young America. As usual, I copped out.

Pressure on me to give public talks for Young America continued, and I finally decided to give in to it and get over my public speaking phobia. I had previously read a great deal of philosophy and psychology, and I was someday going to write a book on the psychology of human happiness, in which I had a great personal interest (because of my anxiety). So I already had an idea based on the writings of that day (1932), on how to handle anxiety and phobias. I had read what some of the great philosophers—such as Confucius and Gautama Buddha—had said about conquering anxiety. I had especially noted what some of the ancient Greek and Roman philosophers—such as Epicurus, Epictetus, and Marcus Aurelius—had said about it. And since philosophy was my great hobby at that time (from the age of sixteen onward), I had read what many of the modern philosophers, such as Thoreau, Emerson, and Bertrand Russell, had said about dealing with anxiety. Finally, I had read, at that time, most of the modern psychologists, such as Freud, Jung, and Adler, who were also interested in curing people of their anxiety. So I was philosophically and psychologically prepared.

But I had also read the famous behaviorist John B. Watson, on his early experiments aimed at curing children of their overwhelming fears and anxieties. Watson and his assistants took children seven or eight years of age who were terribly afraid of animals (such as a mouse or a rabbit) and actually exposed the children to the feared objects, first at a distance and then at closer range. Meanwhile, Watson talked to the children and distracted them, then he gradually moved the feared animals closer and closer. What do you know—after around twenty minutes of exposure, the children would become unafraid and would actually start petting the animals. This deconditioning procedure, which is called in vivo (live) desensitization, worked very well, and in one or a few sessions, he trained the children to rid themselves of their extreme anxieties and phobias.

"Well," I said to myself, "if it's good enough for little children, it should be good enough for me. I'll try it."

So, for practically the first time in my life, instead of avoiding public speaking engagements, I did just the opposite. Every single week, I set up at least one speech that I was to present in public for my organization, Young America, and I made sure that come hell or high water I presented that speech. I was still as scared as I could be; and I was most uncomfortable making the first few speeches. But I knew from my reading and from figuring out things for myself that my discomfort would not exactly kill me. I also reasoned that the dire things that I imagined were going to happen—including my audiences laughing at me and booing me—in all probability would not occur. I would merely give a fairly poor speech, would not by any means convince my audience that Young America was the greatest political group since the United States rebelled against England, and, at worst, few people would join it. Oh, well, that would be bad—but it wouldn't be the end of the world.

In other words, I used a combination of talking to myself rationally—which I had largely learned from philosophers—exposed myself to what I feared most and was uncomfortable doing, and forced myself to speak and speak in public every week for the next ten weeks. Well, it worked! I was very uncomfortable, then I was less uncomfortable, and then, actually—surprise!—comfortable. My heart palpitations, my sweating, and my stumbling over words went down and down and down. I learned to focus intently on the content of my talks—how great a political group Young America was—rather than on how I was doing at speaking and how anxious I was about speaking. I also discovered, much to my surprise, that I really could be quite a fluent speaker, with just as little trouble speaking in public as I normally had in speaking to one person or to a group of my friends. Actually, I was never really poor at speaking, but, because of my anxiety, just terribly afraid of *public* speaking. My vocal cords and my ability to make sensible sentences, had always been okay, and now, with practice, they were getting even better.

That experience, of forcing myself—yes, forcing myself—to speak in public no matter how uncomfortable I was until I got comfortable and began enjoying it, made a profound impression on me. It was one of the main reasons that, nine years later, I decided to become a psychotherapist. At the time I gave my first public speeches, I was not at all interested in becoming a therapist but was obsessed with becoming a writer—and possibly a writer on the subject of human happiness. Perhaps I was hooked on becoming a writer just because I could do it without having to speak in public. In any case, I was not interested in being a therapist, just in being a less anxious, happier individual. And in very short order, I achieved exactly that. I became completely unanxious about public speaking—I lost my phobia totally. Seeing that I had conquered anxiety in this area, I also became somewhat less anxious generally.

I had always, for example, had to accomplish, had to succeed—in school, at sports, at looking well, and at other important endeavors. I tried very hard to succeed and was reasonably good at it. I especially studied hard, did my homework, and got along well in school. But, of course, I was quite anxious about doing so—since I had to succeed to be a worthwhile individual, and there was always a chance that I would fail. Horrors!—that would be awful.

Now that I saw that I could be uncomfortable in public, and at times even speak badly and not put myself down for doing so, I became a lot less anxious about success. I still *wanted* success, but didn't absolutely *need* it.

HOW I OVERCAME MY SOCIAL ANXIETY

To test myself out, however, I decided to do the second great experiment of my life: to try to get rid of my social anxiety—and particularly my fear of being rejected by women in whom I was interested. This anxiety had plagued me all my life and was much more important than my fear of public speaking. Remember, I was aiming to be a writer and therefore could largely avoid appearing at public presentations. But if I were to continue my interest in women—which indeed I intended to continue—my not being able to approach and speak to those I was interested in would certainly be too restricting! I would be reduced to meeting new women through my friends and relatives, and I would not be able to meet them on my own. What a drag!

So, keeping in mind my success with public speaking, I decided to use the same procedures with my social anxiety. The August before I was about to go back to college to finish my senior year, I gave myself the brilliant homework assignment of going to the Bronx Botanical Garden every day. I would talk to strange women no matter how uncomfortable I felt about doing so. I would, I told myself, walk in the park until I saw a suitable woman sitting alone on a bench, and then I would quickly, immediately, sit next to her. No, not in her lap, but next to her on the very same bench on which she was sitting (instead of a bench away). Then, having accomplished that—which I was afraid to do because I feared that she would reject me and quickly walk away—I would do the most dangerous thing that I had always avoided: I would give myself one minute, no more than one lousy minute, to talk to her. Yes, if I died I'd die! I would speak to her within one minute, no matter how uncomfortable I felt, and no matter how foreboding she looked. That was my brilliant homework assignment to myself. Why was it brilliant? Because if I quickly spoke to her instead of waiting and waiting to do so, I knew I would be less anxious, would get the damned thing over with, and would have a better chance of getting somewhere with her.

Well, I did exactly what I assigned myself to do. No matter how anxious I was, whenever I saw a woman sitting alone on a park bench, I immediately—no debate!—sat next to her on the bench. I allowed no excuses as to how she looked, how old she was, whether she was tall or short, and so on. No excuses! I just forced myself, very uncomfortably, to sit next to her, whereupon, immediately, many of the women I sat next to quickly got up and walked away. All told, I think I approached and sat next to 130 women that month of August. Thirty, or almost a third of them, immediately walked away. Very discouraging! But that left me with an even hundred who still stayed—which was good for research purposes!

Not at all daunted, I spoke to the remaining hundred women just as I had planned to do. I spoke about the flowers, the trees, the weather, the birds, the bees, the book or paper they were reading—anything, just to make conversation. Nothing brilliant or clever.

Nothing personal. No remarks about their looks or anything else that might make them afraid of me and make them turn away or leave. Just one hundred ordinary statements.

Well, the hundred women did speak back to me, some very briefly, some for an hour or more. I soon got many of them in animated conversation. When they seemed willing, I asked them about their work, their families, their living arrangements, their hobbies, interests, and so forth. Regular conversations, just as I would have had if I had been formally introduced to them.

As for my primary purpose in talking to them—to ask for a date, see them regularly, go to bed with them, and perhaps marry one of them—I got absolutely nowhere. Nowhere at all. For out of the hundred women I talked with, I was able to make only one date— and she didn't show up for it! She talked with me for two hours, kissed me goodbye when she left, and agreed to meet me later in the park for a date that night. But she never showed up. And, foolishly, I neglected to ask for her phone number, so I never saw her again. How tragic! How disappointing! But I still survived. And thereafter, I always asked for the phone number of the women I met and dated!

Within that month of getting rejected by a hundred women, I completely lost my social anxiety and, especially, my fear of encountering strange women in strange places. For I saw, cognitively, that nothing terrible happened as a result of my rejections. None of the women I talked to took out a knife and cut my penis off. None of them vomited and ran away. None of them called a cop. No, no terrible thing, which I had so often imagined would happen, actually occurred. Instead, I had many pleasant conversations with these women, enjoyed having them, learned a great deal about women that I had not previously known, got increasingly less uncomfortable and afraid to talk to them, and had several other fortunate results. Best of all, I almost immediately got over my fear of approaching women, and for the rest of my life I have been able to speak to and try to date literally hundreds of them whenever I chance to meet them in parks, on trains, at airports, and other public places. I now have no fear of doing so, and even though I normally get rejected for sex, love, and marriage by the vast majority of them, my social anxiety has gone for good. Nothing ventured, nothing gained! My fear of doing poorly with women and being rejected was gone!

Now can you see why, as I note in the title of this chapter, I am so sure that people can control their anxiety before it controls them? It is because I have done this so thoroughly myself, in the areas of public speaking and social anxiety, and I did it without help from anybody, including a psychotherapist. I have indeed used my experiences to learn how to control anxiety and have, as a therapist, taught thousands of people to do so over the last fifty-four years. Moreover, I have put the experience of conquering my own anxiety into my therapeutic theory and practice over the years, and most probably would not have originated Rational Emotive Behavior Therapy had I not experienced it. Knowing that I had been exceptionally anxious about many things, and that I could make myself into a person who now had great trouble becoming tense or anxious about even the most difficult situations, has spurred me to help other people with my therapeutic theory and practice.

The most important thing of all, however, is that I overcame my own overweening anxiety entirely by myself. To be sure, I used the writings of many philosophers and therapists and learned much from them. I also used the experiments of John B. Watson, who was not really a therapist himself but who conducted several therapeutic experiments. With these aids, and by forcing myself to bite the bullet—make myself very uncomfortable and talk to myself about the futility of my anxiety and phobias—I think I can honestly say I was able to become one of the least panicked people in the whole world. Many unfortunate things have happened to me since that time when I was nineteen, which is now some sixty-five years ago. I am still concerned about doing well, accomplishing many things, winning certain people's approval, and being comfortable in life. But I have taught myself merely to be quite concerned, sorry, and disappointed when bad things happen or could happen in my life, and I am practically never anxious, depressed, or enraged.

From being, in other words, one of the more easily disturbed and disturbable people in the world, I have made myself into one who is very rarely seriously upset about anything. As the title of one of my popular books indicates, I stubbornly refuse to make myself miserable about anything—yes, anything.

I still insist, however, that I mainly did it by myself, with no counseling or therapy, with no support group, with no friends and relatives to help me and push me to do what I did. I made remarkable inroads against my anxiety and have maintained this unanxious tendency since that time.

In the meantime, moreover, I have gone on to become a busy psychotherapist and to see perhaps more clients than any other therapist in this country. I have originated a form of psychotherapy that is among the most popular and widely taught and that has been shown in experimental studies to be unusually effective. In various ways, it stresses what works effectively for other systems of psychotherapy—that is, changing people's self-blocking ideas and inducing people to do what they are afraid of doing.

Best of all, perhaps, Rational Emotive Behavior Therapy (REBT), which I created in 1955, and Cognitive Behavior Therapy (CBT), a similar form of therapy which followed REBT in the 1960s, are probably the most efficient forms of self-help therapy that have been devised. Hundreds of books and materials have used REBT, or something very similar to it, to show readers and listeners how to help themselves overcome their serious feelings of depression, anxiety, rage, self-downing, and self-pity. This is because this self-help therapy can be put in simple terms so that almost anyone can understand it, and it can be used by almost any determined person who will take pains to apply it to his or her own personal disturbance. It works!

From my own experience, then, and from the experience of tens of thousands of people who have used the main elements of REBT and of CBT, I am quite sure that you, the reader of this book, can control your anxiety before it controls you. There are no guarantees, of course, that if you use REBT or CBT it will help you remove your anxiety. But there is a high degree of probability that you can succeed if you really work at it. I did it myself, without much help, and without the over fifty years of research and practice that have now been added to it and that make it more effective today than ever. If you attend carefully to the following pages, you can train yourself to do it, too.

Do you tend to be anxious on many occasions and about several things? Yes, practically all people are. Can you work and think differently to minimize your anxiety? Yes, practically all people can. Will you use the thinking and the action that I have used to minimize whatever anxiety you do have? Try REBT and CBT and see for yourself!

2

What Anxiety Is and How It
Often Controls You

Anxiety, believe it or not, is a good thing that helps keep you alive and comfortable and helps to preserve the human species. For you—like all humans who are "normal"—are born and raised with desires, preferences, and goals, and if you had no anxiety whatever, and were totally unconcerned about your achieving your desires, you would tolerate all kinds of obnoxious things—such as lack of achievement, disapproval of others, dangerous pursuits, assaults by others, and even attempts to murder you—and would do nothing to ward them off or escape from them. Anxiety, basically, is a set of uncomfortable feelings and action tendencies that make you aware that unpleasant happenings—meaning things that go against your desires—are happening or are likely to happen and warn you that you'd better do something about them. Thus, if you are in danger of being attacked, and you desire to remain unhurt, you have a choice of several possible actions, such as running away, fighting off your attacker, seeking support from potential protectors, calling the police, talking to your attacker to ward off his or her attack, and so on. But, you would probably do none of these things unless you were concerned, watchful, anxious, tense, cautious, vigilant, or panicked. You would perceive the danger of the attack, perhaps, but do nothing about it.

Similarly, if you thought you were in danger of losing your job, and you definitely desired to keep it, you would normally feel concerned or anxious about losing it and would again choose one or more of several activities: speak to your boss, work harder at getting the job done, look for another job, get friends to intercede for you, plan to go work for yourself, get some additional schooling or training, and so on.

Anxiety, then, stems from your desiring something and seeing that you are in danger of not getting it, or not desiring something and seeing that you are in danger of getting it. If you were truly without preferences or desires or wishes, you would be indifferent to almost anything that might happen to you, and you would therefore not be anxious. You would also probably not live very long, because living and surviving depend very much on desiring to live and desiring to avoid pain, discomfort, trouble, and hassles that are so severe that they would lead to your death. In order for you to survive, you have to fulfill certain functions—especially breathing and eating—and to be somewhat comfortable. For if you were thoroughly uncomfortable—say, in continual pain or deprived of all enjoyments for a long period—you would tend to lose your motivation for living and would perhaps prefer to die.

Virtually all humans, however, are goal oriented. They desire to go on living and to be reasonably happy and free from pain. There may be a few exceptions to this rule, but they are damned few! And the exceptions don't live very long. People's concern or anxiety about living, therefore, and about being relatively free from pain and trouble keeps them alive and kicking. Even young children, not yet able to fend for themselves, strive to live, to enjoy, and to be free from pain. Anxiety helps them do so.

Unfortunately, there are many degrees and kinds of anxiety and some of them are unhealthy or self-sabotaging. Healthy anxiety—which we can call by names like concern, vigilance, or caution—helps you, as we said above, get more of what you want and less of what you don't want. Especially the latter! For what you don't want could literally maim or kill you. Therefore, it is very healthy if your anxiety helps you look when you're crossing the street, drive at reasonable speeds when you're in a car, stay away from poisonous food, and avoid walking at night (or even during the day) in bad neighborhoods.

Healthy anxiety is life-preserving. But anxiety, as I shall show in detail later, can easily be and often is unhealthy—that is, it is destructive and against your basic interests. Take even walking across the street. If you are healthily anxious, you walk cautiously, heed the traffic lights, watch out for cars that might not be heeding those same lights, and walk briskly rather than at a snail's pace across to the other side of the street. This is good!

But suppose you are so enormously anxious about getting safely across the street that your heart is beating wildly, your limbs are quaking, and you look in every possible direction. What will happen if your anxiety is this severe? Quite possibly, you'll run wildly across the street, or stumble as you cross, or look in the wrong direction, or be so frightened that you'll refuse to cross the street at all, or resort to some other crazy behavior and actually bring on an accident. Acute panic is indeed a form of anxiety—but a dangerously harmful form, and one that usually does more harm than good.

The same goes for panic about problems that include no physical dangers. If you think you might lose your job and you are absolutely horrified about the notion that you go into a state of panic, you are very likely, because of your panicked state, to do the following: talk desperately to your boss, show him or her that you are in a state of panic, quit the job precipitately without finding out whether you are really in danger, be too afraid to go for another job, get a new job and panic about that one too, and do many other foolish things that will not help you keep this job or to find and continue to work well at a new one. Concern may help you save your job or to get a good substitute job. Panic will in all likelihood sabotage this job and subsequent ones. This is not so good!

HEALTHY AND UNHEALTHY ANXIETY

The moral of what I have said so far, and the main point of this book, is that healthy anxiety or concern is life-preserving and leads to pretty good results, but unhealthy anxiety can easily do you in. Healthy anxiety, or cautiousness, actually puts you in control of your own feelings and helps you cope with dangerous or difficult situations in an efficient manner. Unhealthy anxiety, or panic, frequently does the opposite: It makes you lose control of yourself and consequently cope poorly, and sometimes disastrously, in the face of risks and problems that you encounter. Healthy anxiety involves caution and vigilance and wards off potential harm. Unhealthy anxiety takes the form of panic, terror, horror, phobias, trembling, choking, numbness, and all kinds of physical and psychosomatic afflictions that alert you, to be sure, to possible dangers, but very often interfere with your coping adequately with those dangers. In this book, I will keep showing you the difference between healthy and unhealthy anxiety as well as the differences between other healthy and unhealthy feelings and emotions.

The theory and practice of psychotherapy that is outlined here is Rational Emotive Behavior Therapy (REBT), and this therapy significantly differs from most other forms of therapy in that it clearly distinguishes between healthy negative emotions when something goes wrong in your life (such as sorrow, regret, frustration, and annoyance) and unhealthy negative emotions (such as panic, depression, rage, feelings of worthlessness, and self-pity) when similar things go wrong. More about this later. Now, let's return to your possible feelings of anxiety.

Healthy anxiety or concern is almost always based on realistic or rational fear. Thus, if you try to walk across a busy highway that has no traffic lights, you will have the realistic fear that you may easily be struck by a car and hurt or killed. Why? Because there is a good, realistic chance that this will actually happen.

Similarly, if you have a good job and keep coming late to work, telling your supervisor or boss that she is a rotten person, and doing very little work on your job, you will have a realistic fear that you will be demoted or fired. For under these conditions, you may well be!

So your realistic or sensible fears stem from your observations that something bad, even very destructive may happen if you act in a certain way, and the fact that this bad thing actually has a good chance of happening. If you act badly to very hostile people, there is a strong likelihood that they will do something to harm you. Watch it! Realistic fears tell you that some harmful thing may happen to you if you act in certain ways, and they may properly warn you not to act in those ways if you don't want this to happen.

Many fears, however, are quite unrealistic or irrational. Suppose you are walking on the sidewalk and are terrified that some car will jump the curb and hit you. Or suppose you are doing well at work, getting praise and raises consistently from your bosses, and are terribly afraid that if you come late to work once or if you make a single minor mistake on the job you will be unceremoniously fired. Or suppose you are afraid to ride in elevators because you think that there is an excellent chance that you will suffocate, that the elevator will fall down and you will be killed, or that you will be trapped between floors and will not be able to get out of the elevator for several hours or even several days. These are unrealistic fears because they are unlikely to happen, and you are taking a slight probability—a one in a million chance—and making it into a great likelihood.

Unfortunately for the human condition, people often devise these kinds of irrational fears, are terrified by them, and do very foolish things in order to cope with them. Those who have such crazy fears may well refuse to walk on sidewalks because the sidewalks are too dangerous. Or these people may panic on their jobs and even quit work when they are doing well and being favored by their bosses. Or they may completely stay out of elevators and walk up and down twenty flights of stairs every day to avoid going into elevators, whether at home or at work.

Unhealthy and unrealistic fears, then, often lead to enormous feelings of anxiety when there is no danger or very little danger around. Almost all people have some of these fears, and they foolishly restrict their lives because of them. Thus, some people are afraid to ride in elevators, on escalators, or in trains when there is exceptionally little danger that any harm will come to them if they do. Or they are afraid of other people's disapproval of them when these other people have no power over them. Or they are afraid when other people may well disapprove of them but they will say nothing or do nothing about this lack of approval. Or they are afraid that because one person whom they loved rejected them, everyone else in the world whom they may love will undoubtedly reject them. Or they think that if they lose a certain job for whatever reason, they will lose all the jobs they will ever have and they will never be able to get and keep a good one.

Irrational fears like these are exceptionally common, and people who are practically fearless in one area, such as competing for good jobs, will be pandemically fearful in another area, such as finding and keeping a mate. What are the reasons for these irrational fears? A little later, we shall consider the main reasons for these irrational fears and how to not let them control you. But at this point, I mainly want to emphasize, that many, or most people have these irrational fears, let themselves be controlled by them, and live miserable lives because of them. Some people even get themselves killed because of such unrealistic fears—as, for example, when they panic in crossing the street, even though the traffic lights are with them and there is a traffic cop to watch over them. They still panic and stumble in front of a moving car.

How can you distinguish between unhealthy and healthy anxiety and between rational and irrational fears? Again, by checking reality and by using the laws of probability. When you ignore what the known facts are—become convinced, for example, that elevators are dangerous even though people who continually ride them are practically never harmed or killed—you are going to get into trouble. Facts are facts, but if something is truly dangerous—like driving a car one hundred miles an hour—there are almost always facts to show that it is.

Secondly, unrealistic fears are exaggerated or overgeneralized. Because you may hear of one person who got trapped in an elevator for three hours, you may wrongly think that this could easily happen to anyone, including you. Because a few people who got rejected by a love partner never found another partner, you are sure that if you get rejected it will lead to a completely lonely life. You exaggerate and overgeneralize about some risks and possibilities.

Thirdly, you see things as black and white, with no grays in between. Thus, if you lose a fairly good job, you see its loss as being completely bad, all black, when actually you may get unemployment insurance for a while; you may use your out-of-work time to get more job training; or you may even get an alternative job that is better than the one you now have.

Unrealistic anxiety, in other words, is a result largely of incorrect exaggerated thinking—and this form of thinking is common to human beings. Because anxiety, as we said in the beginning of this chapter, is protective of your desires, you often make yourself not merely concerned about dangers and losses but tremendously overconcerned or panicked. Then, sadly enough, your panic interferes with your action—stops you from crossing the street safely or keeps you from working more effectively on your job—and actually brings on much of the "disaster" that you are predicting. Because you are panicked about a loss or a danger, you make yourself so disorganized and inept that you actually bring it on.

Why does this happen? Most likely because your self-protective anxiety frequently becomes *over*-protective, hence self-defeating. Thus, there always is a chance, though very slight, that an elevator will fall or will get stuck in between floors for several hours. So, rather than take that very slight chance, you terrify yourself so much about the possibility of it actually happening that you refuse to go in elevators for the rest of your life. Silly! But quite protective. Indeed, overprotective!

One main reason for this is probably evolutionary. Anxiety was built into our heads, hearts, and actions tens of thousands of years ago, when life was exceptionally dangerous. Men and women are thin-skinned animals—as compared to elephants and rhinoceri—and are easily hurt and killed. Therefore, in the good old days—or in the bad old days—we had to be very anxious in order to survive.

Nature, consequently, not only built caution and concern into us, but also extreme anxiety; and this may have protected us from stronger and meaner animals—not to mention other humans—centuries ago. In today's world, such a high degree of anxiety is not necessary for survival, but it still may remain in our biology. Hence, we not only react with caution and concern to realistic dangers, but we react with extreme anxiety and panic to imagined dangers or to little dangers.

Be that as it may, practically every one of us is prone to both realistic and unrealistic anxiety, to rational and irrational fear. We easily are cautious and concerned in the face of risk and danger, but we also are fairly easily overconcerned and panicked. REBT shows you how to keep the former healthy feelings and minimize the latter unhealthy feelings. Thereby, you control your anxiety rather than let it, alas, as it often does, control you.

To help you recognize whether or not you are experiencing feelings of anxiety, I have included table 2–1. This table describes some of the common symptoms of anxiety. You may experience one or more of these when you are anxious. When you are concerned, you may also experience some of these symptoms, but usually to a significantly lesser degree.

TABLE 2–1
SOME COMMON SYMPTOMS OF ANXIETY

Breathing and Chest Symptoms

Shortness of breath
Rapid breathing
Shallow breathing
Gasping
Pressure on chest
Lump in throat
Choking sensations
Stuttering

Skin Reactions

Sweating
Itching
Hot and cold spells
Face flushed

*Heart and Blood Pressure
   Reactions*

Heart racing
Palpitations
Faintness or fainting
Increased blood pressure
Decreased blood pressure

Intestinal symptoms

Loss of appetite
Nausea
Abdominal discomfort and
   pain
Vomiting

Muscular symptoms

Shaking and tremors
Eyelid twitching
Fidgeting
Startle reactions
Pacing
Wobbly legs
Rigidity
Insomnia

Table 2–2 shows you some things or situations that you may be anxious about. The list is not exhaustive, and you may be anxious about some unusual things that most people would not be anxious about.

TABLE 2–2
You May Be Anxious About

Anxieties	*Phobias*
Socializing	Social gatherings
Public speaking	Open spaces
Job seeking	Closed spaces
Working on your job	Heights
Sports	Trains
Educational courses	Automobiles
Traumatic events	Elevators
Post-traumatic stress disorder	Animals
Medical conditions	Bridges
Substance-induced anxiety	Tunnels
Drinking or drugging	
Obsessive-compulsive disorder	
Stuttering	
Feeling anxiety symptoms	
Showing anxiety	
Feeling or showing panic	

Watch for the signs that you may experience when you are anxious, particularly when you are frequently or intensely anxious. Then, note the things or situations that you are commonly anxious about. Don't, however, make yourself so anxious about the possibility that you may be anxious that your anxiety about your anxiety takes over. Then you may find that you are "anxious" about it or about other things when you are actually normally and healthily concerned about them.

3

Luckily, Most of Your Anxiety Is Self-Created and Can Be Uncreated

Fortunately, you create much of your serious, unhealthy anxiety and even more fortunately, you have the power to remove or decrease it. As we have already noted, you are born with the tendency to be concerned or anxious, and you had better not remove it completely or else you will have trouble surviving. You also are born and reared in an environment that keeps you anxiety prone, for your desires and goals may easily be interrupted or blocked by many dangerous things, such as diseases, accidents, opposition from other people, assaults, abuse, rape, stock market crashes, wars, and a host of other difficulties. The fact that so many possible troubles may occur in your life, and that they may easily interfere with your wants and your pleasures, means that you are set up to be wary and that you need anxiety as a form of protection.

As a human person, therefore, you are presented with two major factors that make you prone (as we have noted in the last chapter, healthily prone) to anxiety: first, your biology, or your hereditary tendencies to be cautious and vigilant; second, many environmental factors in your life which thwart and balk your desires and that you need to be concerned about. As a human, moreover, you are especially born and raised with some degree of choice or will. You can make decisions and decide between one form of activity or another. Although you are partially restricted by your biology and your environment, you are an agent in your own right and therefore have choices.

This means that you can decide to go one way or another. When you want to get more of what you want and less of what you don't want, you make a guess as to which road it would be best to travel, and as you go down that road, you discover what is "right" and what is "wrong" for you—meaning, what will fulfill your goals and what will block them. But you are rarely certain, as you choose your path, which is the best path to follow, and you can easily make mistakes along the way that you could not completely see in advance. Changes in the road itself may easily occur.

So, as a human, you are always somewhat in doubt. You rarely completely know—even though you think you may know—what is "right" and what is "wrong" or what is "good" and what is "bad" for you. You have to experiment, take some risks, and, ultimately, discover the "correct" path. But, since you often know what you want and don't want and have to discover what pathway is "correct," you have no absolute certainty, no invariant rules to go by, to ensure your fulfilling your desires. Your very existence is uncertain and, at best, probabilistic. You think you know the right way but you are never absolutely sure. This results from your having some degree of choice: a choice of goals or intentions, and a choice of how to fulfill them. That is why the existentialists talk in terms of your "existential anxiety." Choice gives you doubts and uncertainties. Therefore, you are always somewhat anxious— which largely means in doubt about the outcome of your choices, hoping that you make the right or correct choices, but never absolutely certain what will work for you.

Anxiety, doubt, and uncertainty, consequently, are part of the human condition. You can't completely escape from concern, but you can reduce much of its unhealthy, exaggerated quality if you truly understand what you do to bring about this unhealthy aspect and if you teach yourself to do something different—something that will result in healthy caution.

As we have said, your anxiety has a biological factor, which consists of inborn tendencies to have desires, to make choices that will presumably aid them, to risk not fulfilling these choices, and then to revise and change them. So you are born a chooser and you are born with tendencies—powerful tendencies—toward anxiety. Then, as noted above, the second important factor arises: the environment in which you live, the people and the things that surround you that either aid or block your desires. If these people and things are "good," you will get much of what you want and little of what you don't want and you will have little anxiety or depression. But if these are "bad," you will get less of what you want and more of what you don't want, and anxiety and depression will increase.

Unfortunately, there is often not too much you can do about these two important factors that lead to potential anxiety. You cannot readily change your biology—the fact that you are a special kind of human with various kinds of traits, characteristics, and propensities. Still, you are not by any means completely fixed by your heredity, and you can (with much hard work) change some of the traits and ways that you presumably "are." But only to some extent, and only with difficulty. Some of your characteristics— your "nature"—you just have to live with and adjust to. They are not very easily changed!

As for the environment, the people and the surroundings you grew up with and with which you now live, you can only change them in limited ways, too. You can vote at election time—but you can't completely change the government. You can arrange for a different job, new living quarters, a different kind of mate, and many other environmental things. But not completely! And often hardly at all. To some considerable degree, you are stuck with certain people and things that are not too changeable—people and things that block your desires and provide you with what you do *not* want.

So when you are anxious, let us say, about making more money, it is not easy to change your fundamental skills and talents (say, your ability to learn accounting or to paint well enough to make a living as an artist). Nor is it easy to change your environments (say, the number of jobs that exist in the field of accounting or of art).

You can change these things to some extent—but only in a limited way.

Fortunately, however, there are some major things you can change that have enormous influence over whether you are going to feel moderately concerned or terribly overconcerned or anxious. There are things, the same things, that you can change to make yourself feel healthy anxiety rather than unhealthy anxiety about any predicament you face. These are your own *thinking*, your own *feeling*, and your own *behavior* that largely lead to the kind of anxiety you feel and whether it is healthy or unhealthy. You may think, wrongly, that it is mainly your biology that controls your anxiety. Or you may think, wrongly, that it is mainly the influence of your environment—your upbringing or early conditioning or the events in your present environment that make you anxious. Well, these are important matters, and they both do have a bearing on anxiety. But they are not all-important, crucial. The third factor, you yourself—and how you choose to think, feel, and act—is in many ways more important, more influential in creating your anxiety and the healthy and unhealthy forms in which it manifests itself.

A CASE OF JOB INTERVIEW ANXIETY

This third important factor, as I said in the first chapter, was originally proposed by philosophers and thinkers. People, for the most part, are poor philosophers: They do not think clearly about their various forms of upsetness, and they tend to blame most of their problems on the things that happen to them. This, as we have noted, is partly true. When your drive to fulfill your desires is thwarted, you tend to blame it on the events that happened to you just before you were frustrated. Thus, if you go for a job and the interviewer gives you a hard time and rejects you, you say to yourself, "My desire for the job got blocked by the interviewer." Actually, however, you wanted the job, you picked the firm to possibly work for, you answered the interviewer's questions, and you felt rejected. The outcome, therefore, is not simply a matter of the interviewer rejecting you but largely of your desires, your selection of the firm, your answers to the interviewer, and so forth. You are an *integral* part of the situation. And if you really want a job, you will not only have to find a "good" interviewer but will also have to look for a certain kind of job, find a firm to interview, go for the interview, and do all kinds of other things to get it. The interviewer plays an important role of course, but your desires, choices, actions, and other variables play an even greater role. You may not understand these many factors at play and may therefore not see why you really didn't get the job.

The situation is even more complicated and less understood in regard to your feelings about being rejected for the job.

Your goal or desire is to get it. At point A, Adversity, you meet the interviewer and are turned down for the job. Then, at point C, Consequence, you feel depressed about losing the job and very anxious about failing to get other similar jobs that you may apply for. So we have A, Adversity, and C, Consequence, depression and anxiety. This seems very clear, and almost always as a normal human, you will tend to conclude that A leads to or causes C—that your Adversity leads to your depression and anxiety.

This, however, is the kind of crooked thinking that gets practically all of us into trouble. Whenever something unpleasant occurs and we feel anxious or depressed about it—for we hardly are going to feel very good about something unpleasant that works against our desires—we quickly conclude that this unpleasant event, A, preceded our negative feeling of anxiety or depression, C, and that therefore A must have caused C. This is especially true because if A had not occurred, and instead it had consisted of something pleasant rather than something unpleasant (such as success instead of failure), we would most probably never have gotten anxious or depressed. Therefore, we conclude that because something did occur that was unpleasant, its unpleasantness (which is bad) must have caused our unpleasant (bad) feeling of anxiety or depression. Obvious, is it not?

No, it really is not obvious; and we are actually quite wrong in concluding that A (Adversity) causes C (anxiety or depression). For if this same Adversity had occurred to, say, 100 people, would they all feel anxious or depressed about it? Obviously not. Practically all of them, say 90 percent or 95 percent, would have had some bad feeling about this Adversity—for it is against their interests and they would rather it not occur. But the bad feeling that they would have at C (Consequence) about A (Adversity) would tend to be a variety of different feelings. After they meet the interviewer and are turned down for the job, some of the hundred rejectees would feel disappointed, some angry, some depressed, some frustrated, and some would have other kinds of feelings. Very likely, they would not all feel exactly the same way. They would have a variety of feelings, most of them negative to be sure, but different kinds of negative feelings. Not all would feel depressed, and a few might even feel happy about being turned down for the job by the interviewer. This last group would have concluded that they really didn't want the job or that they wanted it but it had more disadvantages than advantages for them.

The extremely important point is that when bad things happen to you, such as not getting a job you want, these events or Adversities do not directly cause you to feel depressed. There is also an intervening variable—your thoughts or Beliefs (B) about these As have a more direct bearing on your feelings of depression. Just as you choose to want the job (or not want it) and choose to try to succeed at the interview (or not try too hard to succeed at it), you also choose your Beliefs about failing at the interview; and depending on what Beliefs you choose, you can have quite different feelings about a rejection.

For example, suppose you apply for the job, take the interview, do your best to pass it, and still fail to get the job. Then you may Believe, at point B, "Well, I did my best to get this job but unfortunately there were more qualified applicants for it. Too bad, but it's hardly the only job out there. So let me learn by this experience and try for several other similar jobs."

If your Beliefs (B) are along these lines, you will most likely feel sorry, regretful, and disappointed—but not depressed and self-hating. If, however, you take the interview, do your best to pass it, and still fail to get the job, you may have quite a different set of Beliefs (B) about failing, such as: "I really *should* have done better at that interview. I made several mistakes that I *should not* have made. This job was a great one for me and it's *awful* that I didn't get it. I did so poorly at the interview that I'll probably fail again at other interviews for similar jobs. How stupid of me! I *must* get a job like this one, otherwise my life will be wrecked. If I keep interviewing like this I'll probably never get a good job. How terrible! Poor me!"

If your Beliefs (B) are along these lines, you will most likely feel very depressed, perhaps suicidal, and instead of going for several other interviews, you may cop out of the job-getting process and remain unemployed for a long time.

The moral of all this is that you control your emotional destiny. While you do not control what jobs are available, what kinds of interviews you will get, what the interviewer's decision will be, how many similar jobs are available, and many other important aspects of job-seeking, you *do* control how you will react and how you will feel after you gain or lose the job. You, largely, though not completely, control your feelings by being in charge of your Beliefs: what you say to yourself at B, when unfortunate events, or Adversities, happen in your life at A.

Therefore, fortunately, while you often can't control what happens to you in the world, you usually can control how you react to what happens to you. If very bad things happen to you—that is, events that are against your goals and interests—you will most likely first feel healthy negative feelings, such as disappointment, sorrow, regret, annoyance, and frustration, for you don't like being deprived of what you want (or getting what you don't want) and you'd better react somewhat negatively when these unpleasant events occur. This is healthy and good, because your feelings of disappointment and frustration then tend to motivate you to review the Adversities that occur in your life, to think about them, to cope with them, and to try to change them. If you didn't have some kind of negative feelings about them, you would simply let them continue and you would do nothing about them. So you want to act on them, and your healthy negative feelings of regret and disappointment help you do this. This is why, in REBT, we call them healthy or helpful.

If, however, you choose to have *unhealthy* negative feelings (B) when Adversities occur in your life, you will not successfully cope with these problems. For such feelings—like anxiety, panic, depression, rage, self-hatred, and self-pity—are usually disruptive and interfere with the coping process. Such feelings frequently are exceptionally intense. They obsess and preoccupy you. They interfere with straight thinking and problem solving.

They may paralyze you. They often distract you into acts, such as planning to harm others, that sabotage the things you can do to help yourself. They create psychosomatic upsets, such as heart palpitations and headaches, which obstruct you and again make it difficult for you to plan to cope with Adversity.

Let us repeat, then: When unfortunate things happen in your life, such as the loss of a job that you really want to get, and you quickly feel anxious and depressed about these things, it is rarely the things themselves (Adversities) that affect you emotionally and make you react to them. These Adversities may be quite bad, and they are important in creating your moody reaction to them, but just as important, often more so, are B, your Beliefs about Adversities. These Beliefs may cover a wide variety of perceptions, observations, and conclusions. Because they do, your emotional reactions to Adversities also cover a wide range of results. Thus, when exactly the same Adversity happens to you—such as, again, rejection for a job—you may react with weak feelings or strong ones, healthy feelings or unhealthy ones. You don't always react the same way to the same Adversity, nor do any of us. If a very similar Adversity occurs to one hundred people, each person will tend to have some similar bad emotional reactions, but each person will also have some very different reactions.

The same thing goes for your (and other people's) behavioral Consequences. If you lose out on a desirable job at point A (Adversity), this failure may spur you to get many other job interviews and eventually get the job you want. But it may also lead you to feel discouraged and hopeless and never go for another interview. How come? Again, the main difference is what you tell yourself at B, your Belief system. You may say, "Too bad I lost out on this job, but now I see better what the interviewer wants and feel that I am really capable of getting this kind of a job and performing well at it. So I'd better get as many more interviews as I can and finally get a job. It may take awhile for me to get one, but if I keep trying, I'm sure I'll succeed." If you have these kinds of Beliefs (B), you will keep looking for a job and arrange for as many interviews as possible.

On the other hand, you may believe, instead, "Oh, I can see by this interview that I'm going to have a most difficult time getting this kind of a job. I really don't have the qualifications they're looking for. If I do manage to get hired, I won't be able to do very well and they'll probably soon fire me. What's the use of going for more interviews? I'd better go for a much different kind of work. Or maybe there's nothing I can do well. So maybe I'd better go on welfare or get some family members to support me." If this is your Belief system's reaction to failing to get a job, you will most likely not try too hard to get a similar one, or, in extreme cases, you may drop out of the job market entirely.

So, how you act and behave in regard to failing to pass a job interview largely depends not just on the interview and its results but on what you tell yourself about failing to get this job and trying for other jobs. Both your emotional reactions and your behavioral reactions to Adversity, I repeat, largely follow from your Beliefs about this Adversity and not merely from the Adversity itself.

This, we repeat, is very lucky. Most of the time you have a great deal of control over what you believe and what you disbelieve, and can feel and act accordingly.

4

Irrational Beliefs That Make
You Anxious

If you are under very serious stress—as occurs when you are traumatized by violence, rape, abuse, or a major accident—you may quickly become very panicked or explosive, and for a period of time you may lose control of your thoughts, feel off the wall, and act strangely. Even then, you will tend to recover after a period of time and become much more in control of your thoughts and actions than when you first experienced this trauma. But, at least temporarily, you are so shocked, especially by an unexpected traumatic event, that you can't think straight.

These, fortunately, are exceptional cases. For the most part, your brain and central nervous system function pretty well, and you do have a choice of your thoughts, feelings, and actions—that is, if you think that you do! For if you believe you are out of control, and that your thoughts and feelings thoroughly possess you and run you, then you may indeed bring about that result. Theoretically, you are capable of modifying your thinking, your emotions, and your behaviors, but you may be convinced that you cannot do so, and therefore you may give up and let them control you. Thus, you think that there is no way of stopping your anxiety or panic, and you therefore give in to them and let them run rampant. You are really able to do something, even when you are in a severe state of panic, but you believe that you are not able to do anything, and you even panic about your panic. Then all hell—meaning lack of control—breaks loose!

Once you believe that your Beliefs are very important in producing your emotional reactions and behaviors, and once you work at observing the Beliefs that tend to make you disturbed and dysfunctional, you are still not entirely in control of your feelings. No miracle cures here! But you *can* remarkably create, manage, and change your emotional reactions and behaviors to suit your bidding. You are no longer prey to serious anxiety, depression, and rage—as you frequently are without exerting this form of control, for you have a wide choice of Beliefs and can subscribe to many of them and refuse to subscribe to others. As we shall keep repeating in this book, you can think, you can think about your thinking, and you can even think about thinking about your thinking. That's the way normal humans are. They can think in many different ways—good and self-helping ways and bad and self-harming ways. They are born and reared with that ability. If only they used it!

I shall now explain basic principles of Rational Emotive Behavior Therapy and show how its ABCs give you a great amount of control over your emotions and behaviors, and specifically help you to control your anxiety before it controls you. If you use these principles and keep practicing them, you will most probably achieve a degree of control over your feelings that you never before dreamed possible—especially control over your anxiety, but also over any other disruptive feelings that you may be in the habit of creating.

HOW YOU CREATE ACHIEVEMENT ANXIETY

Let us take one of the most common things that often "makes" you anxious. Say you very much want to do well in a task, a sport, a job, or a relationship and you are afraid you won't be able to do so. In failing, you will lose the approval of several people whom you decidedly want to gain favor with. So naturally, you feel very anxious.

In REBT terms, you have the goal of succeeding (G) and there is a good chance that Adversity (A) will occur and that you actually will fail and be rejected. So at point C, the Consequence of your contemplating failing and being rejected (A), you feel terribly anxious. Your anxiety, of course, is not helping you to succeed at this project and to be accepted for succeeding. On the contrary, you worry, worry, worry about failing: You may actually quake and tremble, you may feel weak and insecure, and your planning to do well at the project is seriously interrupted. Perhaps you are so anxious that you feel sick to your stomach and your body is uncoordinated and almost paralyzed.

According to REBT, your anxiety may have several causes—such as that the task you are trying to succeed at is known to be very difficult and the people who are to judge you on this task are very critical. But these external causes are beyond your control to change. So what causes of your anxiety *are* in your control and can be adjusted and changed in a helpful manner? The answer is: mainly your Beliefs (B) about the situation and the possibility of your failing at it and being rejected. These Beliefs are largely in your control and can be properly adjusted in case they are unhelpful. So, let us turn to them.

First, you probably have a set of Rational Beliefs (RBs) about the project you are doing and the approval you may get for accomplishing it well. These Rational Beliefs—or preferences—are likely to be along these lines: "I really hope I do well at this project and thereby win the approval of the people I want to like me. I may do poorly, of course, and that would be unfortunate, for I would not be getting what I want and might be getting the disapproval that I don't want. However, failing and being rejected won't be the worst thing in the world. I can learn by it and always try again. And being disapproved of by those whose favor I want won't kill me, but will only deprive me of some pleasure. Even if I never succeed at this project and at similar important projects, I will merely be frustrated but hardly destroyed. And if I never win these people's approval, I will again only be frustrated but hardly annihilated. Now let me see if I can give my best to this project, and if I fail, to keep trying at similar projects so that in time I will probably succeed and most likely win a fair amount of approval. But if I don't, I don't! I can still be a reasonably happy person."

These Beliefs (B) are rational ones because they will usually help you succeed at your project and win the approval of those you favor. They will create the healthy feelings of disappointment and frustration, in case you do not succeed, and the healthy feelings of encouragement and enthusiasm that will help you succeed. They will also tend to keep you trying to do well at this project and at similar projects and not cop out or give up prematurely. They will also help you to focus your thoughts and energies on schemes and plans that will again help you achieve what you want and not get what you don't want. They are highly proactive Beliefs, and, although they won't absolutely ensure your reaching your Goals, they will greatly increase the likelihood of your doing so. That is why we call them Rational Beliefs (RBs)—because they are helpful and will tend to make you effective and productive.

When, then, your potential Adversity, failing at your project, is followed by RBs, your Consequences (Cs) are likely to be in line with your desires. So your Rational Beliefs more often than not get you your Goals and lead to constructive feelings of disappointment and frustration in case, this time, you fail to reach them. Therefore, you have a good chance of attaining these Goals in the present and/or the future. Rational Beliefs tend to lead to desirable Consequences.

However, when you have the Goals of success and approval and you realize that various Adversities (A) may block and thwart them, you may easily have a set of Irrational Beliefs (IBs) that make you feel emotionally disturbed and very likely will sabotage your Consequences (Cs). Thus, you may irrationally believe, "Suppose I definitely fail at my Goal and am thoroughly rejected by those people I favor? That would be *awful*! I absolutely *must not* fail and be rejected. I *could never stand* that. It would mean that I wasn't good enough to succeed—that I am an *inadequate, worthless person*! If people rejected me for failing, that would prove I am not worthy of their approval, and that I'll keep getting disapproved of for the rest of my life. How horrible that would be! I'd be totally destroyed! I couldn't be happy at all. If I am deprived of what I really want, life is not worth living and perhaps I'd better kill myself!"

These Irrational Beliefs will usually be harmful rather than helpful. They will tend to make you so anxious—indeed, panicked—that you can't function properly and will actually bring about failure and rejection. They will often make you physically ill and weak. The panic created by Irrational Beliefs will interfere with your intellectual functioning; you will have trouble figuring out what plans to make and put into practice in order to bring about success. They will cripple you so much emotionally that if you actually fail at one of your Goals, you will probably be discouraged from trying again, or you will try *desperately* to achieve and therefore will fail again and again. Irrational Beliefs will often lead you to give up your Goal completely and to settle for other goals that you do not really want, or else to become thoroughly goalless and purposeless. They may well impinge dreadfully on the rest of your life and foster your failing at other goals and projects that formerly you enjoyed and did well at. They may, in extreme cases, cause a mental breakdown or drive you to suicide.

What a difference, then, between constructive Rational Beliefs and destructive Irrational Beliefs when you approach an important project and desire to be approved by significant people for succeeding at that project. Your RBs will make you feel enthusiastic and encouraged to pursue the project and will produce sensible concern about it. Concern is a form of anxiety because it contemplates your failing at the project and forces you to be cautious and vigilant about doing it. Concern helps you to plan your project and carry it through. It helps you to put its various aspects in order and to change them around if and when they get out of order. Concern, you might say, is a necessary part of control: For if you were not healthily concerned about doing something, you would not go to the trouble of trying to do it, and especially of trying to do it well. So Rational Beliefs tend to make you concerned, cautious, vigilant, and prepared for eventualities in connection with a project you undertake. Concern, moreover, is interesting and enjoyable: It gets you to really put your head into a venture, figure out the best ways of doing it, and makes you vitally absorbed in it. It leads to what Professor Csikszentmihalhyi of Chicago University calls flow, or the intrinsic enjoyment of something you are working on and the great pleasure of being occupied with it.

Not so anxiety! Anxiety is *overconcern* or *exaggerated* concern. Where concern makes your projects important and exciting to you, anxiety makes them all-important or sacred. Though the two involvements may seem similar—concern and overconcern—in some ways, they are light years apart. For when you tell yourself, "I want very much to do this project and I'll try my best, but if I don't do it perfectly well, I'll still enjoy what I can do," you are duly concerned and involved with it. But when you escalate this Belief to the Irrational Belief, "I absolutely *must* do this project and *must* do it perfectly well or I'm a worthless person," you are overconcerned, anxious, and frantic about it. As we have noted, this kind of overconcern or anxiety will often thoroughly upset you and make you much less likely to accomplish the project well.

How do you know when your Beliefs, at point B, are irrational or self-defeating? There are some fairly simple ways of looking for these Beliefs, finding them, and then later Disputing them if they are Irrational (at point D) and changing them back to Rational Beliefs. I shall describe these ways shortly. But first, take a look at C, in the ABCs of REBT, to see how anxious you are. Anxiety is a feeling in your gut, a feeling of insecurity, doubt, and indecision. You usually know it by your physical sensations—by the butterflies in your stomach. But it takes various other forms, such as shortness of breath, trembling, shaking, twitching. We outline some of the main forms it may take in table 2–1 on page 21. If you are not sure whether or not you are anxious, check this table to see whether you have one or more—and sometimes quite a few—of these signs. When you have determined that you are anxious and not merely properly concerned, cautious, or vigilant, then try to determine what you are mainly anxious about—A or Adversity in the ABCs of REBT. Usually, you will find that you are anxious about possibly failing at one of your major Goals, or being disapproved of by people that you would like to favor you, or various kinds of losses, or certain forms of discomfort, or physical diseases or dangers, or dying. Some of the main things you may be anxious about are listed in table 2–2 on page 22.

DEADLY DEMANDS AND MUSTS
THAT LEAD TO ANXIETY

Now that you are pretty sure you are anxious and have some indication of what you are mainly anxious about, look for the Irrational Beliefs that are leading you to feel anxious. Theoretically, there are hundreds or thousands of these Beliefs. But after a great deal of research by practitioners of REBT and other kinds of Cognitive Behavior Therapy (CBT), it has been found that almost all the specific IBs you have can be listed under one or more of a few major headings. So all you have to do at first is to check the major headings to see if any of your personal IBs fall under them. These major headings are as follows:

Absolutistic Musts, Shoulds, Oughts, and other *Demands.* When I first researched the Irrational Beliefs of my clients, I came up with twelve common ones, all of which had many variations. These Beliefs and their variations were put into tests of IBs and these tests were given, in hundreds of published studies, to all kinds of people, both disturbed and nondisturbed. It was generally found, just as I had predicted, that when individuals held more of these IBs and held them very forcefully and rigidly, they generally turned out to be more anxious and otherwise disturbed than when they held less of these Beliefs and held them only lightly or moderately. That was an important finding which showed that the theory of REBT was probably sound and that people's emotional disturbances were related to their Irrational Beliefs.

When I did further clinical work and research into people's Irrational Beliefs, however, I was somewhat surprised to learn that my original twelve IBs held up, and so did many variations on them. I also found that they could be condensed into three major IBs and that virtually all the other IBs—hundreds of them, in fact—could be put under these three major headings. I was somewhat surprised to see—although I had suspected for years that it was true—that every one of these three basic irrationalities that led to emotional disturbance was an absolutistic demand or command: an unconditional should, ought, or must. Karen Horney, an unusual analyst, had pointed out something similar in 1950, when she spoke about the "tyranny of the shoulds" that made people disturbed. But I more specifically zeroed in on these absolutistic shoulds and musts as I used REBT with my clients in the mid 1950s. The three powerful musts that I found, and which I labeled *must*urbation, were these:

1. *Musts directed against oneself* Examples: "I *absolutely must* be successful in every important task I undertake." "I *must* be loved *completely*, or at least thoroughly approved, by people whom I find significant." "I *must* be outstanding or perfect at certain projects that I select to do." This very common form of musturbation, which people all over the world often have at many points in their lives, leads them to feel anxious, depressed, worthless, self-hating, and insecure when they do not achieve various Goals in their lives.

2. *Musts directed against other people* Examples: "Other people *must* help me to get whatever I want and help prevent me from getting what I don't want." "Other people *must* love and approve of me when I want them to do so." This form of musturbation leads to anger, rage, fury, violence, feuds, wars, and genocide, when other people do not follow your commands and treat you precisely as you *demand* they should.

3. *Musts directed against environmental or world conditions* Examples: "Job conditions *must* be established so that they make sure that I get the kind of employment I like and that it pays very well." "The weather *must* do my bidding and bring me exactly the kind of day I demand." "Politico–economic conditions *must* be at all times the way I want them to be and must not work against my personal interests." This kind of musturbation produces low frustration tolerance, depression, procrastination, addiction, and various other kinds of poor consequences.

As I said, I was somewhat surprised to see that these three major musts covered the field and that they consequently produced many different kinds of disturbed emotions and dysfunctional behaviors. I still haven't found any major musts or Irrational Beliefs that do not include these three musts that lead to human malfunctioning.

Each of these musts and demands, again, has numerous subheadings, but the subheadings in turn seem to definitely include, directly or indirectly, an absolutistic demand.

This means that whenever you have a specific Goal in mind and you clearly want to achieve it, and refrain entirely from musts and demands about it, you will feel the healthy emotions of sorrow, regret, frustration, and displeasure whenever you do not achieve your Goal, but you will practically never make yourself seriously upset. For a preference statement always seems to imply a *but* or *however* that wards off emotional disturbance about its not being fulfilled. Thus, if you tell yourself, I very much want to succeed at this project but I do not have to succeed at it and can still be reasonably happy if I don't, you may have normal disappointment without experiencing serious trauma if you do fail.

But an absolutistic must does not include a preference or a however. It means what it says: that under all conditions and at all times you absolutely *must* do well and *must* win people's approval, which of course, is completely unrealistic. For there will be times when you will not do as well as you would like to do and you will gain people's disapproval. Then where are you? Answer: anxious or depressed.

There are, of course, conditional musts that are perfectly sane and sensible. For example, if you say that to buy a book you must pay for it and to get through college you must register, must pay tuition, must take courses, and must pass them, then your musts are sensible. In order to accomplish something, you frequently have to do something else. So you must do that thing in order to reach your goal. But to say that under all conditions and at all times you *must* buy a book, whether or not you have the money for it, is silly. Your unconditional *musts* simply won't work and are likely to bring you misery.

So, although it may be most desirable that you finish a project well and win the approval of other people for finishing it, there is no reason why you *absolutely must* succeed in these respects and must succeed just because you *prefer* very much to do so. Your preference to succeed leaves you a way out in case you don't fulfill your desire, but your absolutistic demand that you *have to* fulfill your desire, no matter what, is very likely to get you into trouble. Absolutistic musts rarely work, and you would think that intelligent humans would not make them. But people do continually insist on them, and, as REBT makes clear, such behavior frequently leads to anxiety, depression, and self-downing. So if you want to undo your emotional upsetness, first look for your musts and then dispute them and give them up—turn them back into realistic preferences.

Do you hold these possible musts consciously when you are emotionally disturbed or are behaviorally dysfunctional? You may, but you also may not. Thus, you may consciously tell yourself, "I must pass this math test or else I am a hopeless idiot!" or "I must treat my parents nicely or else I am a rotten child and a bad person!" If you think either of these thoughts, you will obviously make yourself anxious at the thought that you may *not* pass the math test or *not* treat your parents nicely. Your *must* is conscious, and you can see what it is and either hold on to it and create anxiety or you may change it to a preference ("I *prefer* to pass this math test, but I really don't *have to* in order to accept myself"). Then, REBT says, you will make yourself healthily sorry and frustrated if you fail, but not anxious to the point where you lose your ability to function.

Often, however, you are not aware of your musts and demands and wrongly think that you only *prefer* to pass the math test and do not also believe that you absolutely *must* pass it. But if you look at your *preference* to pass the test and examine it closely to see if it *also* includes a *must* or a *demand* which is hidden just below the surface of your preference or want, you will almost always find this must. For, according to the often tested theory of REBT, it is really there and you are merely unaware of it—that is, until you look for it!

Assuming that REBT is correct, and that your wants and preferences do not create anxiety when they are not fulfilled but that your musts and demands often do lead to it, you may then see that accompanying your anxiety-creating musts are several corollary or derivative Beliefs that strongly tend to go with them and that increase your anxiety. Among them are the following:

Self-Downing or Personal Inadequacy Beliefs   "Because I absolutely *must* pass this math test, and there is a possibility that I will fail, failing it will make me a complete failure, an inadequate worthless person." This Irrational Belief produces one of the main forms of severe anxiety. It often consists of performance anxiety but may also include the IB that if you fail at the math test, people will despise you for failing and that because you *must have* their approval and actually may not get it, that also will make you a despicable person.

Downing or Damning Other People for Their Failings   "Because people must treat me nicely and fairly, and some don't, this makes them utterly rotten people who deserve to be damned and punished." This Irrational Belief is an overgeneralization that condemns people for what they do, and it can lead to an enormous amount of rage, feuds, wars, and even genocide. Then, the usual result is that others become equally enraged: They naturally condemn *you* for your anger and not merely condemn your anger itself. So anger begets anger and damnation begets damnation; and there is almost no end to this reciprocal form of overgeneralization.

Awfulizing and Terribilizing   If you believe that you must treat your parents very nicely and kindly and there is a possibility that you won't, you may tend to put yourself down and feel like a worthless person. But you may also have the accompanying Irrational Belief, "Treating my parents badly is *awful*. How *horrible* of me to even think of doing this, let alone doing it." If you awfulize, terribilize, or horribilize in this manner, you will again tend to feel quite unhealthily anxious rather than merely healthily sorry, disappointed, and remorseful in case you do treat your parents badly. Awfulizing tends to add considerably to your anxiety.

I-can't-stand-it-itis   When you insist that you absolutely *must* have people treat you fairly, you frequently conclude (that is, derive from your must): "I *can't stand* their unfair treatment of me! I *can't bear* it." Your I-can't-stand-its reinforce your musts and make you very angry because they both imply that the people who treated you unjustly are stopping you from having any happiness *at all* and that you might as well be dead. I-can't-stand-it-itis magnifies your rage—or your anxiety—when you say, "I *must* succeed at this project, and I *can't stand it* if I don't."

All or Nothingness, Black and White Thinking, and Other Forms of Overgeneralizing When you demand of yourself that you do well, that other people treat you nicely, and that things are terrible unless they are exactly the way you want them to be, you resort to overgeneralized, black-and-white thinking that gets you into trouble. Thus, you come up with these Irrational Beliefs: "Because I failed pretty miserably at this important project, that means that I'll always fail and never succeed at important things." "Because I lost out on a few significant relationships, I'll never have one that I really want and will keep failing at just about all good relationships." "Because unfortunate things keep happening to me, they'll continually happen and make me miserable."

Absolutistic shoulds, musts, and other demands, then, lead to self-downing, damning of others, awfulizing, I-can't-stand-it-itis, and inaccurate overgeneralizations. But, in turn, these kinds of Irrational Beliefs also create and reinforce your musts. Thus, if you strongly believe "It's awful for me to fail at important projects and I can't stand doing poorly at them," you will tend all the more to think "Since it's so awful to fail, that means that I *absolutely must* succeed and that I'm a thoroughly inadequate person if I do not!" Musturbation encourages awfulizing and awfulizing encourages musturbation. Your Irrational Beliefs tend to reinforce each other and to lead to still more IBs.

Why do humans think so irrationally so often? Again, partly because they're raised to do so by their parents and by their culture. But also because they seem to have a biological tendency to take their strong preferences and make them into insistent demands. They don't always do so, but they very often do. That is part of being human.

To sum up what I have stressed so far: You are naturally a concerned or moderately anxious person, for you are confronted with many problems, hassles, and stresses in the course of your normal life. If you were not concerned about dealing with these and did not attempt to remove them, you would hardly survive. So you have a biological and a social tendency to meet up with difficulties and to react to them, and, to some degree, you have to be concerned, cautious, and vigilant.

Over and above this, you easily become overconcerned or unduly anxious, and this tendency makes it difficult to cope with the many stressors you encounter. Your tendency to become more anxious than you need be is partly biological, and evolves from the overly cautious and vigilant tendencies of primitive men and women; but it is also socially learned from your parents, teachers, and culture. It largely consists of your taking your strong desires for success, approval, and comfort and turning them into dysfunctional, exaggerated demands. When you want to do well and to be approved by others, you frequently make your preferences into unrealistic and arrogant demands, particularly three grandiose musts: (1) "I *must absolutely* perform well, or else I am not an adequate, good person"; (2) "Other people *absolutely must* treat me nicely and fairly, or else they are damnable"; (3) "The conditions under which I live *must* be arranged so that I get everything I want and practically nothing I don't want, or else the world is going to be a pretty *horrible* place."

These three irrational musts tend to take your moderate tension and anxiety and turn them into severe anxiety and panic. The first must creates ego anxiety, and the second and third musts create anger and low frustration tolerance, which are forms of discomfort anxiety. Without your having such conscious or unconscious musts and demands, you would still feel quite cautious and vigilant, especially in the face of real risk or danger, but you would seldom be out of control and would be able to handle your stress reactions adequately.

Panic or panic attacks are defined by the Diagnostic and Statistical Manual of Mental Disorders (DSM-IV) of the American Psychiatric Association as attacks of anxiety having sudden onset that may build to a peak rapidly (usually within ten minutes) and are often accompanied by a sense of imminent danger or impending doom and a strong urge to escape, to run almost anywhere. The somatic or cognitive symptoms mainly are palpitations, sweating, trembling or shaking, nausea or abdominal distress, dizziness or lightheadedness, a feeling of choking, chest pain, depersonalization, fear of losing control or "going crazy," fear of dying, abnormal sensations of burning or pricking on the skin, and chills or hot flushes. These conditions also occur with severe anxiety, but they are likely to be experienced in a heightened way in panic states.

Once you make yourself panicked—or even quite anxious without severe panic—you frequently tell yourself, "I *must* not be panicked!" "I *can't stand* the terrible feelings and sensations that go with panic!" "It's *awful* and *horrible* to be panicked!" Then, you frequently make yourself panicked about your panic—which, of course, increases the original panic and sustains it much longer than it normally would last.

In fact, once you panic about your panic, you may become so obsessed with the "horror" of your feelings that you may bring them on simply by thinking about how "awful" it would be *if* they occurred. When this happens, your first set of panic symptoms—which may have been brought on by your awfulizing about almost anything—are preempted and the second set, panic about panic, takes over and you may feel "free floating anxiety." Actually, you are making yourself panicked (secondary symptom of anxiety) about your panic (primary symptom of anxiety), and that is the main cause of your problem.

Suppose, however, you do let yourself get out of control and let your anxiety and/or your panic control you instead of your controlling it. What do you then do to surrender your grandiose musts and change them back into sensible, and sometimes quite strong, preferences? Turn to the next chapter and see.

5

Disputing Your Anxiety-
Creating Irrational Beliefs

Assuming that the Rational Emotive Behavior theory of anxiety is correct, you can control your anxiety, and still preserve your self-protective caution and vigilance, in a fairly simple manner. Simple—but not necessarily easy.

Basically, you simply keep your preferences to do well, to be approved by others, to be comfortable, and to be free of physical accidents and ailments—but rigorously refrain from escalating them into musts and demands. Whatever your desires, goals, and values are, it is most unlikely that you will have to radically change them—if you keep them just that way, as desires. But as soon as you make them into insistences and imperatives, then it's time to stop and think how destructive such insistences are and return them to the state of wishes and wants.

Simple enough? Yes—but, again, not easy. Let us be very specific so you can see exactly how you can do this.

ANXIETY ABOUT LOVE RELATIONSHIPS

Take a most common case. Let us say that you are sincerely in love and there are strong indications that your beloved does not especially return your affection. He or she is pretty indifferent to you or even seems to dislike you. But you still very much want this person to return your feeling of love, and you are consequently quite anxious that she or he will not. How can you alleviate your anxiety?

First, assume that you are more than desirous of winning this beloved's affection. Assume that you have a *must* as well as a strong desire. Why? Why assume this? Because you are following, at least tentatively, the REBT theory that says that when you are exceptionally anxious, you most probably have a must. So assume that you do.

Your preference or desire, obviously, is that your beloved return your affection. But assume that since you are very anxious, this desire has escalated to an insistent must. So you look for and fairly easily find this must: "Not only do I strongly prefer that my beloved loves me, but I think that he absolutely must do so. But, because he doesn't seem to do as he supposedly must, and may well never love me the way I love him, I'm very anxious. I have no guarantee that I will get what I ostensibly must get, so I am very anxious, maybe, in fact, panicked."

Okay, now we have a very likely must that you are telling yourself about your beloved, and this must in all probability is making you anxious. Simple, isn't it? If you look for your must, you will probably easily find it.

Well, now, what are you going to do about the must that says "My beloved must, absolutely must, love me as I love her?" How are you going to change it?

The answer, if you follow REBT, is to dispute it. Your goal is to win your beloved. At point A, Adversity, she doesn't seem to care very much for you, and may never. At B, your Irrational Belief, you are telling yourself that she absolutely must care. So at C, your emotional Consequence, you are anxious. Isn't that all pretty clear?

So, still following the REBT route, you proceed to D. D stands for Disputing, perhaps the most powerful therapeutic method ever invented—and invented thousands of years ago by various philosophers, some of them Asian and others Greek and Roman. D, Disputing, questions and challenges your Irrational Belief, "My beloved *absolutely must* love me!"

Now you can Dispute your IB, "My beloved absolutely must

love me!" Here, I will emphasize three thinking methods for disputing IBs. Then, later on, I will present you with several other cognitive, emotive, and behavioral techniques of challenging this or any other self-defeating Irrational Belief.

REALISTIC OR EMPIRICAL METHODS OF DISPUTING IRRATIONAL BELIEFS

The first, and in some ways the basic, method of Disputing your Irrational Beliefs is called the realistic or empirical method, because the main reasons these Beliefs won't work is that they are against social reality. They just do not accord with the facts of life, and if you stubbornly stay with them when they contradict social reality, they will often sabotage you.

Thus, when you have an Irrational Belief like "My beloved *absolutely must* love me," you first Dispute it realistically or factually. You ask yourself, and persist in asking yourself until you get a suitable answer, "Why *must* my beloved absolutely love me?" Where is the evidence that she must do so? Is it realistic to assume that she absolutely must love me? What are the facts in this regard? Is there any reason whatever why she *has to* love me?"

The answer to all these questions or Disputes is, of course, a resounding No. Your *beloved* has the *choice*, in reality, of loving or not loving you. Therefore he doesn't *have* to do so. Actually and factually, he may *not* love you. There is no evidence that he absolutely must love you, but there is a great deal of evidence that he may not do so, and, in fact, you tend to be upset because you demand that he love you, and actually, he may not or does not. So there is clearcut evidence that he must *not* love you if, indeed, the facts show that he doesn't.

Again, it is not realistic to assume that your beloved must love you when she may decide to love you, hate you, or be indifferent to you. So, too, it is unrealistic to assume that she cannot decide not to love you. What are the facts in this regard? Well, the facts clearly are that sometimes she loves you and sometimes she doesn't. She can and sometimes does change her mind about you. Clearly, these facts show that she doesn't have to unconditionally love you at all times and under all circumstances.

Again, there is no reason you beloved *has* to love you. There are many reasons why he may love you—for example, you may be very nice to him. But he still may not love you despite your niceness, and in fact he may not love you because you are too nice to him and therefore he considers you weak or needy.

No matter how you slice it, there is definitely no point in your unequivocally stating that your beloved *must* absolutely love you because that obviously may not be her *choice*, and her *choice* may not be the same as your *demand*. She is a creature in her own right who may or may not love you. So when you insist that she *absolutely must* at all times and under all conditions do so, you are denying the reality that she may or may not love you and that at one time she may love you dearly and at another time may not. Her nature may be volatile and changing, and you are insisting that she be absolutely consistent in her love for you in a way that is not true to her nature. How unrealistic! If you demand that she must always love you when it should be clear that she will not, you will live in a constant state of anxiety.

Similarly, you can realistically and empirically Dispute some of the main corollary Beliefs that you tend to have when you say, "My beloved must absolutely love me." Thus, if he doesn't love you (as he supposedly must) you may think that "I am a poor lover and an inadequate person, and that is why he doesn't love me." But this is unrealistic because there may be many reasons why he loves you little, some of which have nothing to do with you and much to do with him. For example, he may actually love no one, he may be incapable of loving.

Again, because you are insisting that your beloved absolutely must love you when in fact she doesn't feel much affection for you, you may conclude, "That is awful and terrible! I can't stand her not loving me!" But, if you question these statements realistically, you will see that it is indeed bad that she doesn't love you—for you are not getting the love that you want and need. But realistically, it is not the worst thing that could happen to you—for example, she might actively hate you and decide to kill you. Her lack of love is hardly so bad that it must not exist, but your calling it awful and terrible implies that it *is* that bad and *should* not exist. Actually, her lack of love will exist no matter how bad you find it. Moreover, when you say that you *can't stand* her not loving you, you tend to mean, first, that her lack of love will kill you. But it is most unlikely that you will drop dead just because she doesn't love you. And your statement, "I *can't stand* it!" means that you cannot possibly be happy at all for the rest of your life if she never loves you. But that, too, is unrealistic, because the main reason you can't be happy under those conditions is because you *think* you can't be happy, and not really because it is impossible for you to be.

You can realistically Dispute not only your Irrational Belief that your beloved absolutely must return your love, but also the derivatives of that Belief, such as the unrealistic beliefs that it is awful not to be loved by her and that you simply can't stand the reality of her not loving you as much as you want her to do. Irrational Beliefs, in REBT, are almost invariably unrealistic or anti-empirical; and you can Dispute them and change them by being rigorously realistic and looking squarely at the facts of your and another's existence.

LOGICAL METHODS OF DISPUTING IRRATIONAL BELIEFS

Your Belief that "My beloved absolutely must love me" and the various corollary beliefs that usually go with it are quite illogical and do not follow from your assumption "Because I love him very much and would be most delighted if he loved me in return, therefore he must absolutely love me and continue to love me forever." If you want to give up this idea and change it to a self-helping, Rational Belief, you Dispute it by asking these questions: "How does it logically follow that because I greatly love my beloved that he must love me equally? Where is the connection between my strong desire to have his love and the necessity of my having it? Does he have to love me just because I would greatly benefit from his caring for me? Does my conclusion stem from this fact?"

When you ask yourself these questions and persist until you get a straight answer from yourself, you will find that none of your demands for your beloved's affection are logical. It is quite logical for you to conclude that because you *want* your beloved to love you, you are frustrated and deprived when she does not, for your wants are obviously not fulfilled. Whenever you want something and don't get it, you are automatically frustrated and can legitimately say to yourself, "I am not having my desires fulfilled and therefore I find that unfortunate or uncomfortable." But you cannot logically go beyond that statement and insist that because you are frustrated you absolutely must not be deprived, and that therefore life is hardly worth living at all. That does not logically follow.

Specifically, let's logically challenge some of your conclusions about your not being loved as you absolutely must be by the person whom you love. First, ask "How does it follow that he absolutely must care for me and continue to love me forever just because I love him very much?" Answer: It, of course, does not follow. There's no connection between your assumptions—that you love him and would be greatly deprived if he did not love you in return—and your conclusion that therefore he absolutely must love you. It would be highly preferable if he did love you, but it doesn't follow that he *has* to care for you. He reserves the right, the prerogative, to care or not to care; and he can, of course, exert this right one way or another. Your very strong preference for his loving you won't make him do so. Indeed, if anything, it may turn him off!

Again, in Disputing your Irrational Belief, you can ask yourself: "Where is the connection between my strong desire to have my beloved's love and the necessity of my having it?" Answer: There is no connection between these two things. No matter how strong your desire for her love is, she obviously doesn't have to be connected with that desire and to follow through on it and love you. Your strong preference obviously, again, is not her command. If it were, she would definitely love you. But she clearly doesn't *have to* accord with your desire. No one in the world has to follow your desire—unless you put a gun to their head and force them to do so. Even then, they may choose to die.

But, in her case, you don't have a gun, and even if you had one, she still wouldn't have to give in to your demand and love you. Indeed, it's most unlikely that she would!

By Disputing your Irrational Belief logically, you begin to understand that, in reality, your wants don't have to be fulfilled. Even if you would literally die of not being loved by your beloved, that doesn't mean she has to care for you. She can, if she wishes, just let you die!

It is important to understand that you can always Dispute your absolutistic musts, shoulds, oughts, and demands realistically, and by doing so you can come to accept that there is never a reason why you must get what you want to get, that it's not awful if you don't, that you can tolerate your not getting what you desire, and that you are not a damnable person if you function worse than you feel you "must" function. At the same time you can also accept that your grandiose demands on yourself, on other people, and on world conditions are not logical: Although you would prefer that you do important things quite well, that others treat you fairly and nicely, and that conditions be arranged in your favor, your preferences in these connections never *have* to be fulfilled. It is illogical to keep insisting that *because* you greatly prefer them, they have to be achieved. This simply does not follow.

"But," you may object, "suppose my own failing, my being treated unfairly by other people, and my living under poor conditions actually maims me and kills me. Isn't it then true that in order to avoid being maimed or killed, I must achieve certain things, that I must be treated reasonably well by others, and that conditions must be decently set up to preserve me?"

Yes, that is quite true and it logically follows. Sometimes your very life depends on your succeeding, your being treated decently by others, and your living under constructive conditions. So if you want to live and keep living, certain things have to exist. But remember!—there is absolutely no reason why you *must* live. You will, of course, eventually die anyway, though perhaps after you have lived to be one hundred. But there is no reason why you must live for a long time, or that you must die peacefully and not in pain, or that you must be happy in your life. All these things are highly preferable, but they are not absolute necessities. If you think they are, or that practically any of the other things you really want are absolutely necessary, you will almost certainly be anxious. Your wants and desires are legitimate and, in a sense, good—just because you want them. But you do not *absolutely need* what you want. Really, you don't. If you think that you do, you will live with constant anxiety!

PRACTICAL AND PRAGMATIC METHODS OF DISPUTING IRRATIONAL BELIEFS

The third major way to Dispute your Irrational Beliefs, especially your absolutistic shoulds and musts, and to turn them back into preferences is called the practical, pragmatic, or heuristic way. To use this method, you take one or more of your IBs and ask yourself: "Where will this IB get me if I keep holding on to it? What results will it bring? Will it, in all probability, make me happy or will it make me miserable? What will most likely happen if I stick to this Irrational Belief and stubbornly refuse to surrender it?"

Take, again, your Irrational Belief "I love this person very much and therefore he or she absolutely must love me in return. It will be *horrible* if he doesn't! I *can't tolerate* his not loving me. My failing to win his affection makes me an incompetent, worthless individual!"

Actively Dispute and challenge this Belief pragmatically as follows: "If I really hold this belief, and especially hold it very strongly, where will it get me?" Answer: It will make me very anxious, when I am assessing whether or not my beloved loves me, and very depressed in case I discover that she doesn't. "Will it really be *horrible* if my beloved doesn't love me as I love her?" Answer: No, it really won't be horrible because it won't be as bad as it could be. But I will think that it is horrible and feel horrible— because I hold this foolish idea. "Will this Belief, if I cling to it, make me happy or make me miserable?" Answer: It will make me quite miserable unless I have a guarantee that my beloved really loves me and will always continue to feel that way about me. But, of course, I can't have any such guarantee. So I will always be on the verge of anxiety and misery. "What will most likely happen if I stick to this Belief and stubbornly refuse to surrender it?" Answer: I will keep being utterly anxious until and unless I find out that my beloved truly, truly loves me. Even then, I'll still be anxious because I will realize that I always can lose her love and that I can't, by my own definition, be at all happy without it."

This pragmatic or practical kind of Disputing is really the nub of REBT and similar methods of uprooting anxiety. Because your Irrational Beliefs about having your love returned—or about achieving practically anything else in the world—dictate that you absolutely must get what you want to be a happy, secure individual, unless you do get what you want, you will be desperately unhappy. Therefore, if you use the pragmatic form of Disputing these IBs, you begin to see that there is no use holding them— unless you really want to be exceptionally anxious and depressed. IBs are ideally suited for this purpose! But if you want to be even reasonably happy, productive, and effective, you can see that your IBs are deadly and produce continual misery. Being not completely crazy, you will then presumably change them for Rational Beliefs or for sensible preferences.

All told, however, we recommend that you steadily use all three of these major forms of Disputing your IBs: realistic, logical, and practical disputing. Keep doing so, moreover, because you as a human tend to easily hold Irrational Beliefs, you have usually held them for many years, you are habituated to, and comfortable with, holding them. Therefore, to give them up and to keep them ineffective, you had better vigorously Dispute them in all three of these major ways.

If you also have anxiety about your anxiety regarding your not being loved, this secondary anxiety is viewed in REBT as Adversity^2. Then you most probably have Irrational Beliefs (IB^2) about this A^2, such as, "I *must* not be so painfully anxious! How terrible! I *can't stand* my feelings of anxiety! I'm *no good* for being so weakly anxious!" You Consequently (C²) have anxiety about your anxiety.

To Dispute your IB²s, you can also logically challenge them: "How does it follow that if I am anxious it is *terrible* and that I *can't stand* it? Answer: "It doesn't. It is most unfortunate that I suffer from anxiety about my anxiety because I don't like feeling that way. But it is not *so* bad that it must not exist. I *can* stand it and still have some happiness. It is foolish to think that a bad *feeling*, like my anxiety, makes *me* bad."

To Dispute your IB²s you would also pragmatically question them: "Where will it get me if I believe that I absolutely must not be anxious and that I am no good as a person when I am?" Answer: "Nowhere! Anxious about my anxiety!"

So you can almost always find the Irrational Beliefs (IBs) creating your original anxiety, and can Dispute and change them; and you can also, if you have any anxiety about anxiety (C²) find your IB²s, Dispute them and thus minimize your secondary symptoms of anxiety.

In the course of Rational Emotive Behavior Therapy, clients are strongly encouraged, as I shall note later in this book, to practice homework—cognitive, behavioral, and emotive homework—and to do so persistently and strongly. To help them to this, the Albert Ellis Institute has developed an REBT Self-Help Form, which you can use to do your own Disputing and to come up with Rational Beliefs or an Effective New Philosophy. This is shown in form 5–1 (page 56).

Form 5–1 outlines some of the thinking homework you can do. You start with your disturbance, your Consequences, that is, your unhealthy major negative emotions and self-defeating behaviors. Then, you ask yourself what Activating Events or Adversities seem to have preceded, and ostensibly brought on, these Consequences. Then you list your Irrational Beliefs (IBs), then you Dispute them (D), and you come up with E, your Effective New Philosophies and Effective Emotions and Behaviors that stem from your Disputing your IBs.

A (ACTIVATING EVENT)

- Briefly summarize the situation you are disturbed about (what would a camera see?)
- An *A* can be *internal* or *external, real* or *imagined.*
- An *A* can be an event in the *past, present,* or *future.*

IB's (IRRATIONAL BELIEFS)

D (DISPUTING IB'S)

To identify IB's, look for:

- DOGMATIC DEMANDS (musts, absolutes, shoulds)

- AWFULIZING (It's awful, terrible, horrible)

- LOW FRUSTRATION TOLERANCE (I can't stand it)

- SELF/OTHER RATING (I'm / he / she is bad, worthless)

To dispute ask yourself:

- Where is holding this belief getting me? Is it *helpful* or *self-defeating?*
- Where is the evidence to support the existence of my irrational belief? Is it *consistent with reality?*
- Is my belief *logical?* Does it follow from my preferences?
- Is it really *awful* (as bad as it could be?)
- Can I really not *stand* it?

© *Windy Dryden & Jane Walker 1992. Revised by Albert Ellis Institute, 1996.*

C (CONSEQUENCES)

Major unhealthy negative **emotions:**

Major self-defeating **behaviors:**

Unhealthy negative emotions include:
- Anxiety
- Depression
- Rage
- Low Frustration Tolerance
- Shame/Embarassment
- Hurt
- Jealousy
- Guilt

RB's (RATIONAL BELIEFS)

E (NEW EFFECT)

New healthy
negative emotions:

New constructive
behaviors:

To think more rationally, strive for:
- NON-DOGMATIC PREFERENCES
  (wishes, wants, desires)
- EVALUATING BADNESS
  (it's bad, unfortunate)
- HIGH FRUSTRATION TOLERANCE
  (I don't like it, but I can stand it)
- NOT GLOBALLY RATING SELF OR
  OTHERS (I—and others—are fallible
  human beings)

Healthy negative emotions include:
- Disappointment
- Concern
- Annoyance
- Sadness
- Regret
- Frustration

A (ACTIVATING EVENT)

A difficult test is scheduled for a course that I really want to pass.

- Briefly summarize the situation you are disturbed about (what would a camera see?)
- An *A* can be *internal* or *external, real* or *imagined.*
- An *A* can be an event in the *past, present,* or *future.*

IB's (IRRATIONAL BELIEFS)

*I absolutely **must** do well on this test. If I do poorly or fail it that will prove I am an inadequate person!*

*It's **awful** if I fail this couirse and don't get credit for it.*

D (DISPUTING IB'S)

Why must I absolutely pass this test?

If I fail it will that really prove that I am an inadequate person?

*Is it truly **awful** – as bad as it could be – if I fail this course?*

If I keep believing I must pass this test and it is truly awful to fail the course, what results will I get?

To identify IB's, look for:

- DOGMATIC DEMANDS
  (musts, absolutes, shoulds)

- AWFULIZING
  (It's awful, terrible, horrible)

- LOW FRUSTRATION TOLERANCE
  (I can't stand it)

- SELF/OTHER RATING
  (I'm / he / she is bad, worthless)

To dispute ask yourself:

- Where is holding this belief getting me? Is it *helpful* or *self-defeating?*
- Where is the evidence to support the existence of my irrational belief? Is it *consistent with reality?*
- Is my belief *logical?* Does it follow from my preferences?
- Is it really *awful* (as bad as it could be?)
- Can I really not *stand* it?

C (CONSEQUENCES)

> Major unhealthy negative **emotions:** *Severe test-taking anxiety.*
>
> Major self-defeating **behaviors:** *Avoidance of taking courses or applying for jobs which require a test.*

Unhealthy negative emotions include:
- Anxiety
- Depression
- Rage
- Low Frustration Tolerance
- Shame/Embarrassment
- Hurt
- Jealousy
- Guilt

RB's (RATIONAL BELIEFS)

> *There is no reason why I absolutely must do well on this test, though it would be highly preferable if I did.*
>
> *If I fail, it would be bad but I would not be an inadequate person.*
>
> *It would not be **awful**, only highly undesirable, if I fail this course.*
>
> *If I keep believing I must pass this course, I will keep making myself anxious but even that will not be truly awful.*

To think more rationally, strive for:
- NON-DOGMATIC PREFERENCES (wishes, wants, desires)
- EVALUATING BADNESS (it's bad, unfortunate)
- HIGH FRUSTRATION TOLERANCE (I don't like it, but I can stand it)
- ·NOT GLOBALLY RATING SELF OR OTHERS (I—and others—are fallible human beings)

E (NEW EFFECT)

> New healthy **negative emotions:**
>
> *Feelings of concern and disappointment but not anxiety about taking the course, and not getting depressed if I fail it.*
>
> New constructive **behaviors:**
>
> *Not rating myself as an inadequate person if I fail the course.*
>
> *Not procrastinating in applying for jobs that require a test.*

Healthy negative emotions include:
- Disappointment
- Concern
- Annoyance
- Sadness
- Regret
- Frustration

A sample REBT Self-Help Form (filled out for a typical client who has test-taking anxiety when scheduled for a course that he or she really wants to pass or when applying for a job that requires him or her to take a test) is presented in form 5–2 (page 58).

If you use these forms regularly, particularly when you are first learning the principles and practice of REBT to help with your problems of anxiety, you will become adept at finding and Disputing your Irrational Beliefs and arriving at Effective New Philosophies and Effective Emotions and Behaviors.

6

Using Rational Coping
Self-Statements

Rational Emotive Behavior Therapy (REBT) has many methods that you can use to control your anxiety as well as to minimize your feelings of depression, rage, personal inadequacy, and self-pity. This is because all humans plague themselves unnecessarily in somewhat different ways, and they can use a variety of techniques to stop doing so. Moreover, as I said in my first presentation on REBT at the annual convention of the American Psychological Association in Chicago in 1956, human thinking, feeling, and behaving are by no means separate processes but are importantly related. You confront Adversity and think about it, but at the same time you have pronounced feelings with regard to it. Your feelings, moreover, include important thoughts and behaviors; and your actions include important feelings and thoughts.

When, therefore, you feel upset about some Adversity or potential Adversity, you need to understand the thinking and the behavioral aspects of your upsetness; and when you want to feel less upset or *un*upset, you had best use several cognitive, emotive, and behavioral methods to achieve this purpose. REBT, again, is a pioneering multimodal therapy and practically always uses a number of varied methods to reduce your disturbed emotions and the thoughts and behaviors that go with them. This chapter and the next few chapters will explore a number of other thinking methods, along with direct Disputing of your IBs, to help you control your anxiety.

The complete ABC's of REBT include Ds and Es. At point D, you Dispute your Irrational Beliefs that lead to your anxiety, and at point E, you wind up with a new set of beliefs, or an Effective New Philosophy, that significantly changes these IBs to Rational Beliefs.

A CASE OF PERFORMANCE ANXIETY

One of my clients, John, a fairly stable and undisturbed person, was successful in his profession, teaching music, and he had a good relationship with his wife and children. But he was exceptionally anxious about giving a violin recital once or twice a year at the school where he taught. His ABCDEs were as follows:

A (possible Adversity)   John was scheduled to give a recital in a couple of months and, although he was an excellent violinist, he was terrified that he might not do so well in this particular recital. He would be heard by his own music students and might be criticized severely by them.

RBs (Rational Beliefs)   "I may give a poor recital and be severely criticized and that would be unfortunate. But that would merely be too bad, and I wouldn't like it, but nothing terrible will happen. Also, I may play quite well and get a good deal of approval for doing so."

C (Consequence of RBs)   Some degree of concern that led John to practice extra hard for the recital in order to do well in it.

IBs (Irrational Beliefs)   "I *absolutely must* do well in this recital! People will laugh at me if I don't and that would be awful! I'll lose a good deal of status as a teacher of music and I can't stand that! If I do poorly, I'm just a rotten violinist, as well as an inadequate person!"

C (Consequences of IBs)   Severe anxiety. Avoiding practicing the violin, because every time he practiced it he reminded himself that he might fail and be criticized severely for giving a poor recital.

D (Disputing his Irrational Beliefs)   "Why must I absolutely do well in this recital just because it would bring me the respect and acclaim that I want?"

E (Effective New Philosophy)   "There is no reason why I absolutely must do well in the recital, though it would be highly preferable if I did."

D (Disputing) "Will people actually laugh at me if I don't perform well?

E (Effective New Philosophy) "Some of them may actually laugh at me, but the great majority will probably shake their heads and say that I wasn't in good form that evening. If some—or even all— of my listeners do laugh at me, why would that be awful? It wouldn't be. It would be damned inconvenient, but hardly the worst thing that could happen in my life. *Awful* means that it would be so bad that it absolutely must not occur. But if it does occur, it has to occur. I certainly won't like it. But I'd better not *define it* as awful."

D (Disputing) "Would I actually lose a good deal of status as a teacher if I played poorly in my recital?"

E (Effective New Philosophy) "No, I probably wouldn't. Just because I don't play the violin well in a recital hardly means that I'm a bad music teacher. Not many people would contend that I am. Even if I did lose a good deal of status as a teacher, why couldn't I stand it?

I definitely could stand it. I would hardly die of it. I most likely wouldn't be fired. And I could enjoy many other things in life if I no longer enjoyed teaching that much."

D (Disputing) "Would it really mean, if I failed in this recital, that I am a rotten violinist and an inadequate person?"

E (Effective New Philosophy) "No. It would merely mean that I was fairly bad in this particular recital and that I might be very good again in other recitals, as I have been in the past. If I were pretty rotten at violin playing, would that make me an inadequate person? Of course not! My playing the violin has nothing to do with my personhood. I have many traits and do a great number of things, some good and some bad. Therefore, if I play the violin badly, I can't be a bad person—just as, if I play it very well, that doesn't make me a good person. To say I am a good or a bad person is an overgeneralization and doesn't really mean anything. I am a person who does good and bad things, including sometimes playing the violin very well and sometimes, particularly when I am anxious, playing it poorly. If I fail to play well this time, I'll practice more and hopefully do better in the future."

If John does his ABCDEs of REBT as I have just described, he will first make himself anxious about his recital and then calm down and probably play pretty well when the recital takes place. Even if he doesn't, he will most probably be distinctly sorry and regretful that he has not done as well as he would like to do—but he will not feel anxious or depressed.

In following up on his Disputing, John has come up with E, a series of Effective New Philosophies. Every time you make yourself anxious and then do active REBT Disputing and carry it through, you tend to arrive at E, your Effective New Philosophy. If you do so, and really believe this E, you will not only become much less anxious about one possible failure or rejection but will help set the stage for your becoming less anxious about other possible failures, rejections, and discomforts in the future.

To solidify your Disputing and your arriving at New Effective Philosophies, you can write down rational coping statements that you can use to ward off your anxiety. You can continue to use these statements in the future when you tend to make yourself anxious: Write them down, think about them, and, through repetition, let them sink into your head and heart. When I worked with John on his fear of giving a poor violin recital, his rational coping statements went like this: "I definitely do not have to do well in my forthcoming recital, though that would be highly preferable. If I don't, it's not the end of the world."

"If some people laugh at me for performing badly in my recital, I don't have to take them too seriously. They may have a problem themselves and be very hostile. But whether they have a problem in this respect or not, I can take their laughing without horrifying myself about it."

"Nothing is awful, including my failing miserably at my recital. It's just highly inconvenient if I do poorly and I can even learn by it and help myself do better in my future recitals."

"People won't usually judge me as a bad music teacher just

because I happen to fail in one violin recital. If they do, they're obviously prejudiced and I don't have to take them too seriously. I think that I am quite a good music teacher, even though I may not be consistently good at playing the violin."

"I probably won't lose status as a music teacher if I fail at the forthcoming recital. But if I do, I do, and I can go on teaching nonetheless and even teach well."

"Playing poorly in one recital doesn't by any means make me a poor violinist. Even the greatest violinists sometimes play poorly. And if by any chance I turn out to be a fairly poor violinist, that still doesn't make me an inadequate person. Violin playing is merely one of the many things I do. There are things I do very well. And I am never a bad person even if I play the violin badly at every recital. I'd just better improve or quit playing!"

Again, when you do the Disputing of your Irrational Beliefs and get to E, your Effective New Philosophy, that philosophy is generally in the form of rational coping statements. You can go over them, add to them, and come up with a number of similar rational coping statements you can use with any current anxiety you may experience, and that will help you to ward off anxiety in the future. These self-statements are a form of positive thinking. You can create them without doing realistic, logical, and practical Disputing of your Irrational Beliefs, but you can also create them over-optimistically and somewhat falsely.

Thus, you can say, as John almost said as he was working out his rational coping statements: "It doesn't matter at all whether I play my forthcoming recital well or badly. Who cares? I'll just play and let the chips fall where they may. I'm a great guy and a scholar, and even if I'm the worst violinist in the world and I lose my reputation as a music teacher and they fire me, who gives a damn?"

This kind of unrealistic positive thinking may work temporarily to quell your anxiety—but not for long. So by all means, Dispute your Irrational Beliefs, and, through doing so, try to come up with some quite realistic and sound rational coping statements. Think them over. Revise them. Then use them to quell your current and your future anxiety.

7

Using Positive Visualization
and Modeling

Just as you can use rational coping statements to cope with your problems of anxiety, so can you also use positive visualizations. To do this, you imagine something that frequently makes you anxious or panicked and you picture yourself facing it very well and not becoming upset about it.

ANOTHER CASE OF PUBLIC SPEAKING ANXIETY

Sandra, a thirty-year-old computer analyst, used positive visualization to cope with her public speaking anxiety, which she had since the age of thirteen. She always avoided speaking before even small audiences for fear that her voice would quaver or she would say the wrong thing and everyone in her audience would see what a hopeless case she was. But when she got a promotion, her job required that she talk to new additions to her group and explain to them some of the revised operating procedures. Although she knew these procedures quite well, she was terrified that she would explain them poorly, that everyone would think she was a dunce, and that she would be demoted back to her less-desirable position. She made up several excuses and postponed her speeches, but finally she had to make an important one. The situation left her too terrified to sleep or eat.

Under my therapeutic direction, Sandra quickly saw the Irrational Beliefs leading to her terror of speaking: "Because I really know how to operate the computer system and earned my promotion as a result of my knowing it and working with it so well, I must be able to explain it clearly and compellingly to my listeners. If I can't do a good job at teaching it to them, as is required of my new position, what good am I? They'll surely think me incompetent and not worthy of this promotion. And they will be right!"

Sandra saw these IBs and Disputed them. She arrived at the Effective New Philosophy that she was not an incompetent person even if she was not good at giving talks, but only a person who, out of anxiety, had public speaking defects. But she wanted to make her effective new philosophy really stick. So she used positive visualization to make her conclusions stronger.

She first envisioned herself talking to her listeners and *not* being anxious. She saw herself as being concerned about her teaching but just concerned, and therefore she almost relaxed about it. Imagining herself that way, she was able to see that she *could* be comfortable with public speaking, and that thought actually made her less terrified of it.

Then, Sandra imagined that her listeners asked her relevant questions about her presentation and that, without quaking, she was able to answer them to everyone's satisfaction. Visualizing this, she saw that she really *was* in control of the content of her talk, and she was also in control of her anxiety. She had a few qualms about being anxious, but only a few. She was concerned without being *over*concerned.

With repeated positive visualization and continued Disputing of her Irrational Beliefs about the *horror* of giving a poor talk, Sandra made her first public presentation with a minimum of anxiety. She soon learned that she could control her panic before it controlled her, and within another few months, she actually began to look forward to her public speaking.

You, too, can use positive visualization by taking your anxiety about something—such as going for a job interview or preparing for a test—and imagining that you *are* able to do it with little anxiety, or that you are able to master the situation and do well at it, or that you first feel anxiety about doing it but manage to cope with this anxiety and control it. At the same time you do this positive visualization, you can examine your Irrational Beliefs that lead to your anxiety—such as, "I must do very well at this task or else I am an incompetent person!"—and actively Dispute these IBs. Positive visualization plus Disputing of your IBs can reduce your anxiety considerably.

USING MODELING METHODS

As Albert Bandura and other psychologists have shown, modeling yourself after other people who are not anxious in situations that inspire panic in you is a good method of controlling your anxiety. To do this, talk to people you know about how they manage to have minimal anxiety. You can read biographies and autobiographies to discover how many noted people overcame their feelings of panic. You can observe and talk to teachers, lecturers, and workshop leaders to see whether they had any anxiety problems and what they did to conquer them. Talk to people who manage to be calm and unstressed under quite stressful conditions and discover what their attitudes were when they faced these conditions. Talk to people who once were very anxious about certain things and who did something specific to reduce or eliminate their anxiety and see if you, too, can use their methods to minimize your irrational fears.

8

Using Cost-Benefit Analysis to Control Your Anxiety

When you are anxious about some feared condition that you will encounter, you will tend to avoid that situation and thus get rid of your anxiety—*temporarily*. In the long run, however, you probably increase it. Thus, if you have a phobia about riding in elevators, even though you have never heard of anyone who was hurt or killed in one, you will avoid going in them. But every time you do, you will tend to tell yourself, "If I went in this elevator, terrible things *would* happen to me! So I *must* avoid it to prevent these terrible things from happening!" You thereby reaffirm to yourself the *horrible consequences* of riding in elevators and you increase your phobia.

If, however, you risk going in elevators and do so several times, you will *see* that nothing terrible does happen and will contradict your catastrophizing Beliefs and usually get over your phobia. Your problem, therefore, is to look at the *disadvantages* of avoiding elevators, make a list of them, and go over them several times a day to convince yourself that the ultimate cost of avoiding elevators is greater than the gains of avoidance. By this cost-benefit analysis, you encourage yourself to take the short-term risks and the long-term gains of acting against your phobias. You then are able to control your unhealthy anxiety before it controls you.

A CASE OF DRIVING ANXIETY

Jeri was extremely afraid of riding in cars, although she was a good driver and had never gotten into an accident, and almost always traveled to and from her job by bicycle, bus, or train. But her friend Joan was in a car accident one day, was not badly hurt, and avoided cars thereafter. Jeri irrationally modeled herself after Joan and became phobic about driving, even though she greatly inconvenienced herself in her work and social life.

I helped Jeri see that her main Irrational Belief was, "I *need an absolute guarantee* that I'll never get in a car accident and cannot have one. Therefore, I must avoid driving or even being a passenger in a car!" She Disputed this IB by showing herself that absolute guarantees did not exist and that there was a high degree of probability that she wouldn't be seriously hurt in a car accident.

In addition, Jeri did a cost-benefit analysis by writing down all the disadvantages of her avoidance of riding in cars and all the advantages of risking the initial discomfort of riding in them to overcome her phobia. In doing so, she found it much more advantageous to be uncomfortable *for a while* by overcoming her car anxiety than to be uncomfortable *forever* by retaining and escalating this anxiety.

Like Jeri, you too can do a cost-benefit analysis to show yourself that it is much less costly to take the short-term discomfort of exposing yourself to unrealistic fears and getting over them than to take the long-term inconveniences of indulging in them, often forever.

Doing a cost-benefit analysis is also very valuable in helping some people get over their anxiety about addictions. For example: they are addicted to cigarettes and promise themselves that they will stop smoking but then they find the discomfort of stopping so "horrible" that they keep returning to their addiction. They first become anxious about not sticking to their resolve to stop because they are afraid that they will fail to follow through with this resolve. So their uncertainty about this leads them to feel anxious.

To make matters worse, they may quit smoking for a while, then take it up again and berate themselves for their "awful" weakness. They become insecure and more anxious than ever as a result of their self-downing.

If you suffer from this double kind of addiction-oriented anxiety, you can use the cost-benefit analysis method in two major ways:

1. To maintain your addiction itself, you are usually focusing on its advantages—e.g., the pleasures of smoking—and deliberately keeping out of mind its disadvantages—e.g., possible emphysema and lung cancer, the expense of smoking, and the offending of nonsmokers. If, therefore, you take several days to make a list of the many disadvantages of smoking—which may add up to ten or more—and make sure that you write them down and seriously focus on them at least five times every day, they will sink into your consciousness, reduce your worry about stopping smoking (or any other addiction), and appreciably help you give it up. You will most likely see that the costs of smoking that you keep looking at every day are hardly worth its benefits. You will thereby reduce your discomfort anxiety about the "horror" of your difficulty of giving up smoking.

2. You can also work on your self-downing about your weakness in quitting smoking (or some other addiction). Even if you are quite ineffectual about stopping and tend to berate yourself for your lack of strength, you can then make a list of the distinct disadvantages of self-blaming, go over this list again several times a day, and really help yourself to achieve unconditional self-acceptance (USA). This will eliminate much of your anxiety, since self-castigation is a paramount source of anxiety.

A cost-benefit analysis will not help you with all possible forms of anxiety, but it can be adapted to several of the worst forms of it—such as that which stems from self-downing—and used beneficially. Self-defeating behavior frequently stems from your refusal to focus on the disadvantages of engaging in this kind of activity. The use of cost-benefit analysis puts your focus, as it were, into focus, and interrupts your tendency to sabotage yourself in the long run by only looking at the pleasure of harmful addictions.

9

Using Educational Methods to Control Your Anxiety

USING PSYCHOEDUCATIONAL MATERIALS

When I first started to practice REBT, in January 1955, I found that some of my anxious clients got as much or more help from my published articles and books than from their therapy sessions. James, for example, who had great anxiety over his sexual ability, was telling himself, "I must maintain a terrific erection and satisfy my fiancée in intercourse or else I am a sexual weakling!" This Irrational Belief often made him impotent, and then he damned himself for his impotence and made himself still more anxious. He had some success during our first few sessions of REBT in Disputing his IBs, but then he read some of my writings on sex in *American Sexual Tragedy* and some of my articles, "Psychosexual and Marital Problems" and "Sexual Inadequacy in the Male."

These writings made it even clearer to him that his *demands*, rather than his *wishes*, for great sexual performance were creating his anxiety, and by vigorously Disputing these demands, soon lost most of his sexual panic. Like several of my other clients, he reported that written material truly helped him. Consequently, at the psychological clinic of the Albert Ellis Institute for Rational Emotive Behavior Therapy in New York, we always give our clients a group of pamphlets on REBT and recommend that they listen to several of our audio and audio-visual cassettes and read some of our books to help them learn the principles and practice of

REBT. For clients who are seriously anxious, we especially recommend my books: *A Guide to Rational Living*, *A Guide to Personal Happiness*, and *How to Stubbornly Refuse to Make Yourself Miserable About Anything—Yes, Anything!* Some of the tape recordings we frequently recommend for anxious people are my tapes "How to Be a Perfect Non-Perfectionist," "Twenty-One Ways to Stop Worrying," and "Conquering the Dire Need for Love." We also recommend Arnold Lazarus' "Learning How to Relax" and Michael Broder's "Overcoming Your Anxiety in the Shortest Period of Time" for tape listening.

We have many talks and workshops at the Institute and recommend that clients attend them. People seem to benefit particularly from my famous Friday Night Workshops, *Problems of Everyday Living*, where I regularly give demonstrations of live therapy to volunteers who come up to the platform to present a serious anxiety or other emotional problem. In showing these volunteers how to deal with their anxiety, depression, or self-downing, I model for the rest of the audience how everyone can handle his or her own difficulties. Many anxious people are helped by this form of modeling.

David, for example, had trouble using REBT with his anxiety about being rejected by women, but when he heard me show two other volunteers how to overcome similar social anxieties, he was inspired to use REBT more forcefully and soon minimized his own social anxiety. Many other participants in my Friday night workshops, and our other workshops, have reduced their anxiety with or without therapy sessions.

USING TEACHING AND PROSELYTIZING METHODS

John Dewey pointed out many years ago that when teaching another person a technique or subject, you frequently learn it better yourself. I have also found that if I teach someone the main elements of REBT and they, in turn, teach them to their friends and relatives, these people not only can benefit greatly from such teachings, but the teacher frequently learns to apply REBT to his or her own problems better and more deeply.

A CASE OF WRITING ANXIETY

Anne-Marie, for example, learned REBT from several sessions in one of my therapy groups and by reading several of my books and listening to some of the Institute's audiocassettes and videocassettes. Her anxiety about writing term papers improved considerably. But she particularly made great inroads when she began teaching REBT to other anxious individuals she encountered. She half-cured three of her female friends whom she sent to me for further work on their anxiety problems; and in the process of helping them, she completely got over her fear of writing term papers and volunteered to write two *extra* papers, which would have previously panicked her. She became so adept at teaching others—and herself—REBT that she decided to go to graduate school to become a therapist.

Try it yourself. Learn the principles of REBT and teach them to some of your receptive friends and relatives. As you help sink these principles into their heads, you will become more adept at using these principles to lessen your own anxieties.

10

Using Relaxation and Cognitive Distraction Methods

USING COGNITIVE DISTRACTION

Many centuries ago, the ancient philosophers discovered that when people are anxious, they can use several forms of meditation and Yoga to distract themselves from their irrational fears and to temporarily calm down. This is because anxiety and worry are preoccupying and often obsessive. But the human mind has trouble focusing on two preoccupations at the same time. If you are very anxious about acting, reciting, or singing in public, you tend to focus on *how well* you are doing: "I absolutely *must* perform well, and if I don't, I'm an *incompetent* person!" You can really obsess about this—and thus perform very poorly.

If, however, you force yourself to focus only on the *content* of your acting, reciting, or singing—on the character you are playing, the poem you are reciting, or the words and music of the song you are singing—you will tend to distract yourself from *how* you are doing, and you will therefore, at least temporarily, be much less anxious. In fact, you can get so absorbed in the content of your presentation that you can completely forget *how* you are doing—and, for the time being at least, you are completely without anxiety. That's the way the human mind often works—to be so absorbed in one thing that it ceases to worry about another.

You can use many kinds of distraction to temporarily stop yourself from worrying. Meditation, Yoga, Edmund Jacobsen's

Progressive Relaxation Exercise, biofeedback, reading, entertainment, watching sports—almost anything will work as long as it requires you to really focus on something other than your worry.

Take Jacobsen's Progressive Relaxation Exercise, for example. You concentrate on relaxing one set of your muscles at a time, from your toe muscles to your head muscles. While concentrating on your various muscles, you find yourself unable to concentrate on how well you *must* perform and how *awful* it is that you're not doing so well. (For more details of Jacobsen's progressive relaxation technique, you can consult chapter 11 of my book with Chip Tafrate, *How to Control Your Anger Before It Controls You*.)

You can also use Herbert Benson's famous relaxation response, which works as follows: You select a word, such as "peace" or "one" or some phrase that has meaning for you. Sit in a comfortable position and close your eyes and relax your muscles. Breathe slowly and naturally. As you exhale, keep repeating the word or phrase you have selected. Focus on your breathing, your relaxing, and on the soothing word or phrase you use. Try to disregard intrusive thoughts, particularly worrisome thoughts. If they intrude, remain relaxed and passive. Try this relaxation response for ten to twenty minutes, once or twice a day.

So, again, whenever you want to stop your anxiety in its tracks, you can use some of the many forms of cognitive distraction that are available. Just focus on some pleasant task or involvement and you will find it difficult to also worry. However, distraction is no miracle cure for anxiety because it rarely helps you change your anxiety-creating *philosophy*. You tend to return to your old ways after your relaxation method has ended.

For more permanent control of your anxiety before it controls you, however, by all means use several of the other methods you will find in this book, especially the vigorous and persistent Disputing of your main Irrational Beliefs that largely create your anxiety and panic.

11

Using Reframing Methods

One of the main reasons you, like other people, become very anxious is that you misperceive or exaggerate the As, the Adversities, in the ABCs of emotional disturbance. Thus, because an airplane crash is dramatic and unexpected, you think that planes are very dangerous. Actually, fewer than 300 people are killed year after year in plane crashes while 60,000 people are killed in automobile accidents. Yet many more people are panicked about taking a plane ride than they are about riding in cars.

Again, practically no one dies or is injured by being rejected in love—though a few foolishly kill themselves. Yet, more people are anxious about such rejection than about the loss of money or a job. It is because they inaccurately think, "Now that my beloved has rejected me, I'll *never* find a good lover again!"

Exaggeration, misperception, and false attributions that frequently lead to your anxiety can be checked and reconsidered. Then, too, they can be reframed.

A CASE OF ANXIETY ABOUT CRITICISM

Marilyn, one of my REBT clients, "saw" that every time someone frowned or laughed, they were frowning or laughing at her personally. She interpreted that as a "terrible" Adversity (A) and, as a Consequence (C), she felt anxious. Of course, there were many reasons why people might be frowning or laughing, most of which had nothing to do with her. But she was so anxious about the possibility of being criticized that she "saw" almost anything people did as reflecting serious criticism of her. So she led a chronically anxious life.

I first helped Marilyn to see that even if people *were* criticizing her, it was not their criticism (A) that made her feel extremely anxious (C). Instead, it was mainly her Belief (B), "I *absolutely must not* be criticized by others! If I am, it means they thoroughly despise me, think I am a hopeless dimwit, and will tell others about me. How *awful*! I *can't bear* their criticism!"

While helping Marilyn discover and Dispute (D) her Irrational Beliefs (IBs), I also showed her how to check up on and reframe her Adversities (As). Did everyone who frowned or laughed really direct this form of expression at *her*? Weren't they quite likely doing so for reasons that had nothing to do with her? Did every frown or laugh actually mean that people despised her?

In doing this kind of reflecting, Marilyn soon saw that most people's frowns and laughs had little to do with her—and some of these people actually favored her, as when they laughed at her jokes and viewed her as being witty. Reframing people's frowning and laughing in this manner, as well as Disputing her Irrational Beliefs about the *horror* of being criticized, helped Marilyn to become much less anxious.

You, too, can check the Adversities that seemingly occur in your life to see if they actually exist or whether you have imagined or exaggerated them. Using REBT, you can also manage to see *real* Adversities, including rather grim ones, as a *challenge* instead of a *horror*. Thus, you can view the loss of a job as an *opportunity* to get a better one or to get some more training for a better career. You can see the "terrible" breakup of a relationship as the possibility of experiencing other relationships and finding a partner who is more suitable for you than the one who left you.

In the final analysis, if you use REBT conscientiously, you can see even the most unfortunate Adversities that may occur in your life—such as being afflicted with cancer or the death of close relatives—as human tragedies but hardly devastating horrors. In this way, you can prepare yourself for the worst possibilities that are likely to plague you and still be determined to cope with them and lead a reasonably happy life. Taking the *challenge* of grim Adversity and seeing that if it happens you can still be proactive is one of the best attitudes you can acquire—a gift you can give yourself.

12

Using Problem-Solving Methods to Control Your Anxiety

Anxiety tends to overwhelm and control you when you have serious practical problems and life stresses and cannot figure out how to deal with them or solve them. When you tell yourself that you *must* find a quick, easy, or complete solution to them, you tend to panic. The less you *demand* absolute solutions to your problems and the more you calmly look for possible solutions to them and experiment calmly until you find some that work, the less severe will be the anxiety you will feel.

REBT also helps you with effective problem-solving methods. Usually, it first enables you to stop your unrealistic demanding that you must find quick and perfect solutions to your problems. Then, when you stop panicking in this respect, it shows you how to do more efficient problem-solving. Can REBT teach you how to teach yourself effective problem-solving? Yes, it shows you how to use several rules and techniques that are frequently employed in business and organizational management when you are confronted with almost any kind of problem-solving or decision-making.

A CASE OF ANXIETY ABOUT MAKING PERSONAL DECISIONS

Let me tell you about Manny, who ran a successful retail business and made decisions fairly easily. After all, it was only money he had to make or lose, and if he lost some today, he was pretty sure he could make it up tomorrow. No problem!

About his personal life, though, Manny sweated blood. He thought that he *absolutely had to* pick the right wife, send his children to the best schools, take care of his aging parents so that they would be in perfect health and live forever, and be the most popular person among his many friends. If he failed to do marvelously well in any aspect of his personal life, he thought he lost status in his own and others' eyes, and considered himself an idiot and a worm. Yes, no matter how competent in business he was, and how much people therefore looked up to him, Manny was anxious about personal inadequacy.

Manny's difficulty in the personal area, as you may suspect by what you have learned about REBT by now, stemmed from his insistence that he *absolutely must* do what he considered the right things or else he was a total failure. His business achievements just didn't matter if his personal decisions turned out to be stupid or wrong. In his REBT sessions, I helped him to see that, especially in the personal area, he couldn't guarantee success, for his personal relations largely depended not only on what he did with other people but also how they individually reacted to him. And, of course, he had no control over their reactions. Thus, he could treat his friends very well—and they could still choose to dislike him and put him down. Likewise, he could pick the "right" college for his children and they could still refuse to do their work and drop out of school. Depending on other people's "good" reactions was, therefore, a futile exercise for him.

Manny used REBT to Dispute his Irrational Beliefs and to overcome much of his anxiety about solving his personal problems. Then, I showed him that he intuitively knew how to solve practical business problems but he hadn't quite systematized his methods of doing so. I examined some of the problem-solving processes he had used to make his better business decisions. Then, I indicated how these same processes could be used to solve personal problems.

The problem-solving processes I showed Manny are ones you can use yourself to make business, personal, and other practical decisions. These processes have been outlined by several cognitive-behavioral psychologists, including Donald Meichenbaum, G. Spivack and M. Shure, Thomas D'Zurilla, and Arthur and Christina Nezu. The processes can be summarized as follows:

Analyze the problem situation. See what the obvious solutions are and where the difficulties lie.

Consider a few solutions but also consider some alternatives.

Try a number of different solutions, first in your head, then, if possible, in practice.

Check each potential solution to see if it works, and if it works better than other answers.

Seek better and new solutions, even if some you have arrived at seem to work.

Keep assuming that at least one solution is possible. Continue to seek alternative solutions. Don't give up easily.

Define a troubling situation or the stressor as a problem that probably can be solved.

Set realistic goals that will solve or reduce a problem.

Imagine how other people might resolve a problem.

Look at the advantages and disadvantages of the solutions you consider.

When you come up with likely strategies and actions to solve the problem, rehearse them in your head.

Experimentally try out what seems to be the best solution. Check your results.

Expect some degree of failure and some disadvantages even for good solutions.

Even if you fail to find a good solution, congratulate and reward yourself for trying.

13

Using Unconditional
Self-Acceptance (USA)

As I have been noting throughout this book, you can easily see and
Dispute your Irrational Beliefs that lead to anxiety, but if you do so
only intellectually—or lightly—you may well have difficulty in
giving them up. This is because you have the ability to hold
Rational and Irrational Beliefs at one and the same time. Thus, you
can *lightly* believe, "I don't *have* to be good at sports and am an okay
person when I fail at them." At the same time, you can *strongly*
believe, "If I am really poor at sports I am a totally inept and weak
person!" If so, your stronger and more persistent Beliefs usually
win out, even though you *also* hold the weaker Rational Beliefs.
What is worse, you may unconsciously hold your IB while you
consciously and awarely hold your RB. Rather confusing, isn't it?

When you have great difficulty Disputing your irrational musts
and changing them to rational preferences, REBT assumes that you
often have strong underlying IBs, of which you may or may not be
aware. Therefore, REBT includes many emotive-evocative and
experiential methods that help you tackle these IBs and change
them. This chapter describes some of the main, vigorous, emotional methods of using REBT. These are not to be used instead of
the thinking methods I have been describing but in concert with
them.

Following the lead of some of the ancient Asian philosophers—
especially, Gautama Buddha, and Lao-Tsu—the Christian phi-

losophy of accepting the sinner but not the sin, and the existential philosophy of Martin Heidigger, Jean-Paul Sartre, Martin Buber, Viktor Frankl, and Carl Rogers, REBT helps people to use unconditional self-acceptance. This is a radically different view from traditional, conditional self-acceptance or self-esteem. Conditional self-esteem is exactly that. According to its concepts, you esteem yourself *on the condition* that you perform well and are approved by significant other people. As noted sociologist George Herbert Mead pointed out, your approval of yourself very much depends on the reflected appraisal of others.

For the most part, this works very poorly. First, being a fallible human, you often perform quite badly. Second, even if you perform well at important tasks, many people may choose to dislike you for one reason or another. Third, even if you perform very well and are generally liked by others *today*, how do you know how successful and well liked you will be *tomorrow*? Conditional self-esteem is always—yes, always—in doubt. It causes more anxiety, and more feelings of personal worthlessness, than probably any other aspect of human living.

THE EXISTENTIAL SOLUTION TO UNCONDITIONAL SELF-ACCEPTANCE

To combat the pitfalls of conditional self-esteem, REBT emphasizes the attitudes of unconditional self-acceptance (USA). It shows you two main ways of acquiring this philosophy. First, you can choose the existentialist position and convince yourself, "I am a person with intentions and choices, as are all humans. As long as I am alive, a member of the human race, and in some ways a unique person, I *choose* to accept myself unconditionally, *whether or not* I perform well and *whether or not* I am approved by others. I *prefer* to succeed in my projects and I *prefer* to have others' approval. But my worth as a person doesn't *depend* on accomplishment or approbation. It only depends on my *choosing* to be alive, human, and unique."

This existentialist solution to unconditional self-acceptance is quite safe, almost guaranteed. For as long as you are alive, you will be human and will be unique. Therefore, if your accepting yourself *only* depends on that, you will always be able to define yourself, or choose yourself, as a "good" rather than a "bad" person. Neat, eh? Your self-acceptance is made to depend on the indisputable facts of your aliveness, your being human, and your uniqueness—not on *anything* else! So your self-acceptance is pretty secure—as long as you live, you can accept yourself.

Unfortunately, the existential solution to the problem of human worth is philosophically and scientifically debatable. For you essentially say, "I am a good person because I am human, alive, and a unique individual." But a philosopher or scientist could object, "Yes, I see that you are human, alive, and unique. Those are facts and can hardly be contradicted. But being human, alive, and unique really have nothing to do with your worth. You are *defining* your worth as a person as good, but it could just as well be defined as bad or as neutral. You cannot prove or falsify your axiom that your humanness makes you good. You can *choose* to believe it but you could also choose to believe the opposite—namely, that you are bad because you are alive and human. *Definitions* like this cannot be factually upheld."

So your contending that you are "a good person" because you are human is an axiom that is not provable or disprovable. You can prove, perhaps, that your existential definition of yourself as "good" is practical, and will get you better results than if you define yourself as "neutral" or "bad." But we cannot prove that it is factual or "true," just that it works. So, again, it is a questionable proposition.

THE ELEGANT SOLUTION TO UNCONDITIONAL SELF-ACCEPTANCE

REBT gives you a second way of unconditionally accepting yourself that supposedly gets around the arbitrary, definitional way of achieving USA. Using this method, you set up your goals and purposes—for example, to remain alive now that you are living

and to be happy (to enjoy relatively little pain and much pleasure)—and then you rate or evaluate all your thoughts, feelings,
and behaviors *in terms of these goals and purposes.* Thus, you rate your
thought "I am a worthwhile person, who deserves to live and
enjoy" as "good" because it is a thought that helps you stay alive
and to enjoy life, and you rate your thought "I am a worthless
person who deserves to suffer and die" as "bad" because it sabotages
your purposes. Similarly, you rate your feelings of pleasure at
succeeding at a task as "good" and your displeasure at failing at this
task as "bad" because this mode of thought helps you to be happy.
Also, you rate your refraining from overeating as "good" and your
indulging in overeating as "bad" because such behavior helps you
survive and be in good health.

In other words, you can rate or evaluate all your thoughts,
feelings, and behaviors as "good" when they aid your basic goals
and purposes and as "bad" when they sabotage these same goals
and purposes. These ratings enable you to live and be happy
according to your chosen goals and desires. If your desire is to be
miserable and to die soon, you would rate each thought, feeling,
and action in pretty much the opposite "good" and "bad" way.

Okay: Your ratings of your ideas, emotions, and actions help
you achieve your basic goals. So they are useful, or pragmatically
"good." Mind you, these ratings are not good in themselves or bad
in themselves—they fully depend on your goals and purposes. You
choose these goals, and you can change them if you wish. But as
long as you have them, you can rate every thing you do as "good"
or "bad" in regard to them. They are "good" because they aid your
desires, and they are "bad" when they block these desires. That's
the way you see things, and you are, of course, entitled to see them
that way as long as you do not insist that your thoughts, feelings,
and behaviors are "good" or "bad" for someone else, who may well
have different goals and values.

All this seems clear. But, now comes the difficult part—the part
that most humans find trouble achieving and maintaining. It is
relatively easy for you to say "My deeds are good when they aid my
goals and purposes and bad when they block my aims." But

because you are human and are influenced by both your biology and your upbringing, you probably won't find it easy to refuse to give yourself a total rating. You tend, like most humans, to believe that "When my deeds and actions are ineffective or bad, I am a bad person" and that "When my deeds and actions are effective and good I am a good person." The tendency is to rate your total self, your identity, your being as all good or all bad when you do what you believe are good and bad things.

Alfred Korzybski pointed this out in his brilliant book *Science and Sanity* in 1933. In common with practically all humans, you tend to use the *I's of identity* and to rate what you *do* as who you *are*. This is a serious mistake, since it is an inaccurate overgeneralization. You do millions of things during your lifetime: good (aiding your goals) and bad (sabotaging your goals). You are an exceptionally variable, inconsistent, and fallible human being. You choose a purpose, then frequently act against it. You choose not to do something—then frequently do it. Obviously, therefore, you cannot really rate yourself, your essence, your being by any one thing or series of things that you do or do not do. Being many things, millions of things, you cannot possibly be "a good person" or a "bad person." Yet, you continually arrive at these conclusions and damn yourself when you do badly and praise yourself when you do well. As Korzybski said, by responding in such a way, you render yourself "unsane" and will get poor individual and social results all your life.

Also, as Korzybski and a good many other psycholinguists have observed, you have a tendency to put your ideas into language, which seems to be largely a human condition; and then your language itself—which has many advantages over the more primitive languages of the other animals—tends to confuse you and do you in. It creates what Kevin FitzMaurice calls thought–things. It often manufactures objects out of mere thoughts. Thus, you do something well, and you have a thought: "This act helps me and therefore I shall call it good." You tend to forget that your thought *defined* the act as good and you incorrectly say, "The act (thing) *is* good (thought)." You see what factually exists (your act) as *being* good, when you merely thought of it, or defined it, as good.

REBT tends to solve the problem of self-rating by encouraging you to rate your thoughts, feelings, and actions only as good (effective) and bad (ineffective) after you first set up goals and purposes that you want to accomplish. But it then strongly encourages you to stop right there, to say: "This behavior is good for my purposes (and bad if I do not do it). But I refuse to give myself a global, *general*, or total, rating for doing (or not doing) it. It may be good, according to my choice, but I am not a good person for doing it. And it may be bad, according to my desire, but I am not a bad person for doing it."

This may seem to be a simple decision to make on your part—but just try to make it consistently! You will, usually, have little trouble rating your thoughts, feelings, and acts as "good" or as "bad," as you usually know your purposes and know whether your deeds will fulfill them. But once you rate your behaviors as "good" or "bad," you will tend to follow the human condition of also rating yourself, your totality. That is very hard to resist! It seems to be built into the human race by the long process of evolution; and it is also encouraged by practically all human societies and cultures. Our parents, teachers, fairy tales, stories, movies, TV presentations, and so on, strongly encourage us to think that John is doing a good thing when he fights off the lion, wins the princess, scores the winning touchdown in the football championship match, or is kind to his mother. But these "media" also powerfully judge John as a "good person" and urge that we look up to him in that global manner. Moreover, if Mary sasses her parents, is hostile to Prince Charming, or fails in school, our media insist that she is indubitably a "rotten person." We have a natural tendency to overgeneralize from our specific deeds to our general character. In addition, society pushes us to do so.

How can we stop that deadly nonsense? REBT says that, ideally, we'd better by all means stay with rating and evaluating what we think, feel, and do and keep checking our behaviors against our goals, purposes, and desires to see if they get us more of what we want and less of what we don't want. REBT goes on to say that we preferably should refuse to give ourselves global or total ratings. We never *are* good or bad. We merely do good and bad things—again, according to our desires, goals, and values. If we stay with this kind of reasoning, we are much more likely to have our desires fulfilled and not falsely give in to the *I's of identity* and to the vast overgeneralization of rating our essence.

If you, however, find it difficult not to give yourself a generalized, global rating, and to see only your behaviors as "good" and "bad," then you can fall back to the existential solution to this problem of self-rating. Merely say, even though it is definitional and said by fiat, "I am a good person because I exist, because I am human, because I am a unique individual. Period." Say that and stick to it. You cannot prove it and you cannot disprove it factually or empirically. But it will work!

Why is unconditional self-acceptance (USA), such as I have been advocating in this book, so important in controlling your anxiety before it controls you? Because conditional self-acceptance or conditional self-esteem is the root of the worst forms of anxiety. Discomfort anxiety or low frustration tolerance is indeed important. Without any of it, you would not survive for very long. For as a physical organism, you are subject all your life to many possible dangers—such as accidents, disease, attacks by other people, attacks by animals, feuds, and wars. Therefore, you have to be cautious and vigilant to survive. What is more, because you are a thin-skinned animal, you have to be more cautious and vigilant than, say, a thick-skinned animal such as an elephant or rhinoceros.

To aid your self-protection, nature has built into you a fair amount of overconcern and overcaution. Consequently, once you get in a car accident, you may give up driving for a while—or even forever. Once you get attacked on a dark street at 2 A.M., you may avoid going out at night—or even during the day. Evolution is arranged so that a species survives, not so that it will be happy while it survives. The survival of the fittest often means the survival of the most cautious and easily frightened.

Discomfort anxiety, therefore, is life-protective. It urges you to take few risks, to avoid pain, to maintain safety. Frequently, it encourages you to take safety and caution to extremes—and to consequently live an overly restricted and relatively dull life. But you still live.

The worst forms of anxiety, however, frequently do not stem from physical overconcern but from ego-overconcern. They result when you are terribly afraid that you will do some important task poorly and consequently be disapproved of by others.

A remarkably good antidote to this common form of ego-anxiety or potential self-downing is—you guess it!—unconditional self-acceptance (USA). When you really are thoroughly in control of your ego, or self-rating, you are remarkably less anxious about failure and rejection.

A CASE OF EGO-ANXIETY

Take Rita, for example. When I first saw her for Rational Emotive Behavior Therapy, she was beautiful, bright, competent, and especially talented at selling insurance. She was the youngest sales-person in her firm and, undoubtedly, the best. She made at least a quarter of a million dollars in commissions every year, was engaged to be married to a handsome professor of economics who was also a management consultant for several large business organizations, and she had a black belt in karate. But, she was exceptionally socially anxious, partly because her fiancé was continually in the company of outstanding academic and business professionals who were unusually competent and well-read and could talk brilliantly on almost any subject. Rita had only a junior college degree and was in a field (sales) that hardly matched the achievements of most of her fiancé's colleagues. She was sure that they looked down on her, and she was terrified about making verbal mistakes in their presence. She imagined them thoroughly despising her.

Rita had very little discomfort anxiety, as she took on problems and difficulties that others shunned, worked long hours at her job, and forged ahead at her karate classes while competing daringly with the men in her group. But she couldn't stand criticism, and she put herself down severely for making a wrong move with her insurance customers or saying the wrong thing to her fiancé's associates.

At first, Rita argued quite a bit with me about the principles of unconditional self-acceptance. She had made it in her selling career and in her karate training largely because she pushed herself strongly to keep doing well, and she was, therefore, able to perform better than most other people, both men and women, against whom she was competing. She therefore held to the idea that achievement was exceptionally important and that one was a good person only if one performed better than other people who were naturally adept and talented. Although I agreed with her that achievement was very important in life (if you made it important) and that you got many benefits (such as monetary rewards) from achieving outstandingly, I insisted that it had nothing to do with your personal worth, unless you mistakenly thought that it did. Why was this a mistake? Because, as shown in Rita's own case, even when she achieved well in many important areas, she was always afraid of not maintaining her accomplishments in the future. And in certain areas, such as academic ones, where she was not an outstanding achiever, she had severe feelings of anxiety about *herself* and not merely about her *performances*, and she was, consequently, very anxious.

I must say that I am pretty good at talking people out of the concept of conditional self-acceptance, because, as I tell them, it won't work unless they are perfect—and will be perfect for the rest of their lives. For, as fallible humans, they can always do poorly—even though at first they may do very well. I wasn't succeeding at convincing Rita of this, for she really did very well at several things and rarely fell back. But I was more successful in showing her that even if she always did remarkably well, her dire need for people's approval would not work. For other people, particularly out of jealousy, could easily turn on her because she performed so well. Several of the other insurance salespeople, for example, disliked her because she did better than they did. Several men at her karate class disliked her when she excelled over them. Several women, including some of her friends, were jealous of her because of her good looks. No matter what she did, she couldn't win with these kinds of people. I pounded away at this and, at first, made good inroads in getting Rita to see that excellence wasn't always acclaimed. Her superiority actually could get her into trouble with people who weren't as good at certain things as she was.

Then, I also showed Rita why, for several other reasons, people might reject her even though she did remarkably well. They might not like her particular kind of looks, for example. Or they might be prejudiced against her for religious or racial reasons. Or they might be angry people who hated almost everyone.

I finally convinced Rita that her perfectionistic philosophy, in which everyone would like her for everything she did, would never succeed, even though she was respected and admired far more than the average woman was. Still, she was anxious that this respect and admiration might not continue; she was actually more anxious than many women who had far fewer talents and were less attractive than she.

As Rita gave up the dire need for social approval, she greatly reduced her performance anxiety. She read some of my books, *A Guide to Rational Living, How to Control Your Anger Before It Controls You,* and *Reason and Emotion in Psychotherapy,* as well as one of my pamphlets, "Psychotherapy and the Value of a Human." These all helped her chip away at her perfectionistic need for accomplishment. She finally "got it," and she said at one of our closing sessions: "It suddenly hit me. I saw that all definitions of goodness and badness are choices that we make, and that we could well make quite different choices. They are all really, as you call it, definitional. Even when we rate our performances, we do so by choosing certain goals—such as to get an A in a course—and then rate whether or not we achieve that goal. Someone else might easily choose to get an A + or a B, and therefore their performance rating would be different from our own rating. So we choose our goals and rate our behaviors accordingly. Then we choose to rate ourselves totally, in regard to how we measure our performances. That is particularly definitional, our general rating of ourselves, for we do it arbitrarily and could choose not to do it. But, as you say, we have a strong tendency to do so, and we do it. Stupidly, foolishly! Well, not me any longer. I'm still going to rate my performances, but I'm going to try very hard to stop rating myself. I don't *have* to do so and I now see how much harm it does me. So I'll do my best not to. I won't always succeed, I'm sure, but I'll definitely do it much less than I've been doing it all my life. Definitely!"

Rita did exactly what she said she would do. She decreased her self-rating enormously, and when she fell back to it, she stopped doing it again. She kept after herself and evolved from one of the worst self-evaluators I had ever met to one of the least. She fully understood both the grim results of demanding approval from others and demanding perfect performance from herself in order to prove she was "a good or bad person." She became a person who constantly performed good and bad acts—acts that helped or hindered her goals—but who rarely rated herself, her personhood, any longer.

If you wish to do so, you can follow Rita's path toward unconditional self-acceptance. Again, you can arbitrarily rate yourself as a "good person" or a "worthy individual" just because you exist, are human, and are unique. But you can also take Rita's more elegant path and rarely give yourself a global rating at all. You just accept your aliveness, your humanness, and your uniqueness without giving it an overgeneralized total evaluation.

By doing so, you will be much less anxious. You still may be over-apprehensival about being hurt, diseased, or killed; you may retain some of your discomfort anxiety; but your performance anxiety and approval anxiety will largely go. You will still, I hope, strive to perform important projects well and to win important people's respect. For in doing these things, you are likely to fulfill more of your desires and suffer fewer frustrations. But *want* doesn't mean *desperately need*. Not at all. Not needing success or approval, while still distinctly desiring them, will remove much of your need for certainty, for guarantees, for absolutely proving your worth as a person to yourself or to others. Try it and see!

14

Using Unconditional Acceptance of Others to Control Your Anxiety

Humans are distinctly social animals and rarely live completely alone. When you are healthy, you tend to get along with other people—with your family, your relatives, your friends, your schoolmates, your neighbors, your coworkers. You were probably born and reared to do so, and your very existence, to a considerable degree, depends on your relationships with others. As an infant and as a young child, you obviously need other people to care for you. As an adolescent and as an adult, you can very largely get along by yourself. But not completely, because you would have a hard time growing your own food, building your own home, weaving your own clothes, and doing innumerable other things that keep you alive and in comfort. As an older person, you frequently lose some amount of self-sufficiency, and therefore, you require more help from others than you did when you were young.

Besides helping you stay alive, be comfortable, and function fairly well, other people often provide you pleasure. You can definitely enjoy speaking with them, loving them, having sex with them, working with them, participating in games and sports with them, and engaging in many other social pursuits. Why? Because you are human, and being human, your life is much better with companionship, sex, love, cooperation. It is your biological nature to be part of the human family.

Given your social nature, it is highly desirable that you get along with other humans and have close relationships with some of them. Although it is true that as an adult you can get by with minimal human relationships, and even survive if you are something of a hermit, chances are you will do much better if you have friendly and loving relationships with others. You will lead a more interesting, creative, fuller, and happier life—and one that will contribute to reducing your anxiety.

CONTROLLING YOUR ANGER BEFORE
IT CONTROLS YOU

Unfortunately, it is not always easy to control your anger. There are many kinds of people in the world, and quite a few of them often treat you badly, unfairly, and angrily. These people may be enraged, depressed, moody, difficult, even psychopathic. They may think they have good reason for mistreating you. Some of them cheat you or do you in competitively because they want to get what they want and don't care whether you get what you want. Others, seemingly without good cause, mistreat you or block your desires. What do you do then?

Well, unfortunately, you have your own angry tendencies, both innate and acquired. You are likely to feel enraged at them, and you may decide to seek revenge. Does this do you any good or right the wrong that others have presumably caused you? Very rarely! Love begets love and rage begets rage. If you feel, rightly or wrongly, that others have used you unkindly, you first of all criticize their behavior and make it clear that you think it's wrong. Second, you frequently condemn them as total persons. That is what your anger almost always is: first, objection to others' "poor" or "wrong" behavior, and second, serious condemnation and damnation of them.

In other words, just as you tend to overgeneralize and condemn yourself for your own "bad" thoughts, feelings, and acts, so do you similarly overgeneralize and condemn others when, in your view, they have acted badly. You make the mistake of condemning the sinner as well as the sin, and you frequently get in trouble when you do so.

First of all, as Chip Tafrate and I show in our book *How to Control Your Anger Before It Controls You*, your anger, rage, and fury negatively affect your own efficiency and health. Anger motivates you to act against things and people you dislike, but it often propels you to do so impulsively, blindly, and ineffectually. When you lash out in a rage against someone or something that you find obnoxious, you hardly plot accurately to change it or remove it. Instead, you do so in an overdetermined, frantic manner that leads to poor choices and inept tactics, so that you don't often effectively correct conditions that you deplore. You frequently make them worse.

Second, anger tends to stir up your entire physical system, which can lead to a host of psychosomatic problems, including high blood pressure, headaches, gastrointestinal problems, muscular ailments, and even the sabotaging of your immune system. The results can be grim. We include a whole chapter in *How to Control Your Anger Before It Controls You* on the physical consequences of rage, and you might do well to read it.

Third, as noted above, anger, for the most part, leads to fights, to feuds, to wars, and even to genocide. Of all the human ills caused by all the human emotions, anger seems to be the leading cause of violence, murder, and a host of other evils. Just read the newspapers and watch television every day!

Various ways of releasing anger have been promoted by many psychologists, most of these ways, dubious. The cathartic theory of the psychoanalysts and many experiential therapists holds that if you let your anger out and really shout and scream and perhaps pulverize a few punching bags, the release will prevent you from doing real harm. I disagree. Several hundred experiments have shown that the more you express your anger, either verbally or physically, the more you tend to elevate it. Other psychological approaches advise you to take a passive, nonresistant attitude toward others' aggression, and they will treat you kindly in return. This approach may stop a few people in their tracks, but others will take advantage of your passivity to abuse you in an even worse manner. Besides, your passive and compliant attitude, instead of truly releasing your anger, will temporarily suppress it, often making you still angrier.

There are also various forms of cognitive and physical distraction, such as meditation, Yoga, and progressive relaxation of your muscles. Will these take care of your anger? Yes, temporarily, for these distractions may divert you from your angry feelings and relax you. Underneath, however, you will still most probably maintain your anger-creating philosophies, and they will return to stir your stomach and raise your blood pressure when the people who abuse you do so once again.

USING UNCONDITIONAL OTHER-ACCEPTANCE (UOA)

The best answer to enraging yourself, however, is largely philosophic—as REBT says it is. Anger is mainly the grandiose demand that people absolutely *should not*, *must not* treat you the vile way that they are supposedly doing. If you will truly give up this demand, you will not only minimize your anger at present injustices, but you will prepare yourself to be much less prone to outbursts of rage in the future. People, to be sure, often cheat you, assault you, and go back on their promises to you. So, almost instantly, you become disappointed and displeased about their actions. But when you are angry, you go beyond that disappointment and displeasure to feelings of rage by insisting that the people who make you angry absolutely must not be the way they are and must not do the things that they do. It is your grandiose insistence that they behave "properly" and "fairly" that creates your anger—and not their poor behavior.

REBT shows you many cognitive, emotive, and behavioral ways of stopping your anger in its tracks and reducing your tendency to incense yourself all over again. As I noted previously, I have an entire book devoted to showing people how to use these REBT methods—*How to Control Your Anger Before It Controls You*. Some of the main points in this book are described in the next few paragraphs.

The main method of minimizing your rage is to learn and practice the principles of UOA—unconditional other-acceptance. USA, unconditional self-acceptance, as we learned, consists of fully accepting yourself, while still acknowledging and working at changing your flaws, failings, and mistakes. You clearly see your errors, because you know you will not beat yourself for having them. You see the things you do to needlessly afflict others, but you never castigate yourself for doing them. As noted in the previous chapter, ideally, you only rate and evaluate your thoughts, feelings, and behaviors in relation to your goals and purposes, but you refuse to rate your personhood as a whole. If you skipped over this chapter, read it now to see the details of unconditional self-acceptance, USA, and how you can achieve it.

Unconditional other-acceptance (UOA) is basically the same concept applied to other people. Yes, all other people, including those you dislike and who treat you and perhaps others badly. In plain English, it means accepting the sinner but not the sin. So when people act immorally, unethically, or badly to you (and others), you observe their thoughts, emotions, and deeds, tentatively judge that they are "improper" and "wrong," but rigorously refrain from rating them as a whole from labeling them as bad, wrong, or inept people.

This is not an easy thing to do. As a human animal reared in a social group, you have learned a great deal about which behaviors are "good" and which are "bad," and you normally rate these behaviors the way you were taught. Thus, you usually rate stealing, disloyalty, laziness, lying, and many other human traits as "bad," and you rate the opposite of these traits as "good."

That is not much of a problem, and actually, it does a lot of good. For, if you see people's improper and antisocial behavior as "bad" or "wrong" and your judgment agrees with most others in your social group, you may be able to encourage, help, and teach people who act immorally to be more moral—that is, providing you do not excoriate them severely for their behavior.

Unconditional other-acceptance is perhaps not the way to abolish all anger, fights, murders, feuds, and wars, but it will go a long way toward solving these very difficult human problems. For if you are willing to accept people but not some of the things they do, and never insist they must not perpetrate some of their more unfortunate and deplorable deeds, your temper will cool, and you can more sensibly consider whether their doings were absolutely wrong and mistaken.

If, for example, you were sure that someone cheated you out of some money, you would criticize her wrong deed but would not, given unconditional other-acceptance, become enraged. Instead, you would feel disappointment. Then, with this healthy negative feeling, you would be able to consider whether she actually *had* cheated you or merely made a mistake in her calculations; would be able to guess at some of the reasons why she had acted this way (say, her child was ill and needed an expensive medical treatment); would be able to figure out some way in which you could get her to reimburse you; and would have the calmness and ability to see several things about her cheating you that at least partially excused the act. You would then have a much better chance of getting her to rectify her behavior, to work out some kind of compromise, to prevent her from becoming your enemy for life, and to help her change her ways so that she would not cheat others. UOA and the feelings of forgiveness to which it often leads aid you in acting more sanely and sensibly about almost any unfairness by others and thereby encourages them to stop acting that unfairly to you and to other people.

Aside from helping you deal with your anger and rage, does UOA have much to say about your feelings of anxiety? Indeed it does. For when you are seriously angry at people, you tend to be anxious about: (1) whether your judgment of their deeds is really correct; (2) whether you were too severe on them; (3) whether your anger will get out of control and make you do some very foolish things; (4) whether the people you are angry at will, in their turn, become angry at you and go to extremes to hurt you; and (5) whether you are a nasty, mean-spirited person who deserves to be condemned for letting yourself become so enraged.

As I have demonstrated in this book, your anxiety very often stems from downing yourself as a person, and it includes feelings of inadequacy. But it often stems from damning other people as persons and not merely judging their poor behaviors. Anxiety and anger, therefore, have much of the same damnation philosophy. When you indulge in anxiety, you also encourage your indulging in anger, and when you indulge in anger, you often encourage your indulgence in anxiety. Both feelings stem from the overgeneralized notion that people absolutely should not do wrong and that they are wholly to be condemned when they do. Sometimes people call self-downing "anger at myself." Sometimes they call anger "downing of other people." The two feelings have philosophical intertwinings, and it is better, if you are prone to demeaning yourself and others, that you avoid both destructive emotions.

A CASE OF ANGER AND SOCIAL ANXIETY

Martin wasn't particularly interested in controlling his anger; he thought it was quite justified and that it did him a lot of good. He worked as a bodyguard for a wealthy manufacturer, and he kept his position largely because his boss, who was assertive enough in his business, was deathly afraid of physical combat. Martin was hired along with two other around-the-clock guards to make sure that the manufacturer didn't encounter any assaults in his rough-and-tumble union negotiations. Martin had been raised on the streets of East Harlem, was a gang leader at the age of 13, spent some time as a prizefighter, and was afraid of nothing—at least physically. Emotionally, however, he had severe social anxiety, and he was especially afraid that women would notice that he stuttered slightly and was very shy. So, although he was 6 feet 3 inches tall, handsome, a great dancer, and was brighter than you would expect a bodyguard to be, he rarely tried to date women and hated himself for not getting into relationships with them, as all his male friends easily did.

At first, Martin had trouble with the idea of unconditional self-acceptance. His familial and neighborhood upbringing had notably emphasized competence and achievement, especially physical prowess. As a youthful gang leader and later as a prizefighter, he had always won respect and approval because he was big, muscular, and addicted to fits of temper. He had strong opinions and was always ready to back them up with his fists. So, his male friends looked up to him and pretty much did his bidding. That is why he thought that his anger did him much good and little harm.

I had trouble, at first, teaching Martin the REBT concept of unconditional self-acceptance. He grasped it intellectually, but he was far from practicing it. He got so much more acceptance from others for his physical ability that he didn't seem to need much more self-acceptance. He also took good care of his mother and father, who were poor and uneducated, and his younger sister, Sylvia, who had lost one of her arms in an automobile accident and who required a good deal of support. So, he felt that he was a fine son and brother, and he had considerable conditional esteem for himself on those counts.

I was soon able to show Martin that his social anxiety with women belied the self-esteem that he seemed to have in other respects and that he was basing his worth as a man, first, on his physical prowess, which worked to some extent. But, second, he was basing it on his inability to talk fluently to women and to be confident in their presence. This didn't work for him; he panicked in their presence and was never able to go on more than a few dates before each woman rejected him. Hence, he defined himself as a total failure and he continued to be socially anxious.

I first helped Martin to see that even his confidence with men was highly conditional. It was based on his unusual ability to handle himself physically. Those like himself looked up to him. I helped him realize that if he were small and puny, or even if he were big and brawny but was not good at mastering other males with his fists, he would quickly put himself down and feel like a ninny. He mainly respected himself for the same reason that certain other males respected him—his physical power. Without it, he would be nothing.

I showed Martin that in his particular circles, it was fine to be admired for his ability to stand up for himself and fight anyone who seriously disagreed with him. His assertiveness in that respect was okay. But, his value *as a person* should not be based on any special kind of competence, as he made it be. While physical strength made him a "real man," in his and others' eyes, his weaknesses in the other important areas of "manliness"—his lack of competence in relating to women—made him a "weak man," a loser. If he was going to base his human worth on his competence in one important area, it could well make him "worthless" in this other important "manly" area, where he lacked competence. He would have to be completely competent in order to be a "good person."

I really shocked Martin when I showed him that his caring for his parents and his sister was again a good trait by almost any regular social standard. But it, too, didn't really make him a "good person"—merely a person who acted very well in that particular area. To be a "good person" by his achievement standards, he would have to act well in practically *all* areas. That wasn't very likely!

I was making some progress in helping Martin to accept himself unconditionally, to enjoy his good traits but not attach his personal worth to them, when I took the risk of tackling his other "good" trait, his being prone to intimidating people with his anger. He was very proud of the fact that, when he was young, he had stood up to his main gang rival, Alfredo, and refused to be intimidated by Alfredo's sneaky, underhanded tactics. Alfredo, unlike Martin, didn't stand up for what he thought was right and back up his views with his body and his fists. Instead, Alfredo got in good with older, organized-crime-like characters and used their power to make himself somewhat powerful. Alfredo lied and cheated, if necessary, to control others with their help.

Alfredo still stayed in their old East Harlem neighborhood and was involved in drug dealing and several other rackets. Martin, after he became a boxer, kept himself clean of gang relations, went straight, and moved to mid-Manhattan. But he still visited his old neighborhood, where he had friends —and he often fought with Alfredo to prevent Alfredo from taking advantage of some of the weaker people in the neighborhood, some of whom were Martin's friends.

On one particular occasion, Martin stopped Alfredo from exploiting Tony, a friend of Martin's. Martin had a physical confrontation with Alfredo, lost his temper, and told Alfredo that if he bothered Tony in any way again, he would cut off Alfredo's balls and leave him bleeding to death. Alfredo, who actually was an inch taller than Martin and physically strong, had stood up to Martin, at first, but then he had shown his cowardly colors and retreated. Martin was enthusiastic about his great, and perhaps final, victory over "this slimy rat."

I acknowledged that, in defending his friend Tony from Alfredo's harassment, Martin was probably doing a good thing. But, I also pointed out that Martin was hating Alfredo as a person and not merely hating his thuggish behavior. Alfredo, I indicated, had always had his severe problems. He had weakly protected himself by kowtowing to older, more powerful hoodlums. He had not, as had Martin, held his own counsel and fought for what he really believed in, but he had copped out instead and taken over the ways and attitudes of organized-crime characters. Though his behavior wasn't admirable, he was a very fallible person, a victim of his innate tendencies and his poor environment, and he need not be totally damned. In fact, Alfredo was himself displaying a bigoted, intimidating attitude to people weaker than he, and he was controlling them with the strength he got from his powerful associates. If Martin, therefore, used his own physical power and his temper to cow Alfredo and put him meekly in his place, he was himself using intimidating tactics, was trying to make Alfredo feel like a worm, and in a sense was taking advantage of Alfredo's weaknesses. Alfredo's intimidating Tony was bad and could be justifiably stopped. But Martin's intimidating Alfredo had a similar unfairness about it and wasn't exactly the wonderful behavior that Martin was making it out to be.

I didn't have an easy time helping Martin to see that his anger against Alfredo wasn't entirely a good deed on his part and that it had real disadvantages. It wasn't fair to Alfredo, since it condemned Alfredo in toto, not merely some of the things he did; and it wasn't fair to Martin, as it made him out a great hero when he was doing a questionable thing. His damnation of Alfredo, like practically all damning of humans, wasn't accurate and, in some respects, was doing harm. Consequently, I advised him not to hang on to his anger.

My persistence paid off. Martin was finally able to see that damning Alfredo for Alfredo's poor performances was neither ethical nor accurate. Martin said he would work on it.

And he did. He gave the matter some real thought, and a few weeks later he came up with an answer. He made an appointment to see Alfredo about Alfredo continually trying to intimidate Tony. Alfredo was visibly frightened at their meeting because he thought that Martin, as usually was the case, was going to physically threaten him and punish him for controlling Tony. But instead of being bellicose and threatening, Martin explained that he didn't like the way Alfredo was treating Tony, and he felt that it was quite wrong. But he decided not to damn Alfredo for his behavior and was merely going to try to convince Alfredo, without anger, how wrong it was. "I know," said Martin, "that you think you're acting rightly, when I think that you're unfairly intimidating Tony. Both of us can't possibly be right, and I'm assuming that I am. All right, so you're wrong. I am going to accept that point, but I'm also going to accept that you're a fallible human who has a right to be wrong at times. So I'm assessing your behavior as bad and trying to get you to change it, but I'm no longer damning you, as I've done for years. As I said, you think that it's right, and you're entitled to that view. I think it's wrong. Let us agree to disagree. But even if you keep it up and continue to act badly with Tony, as I definitely think you're doing, I'm still going to try to convince you to change. But I am not going to waste my time, and disrupt my own feelings, by hating you. As the Bible says, I am going to do my best to acknowledge that in Tony's case, you are sinning, but accept you, the sinner, with the sin. So I'm dropping my hatred against you and will do my very best to just hate what you do."

Alfredo, to say the least, was flabbergasted by Martin's pronoun-cement and especially by Martin's lack of the rage that usually accompanied his differences with Alfredo. Alfredo even admitted that he may have pushed Tony too hard in some respects, and that he would reconsider some of his actions toward him. Martin and Alfredo's conversation ended on a surprisingly amicable and largely cooperative note.

It certainly did wonders for Martin himself. He left Alfredo, thought over their conversation, and for the first time in his life, felt kindly and forgiving toward him. He saw Alfredo as an excep-tionally screwed-up person who could be expected to act in a screwed-up manner. Martin actually felt some pity for Alfredo—for his nature and for the poor upbringing he had had—and Martin was particularly relieved to be able to drop his belligerent, hostile attitude toward Alfredo, which he had carried since their childhood.

Better yet, Martin did some hard thinking about himself and his nonforgiveness toward himself. He saw that his damnation of himself was along almost exactly the same lines as his defaming Alfredo as a person, and it was equally spurious. Yes, Martin did some stupid, wrong things, and he was responsible for doing them. That was bad, and he was not going to excuse it. But he, Martin, was a fallible person who would do stupid and wrong things for the rest of his life—not always, of course, but frequently enough. If he forgave Alfredo for the distinctly wrong things that Alfredo kept doing with Tony and with many other people, then Martin could certainly forgive himself for his own bad acts!

So Martin had a real conversion in regard to the damning of people for their poor behaviors. First, he worked on fully accepting Alfredo with Alfredo's intimidating actions. Then, partly as a result of that, he worked at fully accepting himself and his own misdemeanors. The one change in attitude and behavior logically led to the other change, and then the second change reinforced the first one. In addition, once Martin stopped downing himself for being shy and unassertive with women, he then was able to work on his shyness itself and to overcome it.

You, too, can achieve this remarkable double change that Martin made in his thinking and his feeling, and in his acting on his thinking and feeling. First, as REBT tells us, humans are human. They are quite fallible. During their lifetimes, they will do many things that will harm themselves and others. Work at forgiving them, though not necessarily their deeds. Damn the latter, if you will, but by no means damn the former. Accept them with their misdeeds—or what you think are their misdeeds—and do your best to help them change for the better. But even if you fail dismally, forgive them as persons who do bad acts, but don't damn them for their deeds.

At the same time, acknowledge your own mistakes, errors, and immoralities according to your normal standards. See them as wrong or mistaken, but don't see yourself as a bad person for having made them. If you work very hard at not damning other people for their wrongdoings and not damning yourself for your own, your two philosophies of acceptance, fully accepting others and fully accepting yourself, will tend to reinforce each other. As pointed out above, minimizing your blaming of yourself and your blaming of other people will not stop you from being completely anxious at all times, but it will reduce that part of anxiety that goes with damning. Which is a hell of a large part!

15

Using Rational Emotive Imagery

I keep insisting in this book that if you ever get to the state where you achieve USA and also unconditionally achieve UOA, you will be well on your way to minimizing your needless anxiety. Most of your needless anxiety, however, stems from your being overconcerned about making mistakes and being disapproved of by other people and of having to be absolutely sure that they will approve of you. So, your achieving USA and UOA will largely take care of those sorts of anxieties.

A third major source of anxiety, as I already pointed out, is discomfort anxiety—your need to have a guarantee that you will not be in danger or be deprived of the things that you really want. This might be called event-concern or world-concern. You not only strongly desire that things and events go your way and thereby satisfy your wishes, but you demand certainty in this respect and insist that conditions, many of which you have no control over, absolutely be the way you want them to be or not be the way you definitely do not want them to be.

Unconditional other-acceptance, if you take it to its logical end, also includes unconditional condition-acceptance. Not only do you continue to want things and events to be the way you desire, but you also very much accept the fact that they may not be that way—in fact, will often be the opposite. You therefore realistically accept the undesirable things when they occur, refuse to whine and scream about them, do your best to change them, and if change is impossible, gracefully live with them.

You have now covered the three main pathways that lead to your anxiety: (1) you accept the unpleasantness of your own mistakes and failures; (2) you also accept the frustrations of other people stopping you from getting what you want or making you get what you don't want; (3) you finally accept the blocks to your desires that things and events put in your way. Voilà—what is there for you to get very anxious about? Very little!

That, of course, is the goal of REBT: not to change your desires and wishes but to persuade you to stop demanding that you absolutely must have what you wish—from yourself, from others, and from the world. You can by all means keep your wishes, preferences, and desires, but, unless you prefer to remain needlessly anxious, not your grandiose demands.

Because your absolutist demands lead to anxiety, REBT strongly advises that you Dispute them—question and challenge them—and turn them back into preferences. To do this and do it solidly, REBT gives you several other forceful emotive methods, as the following story illustrates.

Maxie C. Maultsby Jr. came to study with me in 1968 and also studied, just a few weeks before, with Joseph Wolpe, the famous behavior therapist. He told me that he learned a few useful methods of therapy from Wolpe but was more satisfied with the methods, especially the Disputing of Irrational Beliefs, that he saw me demonstrate as he sat in on my individual and group therapy sessions and attended my regular Friday night workshops. He went back to his residency in psychiatry at Mendota State Hospital in Madison, Wisconsin, and became a rational emotive behavior therapist. Being a creative individual, he originated rational emotive imagery, one of the most effective emotive ways of doing REBT.

In doing rational emotive imagery (REI), you first think of one of the worst things that might happen to you—such as a very important failure or rejection—and you let yourself spontaneously feel whatever you feel when you imagine experiencing this "terrible"

Adversity. Usually, you quickly feel anxious, depressed, self-hating, or self-pitying.

A CASE OF PANIC ABOUT IMPORTANT FAILURE

Let us suppose you feel quite anxious, as did Marion, whenever she imagined herself failing to help a patient in her medical practice and being severely criticized by this patient and perhaps also by her medical colleagues. She felt absolute panic thinking that she gave the patient the wrong diagnosis and the patient actually got worse.

When I used rational emotive imagery with Marion and she imagined failing with a patient and being severely criticized, she got sick to her stomach and started trembling. "Good!" I said, "you are really in touch with your feeling of anxiety. Now feel it as much as you can. Really feel it. Make yourself as anxious and panicked as you can be!"

Marion felt very anxious—indeed, horrified. "Good!" I repeated. "Now, keep the exact same image that's making you anxious. You really failed to diagnose your patient properly and she is getting worse and worse—and she and everyone else is criticizing you for your poor treatment. Now, with the same image, make yourself feel only extremely sorry about your mistaken diagnosis and wrong treatment—only extremely sorry and disappointed, but not anxious. No, not anxious or panicked but only sorry and disappointed."

Marion struggled with changing her feelings and took about two minutes to do so. She finally reported, "I'm now feeling very sorry and disappointed, but not really anxious."

"Good!" I said. "What did you do? How did you make yourself feel only disappointed and sorry about what you did with this patient but not anxious and panicked?"

"I pictured her being very critical of me and telling other physicians that I was treating her badly, and also telling her friends and relatives about her poor treatment by me. But I said to myself, 'That's really unfortunate. I've distinctly messed up and I'm very sorry about that. But now that I've seen how I've misdiagnosed and mistreated her, I'm going to learn by this experience, radically change my diagnosis, and treat her much differently. It's certainly bad that I made this mistake. But that doesn't make me a bad physician or a bad person—just someone who has made a real error and who had better correct it.'"

"Fine!" I said. "That Rational Belief will really work. You'll feel sorry and disappointed, but not horrified and self-downing. Now I want you to do this kind of rational emotive imagery every day for the next thirty days or so. First, imagine the worst and let yourself spontaneously feel horrified and panicked. Then change your Irrational Belief, that you're no damned good and the patient and other people see you that way. Change it to the Rational Belief that you now have and several other coping self-statements that will come to you. Do that every day, at least once a day, until you train yourself to automatically feel sorry and disappointed with your behavior instead of panicked and horrified. As you train yourself to do this, you will come to really believe your Rational Beliefs and disbelieve your Irrational Beliefs, and you will truly change your panicked feelings to those of keen disappointment and sorrow. You can manage to change your own feelings and no longer suffer from out-of-control anxiety. Do so for a couple of minutes every day until you are truly in control of your anxiety."

Marion followed my rational emotive imagery instructions and, within fifteen days, was making herself automatically disappointed and sorry about her "medical misdiagnosis and treatment" instead of horrified and panicked about it. Similarly, you can use REI whenever you feel quite anxious about relationships, sex, school, jobs, sports, or almost anything else. First, track down the main Irrational Beliefs that are creating most of your anxiety—your absolutistic shoulds, oughts, and musts—and Dispute them with the usual kind of realistic, logical, and practical Disputing outlined in this book. Persist until you come up with E, your new Effective Philosophy. Then, to make things much more solid, use rational emotive imagery to imagine one of the things that you frequently make yourself anxious about. Let yourself feel real anxiety—even panic. Then work at changing your anxiety to a feeling of concern, caution, vigilance, sorrow, regret, disappointment, or some other quite healthy negative feeling. You do this largely by changing your irrational demands to healthy preferences—that it would be nice, but hardly necessary, to perform well and/or be approved of by others. Practice this regularly for ten, twenty, or thirty days until you automatically begin to feel healthy negative emotions instead of unhealthy anxiety and panic. Train yourself to be able to feel these healthy rather than unhealthy feelings spontaneously, and thereby cope with the things you are most anxious about.

16

Using Shame-Attacking Exercises to Control Your Anxiety

Soon after I began to use REBT with my clients, in 1955, I realized that shame is the essence of much human disturbance. For when people are ashamed of anything that they think, say, feel, or do, they almost always mean, "I've done the wrong thing and other people will criticize me and put me down for doing it." This self-statement, however, by no means has to lead them to feel shame, embarrassment, or humiliation, because they could follow it up with, "Yes, I've really done something foolish, or stupid, or immoral. Yes, many people who discover this will say that I *shouldn't have done* it and will blame me severely for doing it, but I still don't have to take them too seriously and agree with them that I'm a shameful, bad person. Maybe the thing I did wasn't so very wrong in the first place. Maybe people are condemning me too severely for it. As a fallible human, I can't very well be expected to always do the right thing. So I'll learn from this error and see that I don't do this kind of thing again, and then people will start respecting me once more. But even if they do always think I'm no good for acting badly, I don't *have to* agree with them and *also* put myself down. I can forgive my errors and do my best in the future to make fewer of them."

If you thought this way after you acted badly and were criticized by others for doing so, you would feel sorry and regretful and determined to act better in the future. But you would hardly feel ashamed and self-hating. When you do feel ashamed and embarrassed for your errors, however, you are then sending yourself this message: "Yes, I acted improperly, and people are right in calling it to my attention. They are also right about putting me down for my bad behavior. I *should not have* acted that way, because it was the wrong thing to do. I especially should not have hurt others or displeased them by doing what I did. I *should* accept people's blame and blame myself for acting that way. I am really a pretty rotten person!"

A sense of shame, then, acknowledges that you have done something wrong and that many other people would see your behavior as reprehensible and put you down for doing it, that they are *right* in their judgment of what you did and their judgment of you as a bad person. Shame acknowledges your iniquity and your crumminess as a whole person for making such a bad error. Almost always, shame is synonymous with your worminess and your thoroughly bad character. Shame doesn't merely say that you acted poorly but that you agree with the other blamers. You *are* an inferior person for acting that way. To blame what you think, feel, and do may frequently be correct. But your feeling of shame shows that you condemn yourself for committing a flawed act.

REBT, of course, shows you how not to do this. It agrees that when you feel ashamed of some of your deeds, you may well have done the socially wrong thing. After all, there are standards, rules, and laws of human behavior, and you may well have acted against them. In so doing, you may have also needlessly hurt others— which is why the rules were set up in the first place, to stop you from harming other members of your social group. So REBT says that when you feel ashamed of something, you may have actually broken some social rules and done the wrong or immoral thing.

But REBT also says that your shame at doing something wrong is partly illegitimate, for it includes your downing yourself, your whole personhood, for doing it. You are essentially saying, "Not only are other people right about judging my *act* as bad, but they are right about judging *me* as a no-goodnik for doing it. I am therefore a rotten, worthless person. They *should* be condemning me for my act. I quite agree that I am no damned good!"

REBT directs you to question not your behavior, which may have been bad, but whether, because of this behavior, you are a shameful, terrible *person*. It gives you a general, almost invariant, answer to this question: Even when you really act badly and immorally, and people are needlessly hurt by your actions, it is still a mistake to label yourself as bad or terrible. Even in an extreme case, where you injure a person and he or she dies of your inflicted injuries, REBT says that by all normal standards, the deed was wrong and immoral but that you are still *a person who acted very badly*, never a *bad person*.

Now we could of course quibble about this and say that if you are guilty of enough immoral acts—as Hitler or Stalin were—and if these acts harm literally millions of people, you are bad to the core. Many people would accept this argument and agree that no judgment against you would be too severe. Actually, however, it would be almost impossible to prove that Hitler or Stalin's totality, their essences, were thoroughly rotten. For, don't forget, they did some good things in their lifetimes. Also, they *thought* their bad deeds were actually good ones. If they had lived long enough, moreover, they might have changed their ways and become human benefactors. And, perhaps most important of all, they were quite disturbed individuals who were born and reared to be highly fallible and could not very well be expected to be consistently kindly and fair.

You, of course, are hardly a Hitler or a Stalin and are not likely to behave as they did. Yes, you are fallible and do commit some harmful, foolish acts. Let's not exonerate those deeds and say that they were right, proper, or correct. But if we put you, the entire human, down for acting badly, how will that help you to act better? If you are a no-good, worthless, evil person, and we and you are convinced that you are, will it serve to help you act well in the present or future? Hardly!

So, too, goes the argument for shame. If you really act improperly, scandalize people by behaving that way, and get thoroughly damned by them for doing foolish or bad deeds, will their damnation of you as a total person, and your acceptance of that damnation, make you change for the better? In some cases, it might. For if people condemn you and you condemn yourself for acting shamefully, you might take their judgment into account and resolve to change. But their and your condemnation might easily also make you think, "I am totally bad, so how can someone like me change and act better? If I *do* poorly, I can possibly change. But if I *am* a hopeless criminal for *doing* wrong things, how is it possible for me to ever do better?"

REBT says that your feelings of shame, or self-condemnation, have some value, but they usually do more harm than good. If you only feel ashamed about what you *do* and consider your *actions* quite improper, that may motivate you to change the way you act. But if you are ashamed of *yourself* for doing foolish and harmful things, if you excoriate *you* for your *actions*, you are really giving a vote of nonconfidence to yourself and helping block your chances of changing for the better. Shame, if you keenly feel it, had better be attached only to the wrong or harmful deeds you perform and not to your entire *self* or *personhood* for performing them.

How does this relate to your feelings or anxiety? Very strongly! For when you are anxious, you frequently feel ashamed of what you might do, what you are doing, or what you have done. You think of it as wrong, mistaken, foolish, or inept. Much of the time, you may also think of yourself as a terrible person. Consequently, you become anxious, first about shameful acts that you may do— behaving foolishly, for instance, and being criticized by others for doing so. You frequently obsess, "Oh, how terrible that would be! What a thorough ass I would make of myself! I would never be able to live down my behavior and be comfortable in these people's presence again." You worry thus about what would happen—and frequently you are so upset by your worry, that you actually make that "shameful" misdeed happen.

Similarly, while you are doing a "shameful" act—you may notice that your zipper is open or your slip is showing—you are so full of shame you have great difficulty correcting it. Even after correcting it, you wonder, "I'm sure everyone noticed! What do they think of me? That I'm a total idiot! Will I ever be able to get back in their good graces?"

In addition, you may have performed a "shameful" act years ago—such as having sex with your mate when the shades were up so that people could see what you were doing—and years later you're still dwelling on this "horror." You worry about who actually saw you do it. You cannot let it go.

Shame itself, then, is the prime factor in much of your worry about the past, present, and future. The feelings of self-downing which almost always go with shame lead to much continued worry. If, for example, you stole postage stamps as a youngster or lied to your mate when you were courting him or her, or recently had an affair that people would presumably put you down for if they ever discovered it, you may easily wind up loathing yourself for this "shameful" behavior, continually searching for other "shameful" acts that you have done. You then end up considering yourself a really worthless, undeserving person who should be punished for your steady "sins."

Worse yet is the quiet kind of desperation that, according to Henry David Thoreau, most people are afflicted with. Rather than do anything "shameful" and worry and castigate themselves for doing it, they inhibit themselves—and thus seriously curtail the one life they will ever have.

A CASE OF ANXIETY-INDUCED RESTRICTED LIVING

Take Beatrice, for example. She was naturally spontaneous and free during her adolescence. She lived in a highly conventional suburb of New York City and did many things that her parents and her peers thought were "shameful." She was something of a tomboy, had a passionate sex affair with a boy when she was 14, and paid little attention to her schoolwork even though she was quite bright and easily kept herself in an advanced class. At fifteen, however, she became pregnant and her Roman Catholic parents, shocked to the core, were about to put her in a convent school. Fortunately, she had a miscarriage in her fourth month of pregnancy, suffered from postpartum depression for a while, but then straightened out and went to opposite extremes as a result of the trouble she had caused herself and her parents. She became something of a grind at school, refused to date any of the boys who were interested in her, totally gave up drinking and smoking, and led a life that was as monastic as the one she would have led had her parents gone through with their threat to put her in a convent school.

When, at the age of twenty-seven, she came to see me, Beatrice was suffering from severe depression. She was technically in no trouble whatever because she took no risks. She was thoroughly ashamed of the spontaneous—and rather healthy—way she had acted during her teens. She was a conscientious kindergarten teacher, went home after school to listen to classical music all afternoon and evening, and led an exceptionally inhibited, lonely life. Her parents, who had been so shocked by her youthful outgoingness, were now equally shocked at her hermit-like existence and kept urging her to return, at least, to some kind of social middle ground. But no, she was so ashamed of anything which might lead to criticism that she did practically nothing. To her family's horror, it looked as though this bright, attractive young woman would not only end up an old maid, but she would have no social life whatever.

Shame, in other words, had turned Beatrice from a perhaps overly social to an unsocial creature. She stayed out of trouble—since she was as pure as the driven snow—but she led a thoroughly inhibited, incredibly lonely and depressed life.

Beatrice's problem, as I soon saw, was scrupulous do-goodism. She was afraid to relate to people, except for the young children in her kindergarten classes, and therefore risk getting into any trouble whatever. She was ashamed of everything—dressing poorly, speaking badly, doing the improper thing socially, getting involved with the wrong boyfriend, and having sex that might lead to another pregnancy. So she stayed at home, listened to endless music, and even refused to use her excellent musical skills to play in a string quartet that very much wanted to have her as a member. Playing in it would require having social contacts, making possible mistakes in rehearsals and in public performances, and feeling terribly ashamed in case she did something wrong.

Beatrice quickly understood the principles of REBT that I went over with her and which explained her depression and her inhibited life. Although not originally a self-downer, she had developed into one. Beatrice's commanding musts were pretty obvious: "I must not do shameful, criticizable things, for if I do, I'll know that I'm behaving improperly and other people will blame me severely and boycott me, as they once did. To stop this horror from happening, I'll play it safe, make no risky moves, and get by comfortably, if not fulfillingly. Security, not creativity or enjoyment, is the path to follow. Otherwise, I'm bound to make terrible mistakes and feel like a worthless person. What an awful possibility!"

So Beatrice remained safe—and depressed. She didn't overtly put herself down for her mistakes; she simply made sure that she made no mistakes. To avoid possible errors, she chose to make no hits and no runs.

Beatrice agreed, at least in theory, with one of the main rules of REBT: A bad act, no matter how stupid or vile, never makes you a bad person. Your personhood is so multifaceted that even your serious errors are compensated for by your many good and neutral deeds, and therefore, as a person you cannot be given a global, general rating. Fine, Beatrice thought, but she still considered various acts that she might do as "rotten" or "shameful." These, for the most part, were unethical acts, such as treating others unfairly, lying to them, or needlessly hurting them. So she taught herself, as well as her kindergarten pupils, to avoid such acts; and she also taught her youngsters, along REBT lines, to forgive themselves as fallible humans when they acted wrongly or badly and then to work at correcting their behaviors.

But she still couldn't forgive herself. She was bad if her deeds were improper. She *had* to act well to be a "good person." REBT was okay for her pupils and for other people—but not for her. She had to do the right thing to be honored by herself and others. To accept the sinner but not the sin applied to everyone except her. She had to be especially good, and, of course, with her safety measures and lack of risk taking, she was.

So, although she fought and screamed most of the way, I encouraged Beatrice to do some shame-attacking exercises. This involves thinking of something that you and many other people would consider foolish, asinine, and shameful; you then do this thing quite consciously, and do it in public, while you work on not feeling ashamed. You chose an act that you would normally never do, and that other people would think ridiculous if you did it in their presence, but that would not harm them or get you into trouble. Thus, you yell out the stops in a train or the floors in an elevator—and you stay on the train or elevator. Or you wear an outlandish costume, such as one black shoe and one brown shoe. Or you walk a banana on a leash—and feed it with another banana! Or you ask for a grocery item in a shoe store.

Anything like this will do as long as you personally consider it shameful—rather than just a charming joke—and as long as other people are likely to think it shameful, too, and to think you're pretty bizarre for doing it. Then, while you are still in full view of these onlookers and feeling ashamed of the silly thing you are doing, you work on your feeling of shame. You make yourself, instead, feel sorry and disappointed about your behavior and about other's criticism of it, but not ashamed, embarrassed, or humiliated.

If you practice these shame-attacking exercises several times in a row, you will usually find that two things occur. First, you will frequently find that you are more anxious when you think about doing them, and have not yet done one of them, than when you actually act them out. The thought of being disapproved of by several people for acting so foolishly will tend to make you very anxious. For a while, you may keep putting off actually doing the exercise because you are so anxious about doing it. Then, when you actually do it, you will feel much less anxious because you are engaged in acting it out, and that tends to distract you from your anxiety.

Second, you will often find to your surprise that people hardly notice your doing the shame-attacking exercise. For example, when one of our therapists actually walked a banana on a red leash on a bright October day and was seen by scores of people, many of them looked away—for they were embarrassed to stare at her doing such a crazy thing! They were more ashamed than she was!

Third, when you first do the exercise, you will often feel embarrassed. But as you persist in it, your embarrassment will be greatly reduced; you will get used to it and may even enjoy doing it. Thus, one of my shy clients had great trouble in forcing himself to stop a stranger outside of our Institute and say, "I just got out of a mental hospital. What month is this?" But even though the first man he did it with looked at him in horror and quickly moved away, he saw that he could do it, kept doing it with several other people that week, and soon, he was not at all ashamed and enjoyed doing it. His shyness almost magically vanished after awhile, and he had the most unshy week of his life. As he did the same exercise 20 times, he lost his embarrassment completely and was delighted that he was able to startle so many people and yet not feel ashamed himself.

Fourth, you will frequently find that as you do this ridiculous exercise, your regular feelings of shame will significantly decrease. Thus, Beatrice did two things for her shame-attacking exercise that she would never do in regular life. She went out on the street in broad daylight and sang "The Star-Spangled Banner" at the top of her lungs. And she went into the street when the sun was shining brightly and held a large black umbrella over her head, as if to ward off the rain. She felt very foolish, at first, doing both these things, but she got used to doing them and stopped feeling ashamed. Then, because she practiced not feeling ashamed of herself in these ways, she started to do regular things that tended to inhibit her and that she hadn't done for many years. She called one of her old boyfriends, whom she hadn't seen for a long time, and asked him to go to a dance with her. When he accepted, and they actually had a good date, she kept asking him out and had several pleasant dates with him. She went to a bar, for the first time in years, had a ginger ale or two—for she was still afraid to have a single drink of liquor—and talked to several strangers.

Beatrice felt so little ashamed of these activities, none of which she had done in years, that she started to participate in social activities again, to enjoy them, and to stop leading her hermit-like existence. She saw that risk-taking was not only all right but was actually enjoyable, and although she hardly became a social butterfly, she did get some relationships going and began to lead a much more normal life. Her parents were thrilled with the new Beatrice.

You, too, can get over your anxieties and embarrassment if you do some shame-attacking exercises. Whether it is people you are afraid of, or making public presentations, or participating in a sport, you can find your Irrational Beliefs regarding this activity and Dispute them. If you then do some REBT shame-attacking exercises that are relevant to your fear, you will be increasingly able to face the "fearful" music and enjoy dancing to it. Use shame-attacking exercises with your specific anxieties or use them to make inroads against your general irrational fears. The more you do them, the less anxious you will tend to become—and, as I suggested above, you may even enjoy many of the things that now tend to panic you.

17

Some Forceful and Dramatic Methods of Controlling Your Anxiety

When I first became a psychotherapist, in 1943, when I was twenty-nine years old, I always did some Disputing of my clients' Irrational Beliefs in order to help them overcome their anxieties. Because, even though I favored psychoanalytic ways of understanding how they became disturbed, I also sensed, as many analysts probably do, that my clients often held self-defeating Beliefs, and that as long as they hung on to them and acted as if these were sensible, they were going to be anxious.

SEXUAL ANXIETY AND INADEQUACY

At that stage in my therapeutic career, I was already an authority on people's sexual problems. I saw clearly that when a man failed to satisfy his partner or a woman failed to get sufficiently aroused sexually or to come to orgasm, they tended to devoutly believe a number of sexual ideas that were false and that were creating their sexual anxieties and phobias. Men, for example, tended to believe that they must get stiff erections easily and quickly; that they must achieve intercourse with a woman; that they must persist in having intercourse for a long period of time (from ten minutes to an hour); and that during intercourse they must bring their partner to orgasm. If they were sexually weak or inept in any of these vitally important respects, they would be utterly impotent, and their partners would surely despise them and leave them to the great horrors of masturbation or complete abstinence. This, of course, would "indubitably prove" that they were weaklings and would never be considered "real men." So they might as well give up on sex or, at the very best, be nice to some woman who would tolerate them in a sexless marriage.

As for women, they frequently had the idea that they must quickly get aroused by kissing or petting with a suitable partner (usually a male); that they must quickly want to have intercourse with him; that they must thoroughly enjoy having intercourse; that they should promptly (say, in ten minutes or less) come to an explosive orgasm in intercourse; and that within another ten minutes, they must be eager to have intercourse again, and be able to have another terrific orgasm (or two or three) within a short period of time. If indeed they were unable to be instantly arousable and to have at least one stupendous climax in intercourse, they were unsexy, inadequate women, and they might just as well remain dried-up prunes for the rest of their lives—or, at the very most, let their male partners use their bodies for their own purposes. They could sometimes even manage to have several children, but pitifully not be able to have orgasms in intercourse. So be it.

When I saw that literally scores of my clients, both men and women, had these foolish notions about sex, and specifically about intercourse, I managed to attack their Beliefs fairly vigorously and, within a few sessions of psychotherapy, was able to have the great majority achieve sexual enjoyment and competence. I mainly disabused them of the ideas that sex equals intercourse and showed them how to satisfy themselves and their partners in a number of noncoital ways. I even helped them have more enjoyable intercourse—once I thoroughly convinced them that penile–vaginal copulation was not the be-all and end-all of sex and that all kinds of human sex play were to be prized. Yes, I explained, sex was okay, even when it consisted of so-called "perversions," such as husband and wife consistently petting each other to orgasm and only perhaps once in awhile coming to climax in intercourse.

Where did I learn my techniques of sex therapy, that helped hundreds of individuals and couples, from 1943 to 1948? Mainly from the old sexologists, such as Havelock Ellis, Iwan Bloch, August Forel, and W.F. Robie, all of whom were active in the early part of the twentieth century, and most of whom were physicians who specialized in sex therapy. Sigmund Freud and his followers, alas, were not among those sexologists and, in fact, led the medical profession and their psychoanalytic patients astray by deifying intercourse as, unfortunately, did most of their patients, and stressing copulatory sex skills instead of noncoital as well as coital methods. Freud and the Freudians were wrong and did a great deal of harm to their sexually troubled patients, while the early sexologists I mentioned above were pretty much on the right track and did a great deal of good.

After I had been practicing as a psychotherapist and sex therapist for five years, Alfred Kinsey and his associates came along, in 1948, to confirm my and the early sexologists' teachings. Surveying thousands of men and women for the first time in human history, Kinsey rediscovered noncoital sex and said so very clearly in the first two volumes of his studies, *Sexual Behavior in the Human Male* and *Sexual Behavior in the Human Female*. His books supported all that I had been teaching my clients for a number of years and what I had been saying in my professional articles in *The International Journal of Sexology* and in my popular writings. It was heartening to be backed by Kinsey's scientific researches.

Then, in the 1960s, William Masters and Virginia Johnson began to conduct actual observations of the sex life of many subjects, including many female subjects, and published their revolutionary books, *Human Sexual Response* and *Human Sexual Inadequacy*. Their researches again confirmed what the early sexologists had pointed out and what Kinsey and his associates had found: That sexual behavior of both men and women went far beyond intercourse and included all kinds of petting and noncoital sex acts. In fact, when orgasm did occur, particularly in women, it seemed to be very often noncoital and only partly the result of penile–vaginal intercourse.

In the meantime, shortly after Kinsey's main findings about men and women's sexuality, and before Masters and Johnson even got started on their notable researches, REBT came along, in January 1955. It was much more specific in its theory of sexual inadequacy than was the work of the previous sexologists. For the REBT theory of the ABCs of emotional disturbance seemed to fit neatly into the theory of many sexual disturbances, and the techniques of cognitive, emotive, and behavioral therapy that REBT introduced in the 1950s seemed to cover much of the treatment of people's sex problems.

Specifically, REBT holds that when men and women have sexual difficulties of a psychological nature—for they often have physical and medical problems as well—these fit nicely into the ABC network. Thus, a man desires to have enjoyable sex with his partner, tries to have it with her (or him) at point A (Activating Event), and has the choice at C (Consequence) of succeeding or failing to please himself and his partner. When he fails at C, it is frequently because he not only tells himself, at his Rational Belief (RB), "I would very much like to succeed sexually and bring my partner a great deal of pleasure," but he adds to this the Irrational Belief (IB), "I *absolutely must* succeed sexually. I must get a firm erection, maintain it for some time, and keep thrusting it into my partner's vagina until I fully arouse her and bring her to orgasm and she practically begs me for more orgasms and dotes upon me as the best lover she ever had! Fully pleasing myself and my partner is *absolutely necessary* and unless I do so I am sexually incompetent and hardly a real man!"

These kinds of IBs will tend to make this man very anxious before he has sex, will continue his anxiety while he is having it, will make him keep spying on himself (as Masters and Johnson accurately put it) to see if his penile apparatus "really works," and will make him put himself down as a weakling in case it doesn't. Then the next time he has sex with this same woman (or man), he will be more anxious than ever—and more prone to fail to achieve and maintain his erection. He will have performance anxiety with a vengeance!

As for the woman who has psychological sex problems but who is really quite capable of being aroused and coming to orgasm with her partner, the ABCs frequently go as follows. At A (Activating Event), she wants to become aroused and bring herself and her lover to orgasm. But at C (Consequence), she is not aroused, loses arousal after awhile, finds it difficult or impossible to climax, perhaps has painful intercourse, and may not be able to satisfy her lover and bring him to full climax in intercourse. At B, she starts off with Rational Beliefs (RBs), "Sex is fine and I would like to enjoy it and have my partner greatly enjoy it." But she adds to these the Irrational Beliefs (IBs), "I *absolutely have to* be easily aroused by my partner and *must* have at least one terrific orgasm. What's more, I must be thoroughly able to enjoy his powerful penile thrusts and come to climax while he is energetically copulating with me and driving me to ecstatic satisfaction. I also *must* be able to arouse him fully with my tongue, hands, and vagina and give him at least one, and preferably several, great orgasms so that he loves sex with me completely and keeps begging me for more. Otherwise, if I fail him and fail myself sexually, I am an inadequate woman and hardly deserve to be loved."

There are many variations on these ABCs of male and female sexual disturbance, but most of them tend to follow the above lines. Both sexes not only prefer but demand what is considered to be "proper" sex—usually greatly arousing intercourse leading to stupendous or mutual orgasms. Because of each person's demands, they make themselves anxious or panicked and frequently can hardly perform at all. Even though they definitely care for each other, they often wind up having little sex, or not very enjoyable sex. Sometimes they find other partners, including those for whom they care less. But frequently, if they start failing with one partner, they take similar Irrational Beliefs to the next partner, or to a series of lovers, and fail with them, too. Although they are biologically capable of a variety of good sex, they may actually experience little.

A CASE OF SEXUAL PANIC

As you might guess, the first part of the REBT solution to a male and female psychological sex problem is to find the individual's specific Irrational Beliefs and to vigorously and actively Dispute them. Roland was a highly sexed man of thirty who could get an

erection very easily, masturbate to orgasm every day, and sometimes twice a day, and satisfy almost any woman if she could come
to orgasm within one minute of intercourse. If she took two
minutes or more, it was usually no go. Roland rarely took two minutes to come in masturbation and with an attractive woman,
especially a new partner, he got so greatly aroused that a minute of
intercourse was tops. Then, when he came, his penis was so
sensitive that he had to quickly withdraw from her vagina, and it
took him thirty or forty minutes to get another erection—and that
one also only lasted a minute or two in intercourse. Most of his
partners were physically drawn to him at the beginning of their
relationship, but they soon were left hanging sexually. They grew
disappointed and sometimes resentful and often discontinued having sex with him. One woman, Jill, had little sexual desire and
practically never came to orgasm with any man, but she was willing
to keep seeing and having sex with Roland because she liked him as
a companion. But he found her much too thin and unsexy looking,
and he rarely made a date with her.

Roland was particularly desperate in the case of Laura, who was
very attractive and bright but who insisted that she really enjoyed
sex only when she had intercourse that lasted at least five minutes.
If he couldn't get it up and keep it up for that long, he wasn't for
her. She could get plenty of men who easily stayed erect for ten or
fifteen minutes, and if he wasn't one of them, too bad. She gave
Roland a chance, however, even after she knew about his ejaculation problems. But with her, his problems only got worse. He *had
to* last, just *had to* last in order to please her. So, of course, he didn't,
and he came within a few seconds. She said they could be friends,
but that was it—nothing more.

Roland, who really was taken with Laura, felt very depressed
about her rejecting him. With other women, especially attractive
ones, he continued to be very anxious. "Although I might not be
the greatest lover in the world," he kept telling himself, "at least
I've got to be average. Two or three minutes is all I ask. Some
women are satisfied with that. But it must be more than one
minute! I *absolutely must not* come that quickly! I'm a real loser if I

do. Most women just don't come in a minute. So I'll continue to be a real loser!"

Just to experiment, I tried several slow-down techniques with Roland. I had him use a condom, and sometimes two condoms, to reduce his sexual sensations. I had him try Nupercainal cream, which has some nerve deadening ingredients in it. I had him masturbate to orgasm just before he had a date so that he would be less sexually aroused by the time he and his partner got around to intercourse. No go: Whatever mechanical means he tried didn't work at all because of his ejaculation-triggering anxiety. As he kept spying on himself and his penis to see how long it would take him to come, he became even faster on the draw. He soon was ejaculating only a few seconds after intromission.

He could, as I suggested, have satisfied Laura with his fingers or his tongue, but she insisted that he must do so in intercourse. So, agreeing with her *must*, he made himself very anxious.

We therefore worked steadily on Roland's *shoulds* and *musts*. I helped him ask himself, over and over again, "Why *must* I satisfy a woman with my penis, when there are obviously other ways to do so? Where is it written that she absolutely *should come to orgasm* in this one way? Where is the evidence that I'm a hopeless lover and a weak man because some women, like Laura, are hung up on intercourse and won't allow themselves to be satisfied with clitoral manipulation or other means of sexual contact? Why can't I merely accept myself as a fast ejaculator and find a woman who can easily put up with that but is still bright and attractive? Why must I remain obsessed with getting a woman who deifies my penis—as I am obviously doing myself?"

These Disputing questions helped Roland see more clearly what his psychological problem was. He saw that if he kept *demanding* rather than just strongly *wanting* prolonged penile–vaginal copulation, he was going to be so anxious that he actually wouldn't achieve it. That appeared fairly obvious.

Still, Roland wouldn't accept himself with his coital limitations. He particularly wanted Laura, and he felt that he *couldn't stand* being deprived of her. But, he also demanded that he have several other good choices—women who were able to have orgasms very quickly in intercourse or who preferred to climax in noncoital ways. When he found such women, however, unlike Laura they were wanting in other important respects. So he had low frustration tolerance about that and kept *defining* his sexual predicament as *awful* and *horrible* and not just highly *inconvenient*.

As Roland began to lightly agree with me—or rather with himself—that he didn't *need* to last longer in intercourse, though that would be highly *preferable*, and as his light agreement still didn't work to curtail his anxiety, I started to show him how to use several forceful Disputing techniques. The trouble, again, with light Disputing is that as a result of it, you can tell yourself, as Roland did, "It really *isn't* so awful that I am not great at sexual intercourse, it's just a bother and it doesn't mean anything about me as a person." But, underneath this rational philosophy, you can still tell yourself quite strongly, "But it *is* awful! And it *does* really make me a sexual weakling and less than a man!" Then, you'll still be very anxious.

SOME FORCEFUL AND DRAMATIC METHODS OF DISPUTING IRRATIONAL BELIEFS

The first forceful disputing technique I taught Roland was the recording of his Irrational Beliefs and the very powerful Disputing of them. That is, he recorded his main IB—"I *absolutely must* manage to come more slowly in intercourse or else Laura and every good partner I find will utterly reject me and that will prove I am not a good sex partner and a real man!" I had him put this Belief on a recorded cassette and then vigorously Dispute it for several minutes to show that it was quite irrational and that he could give it up. After strongly Disputing it on tape, he was to let me and several other people who knew about his sex problem listen to his tape, not only to see whether the content of his Disputing was accurate but whether he was doing it *vigorously* and *forcefully* enough rather than in a weak, namby-pamby manner.

Roland did some quite good Disputing on the first tape he made.

His Rational Beliefs suggested there was no reason why he absolutely *must* come more slowly in intercourse; that Laura might well reject him if he didn't come more slowly but that not every possible good partner would leave him; and that if he continued to come more slowly that would only prove he was sexually deficient for some partners but not for every one. It certainly wouldn't prove that he was not a real man. He would be a man, and a real one, no matter how deficient he was in satisfying some women sexually.

Roland's Rational Beliefs were on the mark, but at first they were stated lightly, passively, and without any firm conviction. So he made another tape recording with the same Irrational Belief on it and attempted to make his Disputing and his answer to the Disputation much more forceful. He still didn't succeed, though he improved somewhat. Finally, on his third try at recording, he powerfully Disputed his IBs and came up with Effective New Philosophies (Es) that were much more convincing. His friends and I, listening to the tapes, thought he was now making vigorous Disputes and actually beginning to believe them.

Role-playing was the second forceful emotive technique I used with Roland. He played himself in the role-play and a woman friend, aware of his sex problem, played Laura, the woman who had rejected him sexually. In the role-play, he tried to convince "Laura" that intercourse wasn't sacred and that if she would only be patient with him, he would first satisfy her sexually in noncoital ways and then later would probably be able to last longer and satisfy her coitally. The woman playing Laura deliberately resisted his arguments, refusing to change her mind and be persuaded. He did a good job in the role-playing, but he still got rejected. Whereupon, at one point, he got anxious and hesitant in his arguments. The role-player then took time out, as people often do in REBT role-playing, to learn what he was telling himself to produce his anxiety. He was saying to himself at this point, "What's the use? It's really hopeless! I can't possibly convince her. Nor will I be able to convince any good woman to take a chance on me sexually. So maybe I'd better forget the whole thing and not only give up on Laura but on all women who want prolonged intercourse."

These Irrational Beliefs, which came out in the role-play, were then examined and promptly refuted, and Roland was able to go on with the role-play convincingly even though he continued to get nowhere in his effort to convince the friend who was playing Laura. After he failed to convince her, he felt healthily sorry and disappointed rather than, as he often felt, unhealthily depressed and anxious.

Reverse role-playing was the third forceful emotive technique I used with Roland. A male friend took over Roland's Irrational Beliefs about being no good at sex with Laura or any other women and rigidly held on to these Beliefs while Roland tried to talk him out of them. The role-player wouldn't give up Roland's Irrational Beliefs, no matter how well Roland argued against them. So, in this kind of reverse role-playing, Roland got a good deal of practice in vigorously Disputing his own (played by the friend) Irrational Beliefs and in becoming more able to surrender them.

Vigorous rational coping self-statements was a fourth forceful emotive REBT method I used with Roland. He had no trouble making up several of these statements and telling them to himself, but he had great trouble actually believing them.

So I had him write down several rational coping statements a number of times each and then go over them until they sank into his head and heart. Some of the rational coping statements he used in this emphatic, powerful manner and that seemed to work well were these: "Even if I never overcome my fast ejaculation and I completely lose Laura and other women who demand prolonged intercourse, I'll *never, never* be totally rotten at sex and a real failure. I'll merely be less sexually adept for THOSE women, but hardly for ALL the women in the world." "I really want very much to last longer in intercourse, because I would enjoy it a lot more and so would some of the women I go with. But I DON'T, DON'T, DON'T NEED WHAT I WANT! I only PREFER IT. I CAN, yes I damned well CAN, live a good life without perfect intercourse. And I'm really determined to make myself a good life, whether or not I become a much slower ejaculator."

By using all these forceful emotive REBT methods at various

times, Roland managed to give up his dire need to last much longer in intercourse. As he did so, his anxiety greatly diminished, and within several months more, he was usually able to last in intercourse for from three minutes to five minutes. Not as long as he would have liked to last, but a distinct improvement.

18

Firmly Convincing Yourself
of Your Rational and
Self-Helping Beliefs

I had better repeat again, because it is crucial to understanding your disturbed emotional reactions such as severe anxiety, that you rarely, if ever, have pure emotional reactions. What we normally call your feelings consists of a combination of your thinking, your emotional reactions to that thinking, and the way you react to that thinking and emoting. Thus, when you see something (such as a man with a gun) as "dangerous" and conclude that your safety is at risk, you feel anxious and you tend to run like hell, call a cop, or take some other protective action. Your feeling of anxiety, therefore, is a complicated blend of perception, thought, emotion, and action; it is not merely pure feeling without any other components.

One of the main factors in your feelings, especially your feeling of anxiety, is the *strength* of your belief in the danger of what you observe. Thus, if you see a man with a gun and you believe that it is a toy gun, or that it isn't loaded, or that he is just keeping it in his holster, or that he looks like a police officer, or that he is going to use the gun to protect you from possible assault by others, you will tend to have feelings of mild concern or caution—since your perceptions and thoughts may be wrong and the man with the gun may actually be dangerous. But, if the man with the gun looks frightening to you and you're strongly convinced that he is out to get you, even though most onlookers might see it differently, you may completely panic and attack him before he attacks you, which, of course, he might not do.

It is your *conviction* that the man with the gun is dangerous, and not the real danger that he and his gun actually present, that makes your anxiety about him mild, moderate, or severe. If you weakly believe that he is dangerous, you will usually have little anxiety, but if you strongly believe, even without any evidence, that he is harmful, your anxiety may be overwhelming. So it is not only your Belief in his dangerousness that counts, but the powerful conviction with which you hold this Belief.

This is important to know if you want to control your anxiety before it controls you. When you rationally tell yourself that the man with the gun is not dangerous because he is dressed like a cop and seems to be interested in protecting you from harm, but at the same time you irrationally tell yourself that anyone who carries a gun is dangerous and that therefore this particular gun carrier is out to kill you, your strong irrational conviction of danger will most likely win out over your weak rational conviction of nondanger. You will react to the man with the gun as if he were really a thug who is out to kill you. Your strong convictions, in other words, frequently lead to your strong emotional reactions—even when they do not have any evidence to back them up and when they are most probably false.

Seeing that this is so, and that strong Irrational Beliefs may easily override your weak Rational Beliefs and create in you deep-seated feelings of anxiety that are hardly related to social reality, REBT has a number of emotive methods that help you to challenge your strong irrational convictions and to replace them with strong rational ones. One of these is Windy Dryden's paradoxical technique of checking and disputing your Rational Beliefs to make reasonably sure that you hold them and that they are really effective. Windy Dryden, a professor of counseling at Goldsmith's College of the University of London, has written more books on REBT than even I have done and is a prime innovator of useful REBT techniques.

A CASE OF PANIC WHEN PRESENTING
AT STAFF MEETINGS

When you are feeling unhealthy anxiety and are Disputing your Irrational Beliefs that tend to make you anxious, you frequently will come up with an Effective New Philosophy that you partly believe but hold only weakly. Caroline, for example, was a very competent copywriter for a large advertising agency, and she was steadily praised for her work. She had been employed by her agency for eight years, had received several raises and bonuses, and was practically a fixture at her firm.

Nonetheless, for all of her acknowledged value to her agency, Caroline was terrified about speaking up at staff meetings. She would have good ideas and receive welcome feedback on them, but panicked about her manner of presenting her ideas in public. She might stutter, slur her words, say something stupid, or actually go dumb in the midst of her presentation. Then, everybody present would know she was an incompetent who didn't know how to express herself, and they would conclude that her ideas were stupid and useless. As a copywriter, she was good and knew that she did well. But at expressing her ideas orally, she was a dud—and knew it. So, except when a question was directed her way, she rarely spoke up at staff meetings, refused to risk presenting some of her excellent ideas—and then beat herself mercilessly for appearing such a silent dope to the other staff members.

Caroline's Irrational Beliefs, as we quickly discovered in our therapy sessions, mainly were: "I *must* speak up very clearly and well. I *absolutely must* show them how brilliant I am, and not merely at copywriting, which they already know. I must impress the staff with my ideas, and the clarity of my presentation. If I come off hesitatingly and poorly, they will think I'm only good at copywriting, that I'm really a dunce, and will tolerate me for what I do well but really despise me and talk negatively about me behind my back. I'm sure they already do that. I'm sure they already consider me a hopeless incompetent, and they probably keep me on largely out of pity and not because I'm that helpful to them in these conferences."

Caroline soon saw these Irrational Beliefs and started Disputing them. She wrote down her Disputations and her consequent Effective New Philosophy and did very well with that—for, after all, she was a copywriter and knew how to write. She came up with these Rational Beliefs: "I don't have to speak up clearly and well at the staff meetings, though that would be highly preferable if I did. It would also be lovely if I would show them how brilliant I am, and not merely at copywriting, but I certainly don't have to and if they think I'm only good at copywriting and nothing else, that's all right, too. I would like to impress them with the clarity of my ideas. That would probably make them think more highly of me than they now do. But, again, that is only desirable, not in the least necessary. If I still stumble at staff meetings, and they think I'm a dud and talk disparagingly behind my back, I can live with that. They're clearly not going to fire me, just look down on me. Of course, they may not even do that, but if they do I can stand it and still go on functioning well at my copywriting and be a reasonably happy person. Even if they think I'm a dunce and keep me on the staff only because of my copywriting, I can take their kindness and pity and not put myself down because of it. So I can refuse to down myself if I never make any significant contributions at the staff meetings. I will accept myself with my limitations and not denigrate myself as a person even if they clearly do. I'm still glad that I'm an excellent copywriter, even if I'm not the most brilliant presenter of my ideas."

Caroline's Effective New Philosophy, which she arrived at after a good deal of REBT Disputing of her Irrational Beliefs, was excellent. Normally, if she really believed it, it would have stopped her performance anxiety. Second, her Disputing would have gotten her over her refusing to speak up. For with a New Effective Philosophy, she would not be afraid to speak up at the staff presentations, would get practice in doing so, and see that nothing terrible happened even when she spoke up hesitatingly and badly.

Unfortunately, however, in spite of Caroline's arriving at this New Effective Philosophy, she didn't really believe it—or at most believed it very lightly and nonconvincingly. She saw that it was good in general and would be good for others to hold, but she didn't really believe it herself. So she remained terrified, though less so, about presenting at staff meetings. She still said practically nothing and continued to castigate herself when she failed to speak up as she thought she should. I therefore used Windy Dryden's forceful countering method and had Caroline vigorously and powerfully prove to herself, and thereby reaffirm, her partially acquired Rational Beliefs. For example, I had her take her RB, "I don't have to speak up clearly and well at the staff meetings, though it would be preferable if I did." She then firmly questioned this RB by asking herself, "Why don't I have to speak up clearly and well at the staff meetings? In what way would it be preferable but not necessary if I did?"

Caroline's answers to her own questions were, "Obviously there is no law that says I have to speak up clearly and well at the staff meetings and since this law doesn't exist, I don't have to follow it. It would be preferable if I spoke up at the staff meetings because the other people might benefit from what I have to say and might approve of me for saying it. I would benefit from being a valuable team member. They would think that I'm much more than a good copywriter and that would be fine. But obviously I have not spoken up for a long time and still manage to get by and win some of their approval. No matter how many reasons there are for it being preferable to speak up and do well at the staff meetings, I clearly don't have to do so. What I strongly desire doesn't have to be fulfilled."

Caroline then argued with some of her other Rational Beliefs to see if she could solidly sustain them. For example, she took her RB, "I don't have to speak up clearly and well at the staff meetings, though it would be highly preferable if I did. It would also benefit me if I would show them how brilliant I am and not a mere copywriter, but I certainly don't have to. And if they think I'm only good at copywriting and nothing else, that's all right, too." She questioned this Rational Belief by asking herself, "Why don't I have to speak up clearly and well at the staff meetings though it would be preferable if I did? Why would it benefit me if I would show them how brilliant I am and not a mere copywriter? But why don't I have to?"

Doing this kind of arguing with her Rational Beliefs, Caroline came up with these answers: "I don't have to speak up clearly and well at staff meetings because I simply don't have to. I obviously haven't done so for years and they still put up with me—and even give me raises. It would be preferable if I did speak up well because I would like that and they would probably think better of me. But preferable is a long way from necessary. Death and taxes may be necessary, but winning the great approval of my coworkers obviously is not."

Caroline kept arguing with her Rational Beliefs until she solidly believed them. Her light acceptance of them, which was ineffective, was replaced by a firm, powerful acceptance—and that really worked. She at first, again, fully accepted herself for not speaking up at group presentations, and then she later was able to unanxiously do much better at speaking up.

Like Caroline, you can question your Rational Beliefs and your Effective New Philosophy when you say them to yourself and you even teach them to others without really believing them. It is easy for you, as for practically all humans, to parrot Rational Beliefs, because you realize that they really would work if you truly believed. Sometimes, as a matter of fact, you say that you believe them in order to get yourself off the hook. You know you are being irrational because your Beliefs do not work, so you figure out some Rational Beliefs and act *as if* you truly believe them. Then you can claim that you are really rational when you actually aren't. You can also falsely claim that your thoughts have little to do with your feelings and that you are just having unhealthy emotions—like anxiety, because your feelings spontaneously overwhelm you—and that these feelings really don't have Irrational Beliefs behind them.

Anyway, when you seemingly have Rational Beliefs, and you still have unhealthy feelings and behaviors, use the Windy Dryden method of questioning them until you see—and feel—that you really hold them. Then you will more likely produce healthier and more productive emotions and actions.

19

Using a Sense of Humor to Control Your Anxiety

One method of challenging your Irrational Beliefs and the unhealthy negative feelings that go with them is to view them in a humorous light. The human tendency is to take actual Adversities much too seriously—and thereby plague yourself. Thus, if you are cautious about walking alone at night on dark and deserted streets, you take the situation seriously and in that way help protect yourself. But if you are panicked about going out of the house unless the sun is brightly shining, and you only go out when there are many people on the street, and you refuse to leave your house at night even when it's on fire, you have lost your perspective entirely about darkness and have taken it much too seriously.

Similarly, very anxious people lose their sense of perspective and have no sense of humor whatever as they designate particular dangers as *awful* and *horrible*. They cannot see how silly or funny that is. An elevator phobic, for example, is certain he will suffocate every time he gets in an elevator or that the elevator is sure to crash. He fails to see that elevators are probably the safest form of transportation in the world and that millions of people ride in them every day without incident. He loses his sense of perspective and humor completely about elevators and imagines thousands of potential accidents that, of course, never actually occur.

Humor lightens things up—including some quite serious things. If you are afraid of speaking in public because you're sure all the members of your audience are glaring at you and waiting for you to blunder, a therapist who specializes in public-speaking phobias will often advise you to envision all the members of your audience sitting on the toilet with their pants down or their skirts up and having a hard time moving their bowels. That humorous picture may well alleviate your anxiety.

Again, if you are anxious about the couple next door hearing you and your sex partner making noise while copulating and putting you down and laughing at you for being so obsessed with lovemaking every night, imagine that same couple swinging from the chandelier and beating each other with heavy chains whenever they have sex and you will soon see how ridiculous your own fears are.

REBT often uses humor to help you defeat your anxieties. It shows you, for example, how funny it is for other people to spy on you to see how poorly you're doing and to laugh uproariously at you. It shows you that while few people may share your particular shameful phobia—such as your horror of having one or two gray hairs when you're in your twenties—they have lots of foolish fears of their own. It shows you that others are so preoccupied about how you view them and their own stupidities that they're probably not thinking of you and your behavior at all. Moreover, when you do appear to be very anxious in public and are afraid that people may ridicule you, most of your onlookers are actually empathizing with you and are glad that, at the moment, they're not as publicly anxious as you are.

As REBT emphasizes, it is not what you do that makes you miserable, it is your *view* of that Adversity. If you take a tragic, overserious view of it, you will become anxious or depressed. If you take a humorous view of exactly the same Adversity, you may be thoroughly amused and actually enjoy it.

If, instead of being overly serious, you learn to take things with a grain of salt and a sense of humor, you tend to help yourself gain distance from trouble. You distract yourself from some of your intensely serious and disturbed thoughts. You puncture your grandiose thinking. You learn to accept human fallibility. Humor helps you see that you can often laugh at many of life's foibles.

Instead of taking yourself with grim seriousness, which brings on fairly constant feelings of anxiety and depression, try to look at what you think, feel, and do with a conscious sense of humor. You can deliberately see the humorous or funny side of life—yours and other people's. Thus, you can see humor much of the time even if you get rejected for a job, or in a relationship—and if you keep trying, acceptance may come. Humor lessens anxiety at the same time that it increases optimism.

Failing and being rejected, to be sure, has its rough points. But it also has its humor and its advantages. People will reject you, for example, when you do well—and especially when you do better than they do. Looking at the dark side of things with a humorous slant has the great advantage of lightening them up.

For example, you can laugh at your failings and refuse to take any of them too seriously. You can see that expecting yourself only to succeed and never to fail is ridiculously grandiose. You may fail, but if you take your failure lightly, it will actually help you succeed next time. When you look at your failings with humor, you will understand that failing as well as succeeding is part of the human condition. It shouldn't be judged too harshly or taken as a prediction that you will inevitably continue to fail.

If you look at your shortcomings from a critical but still humorous angle, you will see that you can control their disruptive aspects and reduce them in the future. If you do not down yourself but ironically observe your faulty behavior and do your best to learn from it, you can accept the challenge of failing without awfulizing or catastrophizing about it—which often will bring on greater failure and prevent you from learning from your present errors.

USING RATIONAL HUMOROUS SONGS

To encourage your utilizing humor to deal with your failings and your losses, I have composed a number of rational humorous songs that promote this kind of attitude. I first used these songs at the American Psychological Association Annual Convention in Washington, D.C. in 1976, at a symposium on psychologists' use of humor and I got my audience of psychologists to sing along with me. The songs were so successful that I have been singing them, along with my audiences, ever since at the talks and workshops I give on REBT. I sometimes also sing them at my famous Friday night workshops at the Albert Ellis Institute in New York.

I found that the songs were so effective with my audiences that I decided to use them with my regular psychotherapy clients. So, the Institute has printed a song sheet, which is given to all our psychotherapy clients at our clinic. Whenever they are anxious, they can choose to sing an antianxiety song to themselves. When they are depressed, they can choose to sing an antidepression song. Doing so, many of them quickly reduce their anxious and depressed feelings.

Here are some of the antianxiety rational humorous songs that you can use yourself. First, several songs that humorously attack your ego anxiety:

PERFECT RATIONALITY

(to the tune of "Funiculi, Funicula!" by Luigi Denza)

Some think the world must have a right direction,
And so do I! And so do I!
Some think that, with the slightest imperfection,
They can't get by—and so do I!
For I, I have to prove I'm superhuman,
And better far than people are!
To show I have miraculous acumen—
And always rate among the Great!
Perfect, perfect rationality
Is, of course, the only thing for me!
How can I ever think of being
If I must live fallibly?
Rationality must be a perfect thing for me!

I Like Musturbation

(to the tune of "Yankee Doodle")

Some folks like a happy state,
And strive for real elation,
Some folks like to masturbate,
But I like MUSTurbation!
MUSTurbation keep it up!
MUSTurbation dandy!
Mind the got-to's, yup, yup, yup!
And with the shoulds be handy!

Yes, I know I could create
Greater satisfaction
But I would rather MUSTurbate
And keep my mind in traction!
MUSTurbation, keep it up!
Let its message fit good!
Mind the got-to's, yup, yup, yup!
As shouldhood leads to shithood!

I'm Just Wild About Worry

(to the tune of "I'm Just Wild About Harry" by Eubie Blake)

I'm just wild about worry
And worry's wild about me!
We're quite a twosome to make life gruesome
And filled with anxiety!
Oh, worry's anguish I curry
And look for its guarantee!
Oh, I'm just wild about worry
And worry's wild about
Never mild about,
Most beguiled about me!

OH, SAY CAN YOU SEE WHO I AM?

(to the tune of "Stars and Stripes Forever" by John Philip Sousa)

Oh, say can you see who I am?
I'm the one that the universe runs for!
The gods that you worship are sham
Compared to the great I AM!
I act like a battering ram
To prove I'm a mover and a shaker!
But beneath you can see what I am—
A woebegotten candy-cotton,
Rotten faker!

YOU ARE NOT THE GREATEST

(to the tune of "Funiculi, Funicula!" by Luigi Denza)

Some think that you are not the goddamned greatest—
and so do I, and so do I!
Some think that you come in the very latest—
and so do I, and so do I!
For I, I really hate your self-inflation
And find it odd that you are god!
I try to pry apart each indication
That you suggest still makes you best!
I can't stand your grandiosity!
I demand that you more humble be!
How can I ever think you're godly
When it's clear as clear can be
All the earth and sun is really run
By me, me, me!

As you have presumably been learning in this book, you also have feelings of discomfort anxiety or low-frustration tolerance. You can interrupt these feelings with the following rational humorous songs, which satirize discomfort anxiety:

Love Me, Love Me, Only Me!

(to the tune of "Yankee Doodle Dandy")

Love me, love me, only me
Or I'll die without you!
Oh make your love a guarantee,
So I can never doubt you!
Love me, love me totally—really, really try, dear.
But if you demand love, too,
I'll hate you till I die, dear!

Love me, love me all the time,
Thoroughly, and wholly!
My life turns into slushy slime
Unless you love me solely!
Love me with great tenderness,
With no ifs or buts, dear.
If you love me somewhat less,
I'll hate your goddamned guts, dear!

Whine, Whine, Whine!

(to the tune of "Yale Whiffenpoof Song" by Guy Scull—a Harvard Man!)

I cannot have all of my wishes filled—
Whine, whine, whine!
I cannot have every frustration stilled—
Whine, whine, whine!
Life really owes me the things that I miss,
Fate has to grant me eternal bliss!
And since I must settle for less than this—
Whine, whine, whine!

I'm Depressed, Depressed!

(to the tune of "The Band Played On" by Charles B. Ward)

When anything slightly goes wrong with my life,
I'm depressed, depressed!

Whenever I'm stricken with chickenshit strife,
I feel most distressed!
Oh, when life isn't fated to be consecrated
I can't tolerate it at all!
When anything slightly goes wrong with my life,
I just bawl, bawl, bawl!

You for Me and Me for Me

(to the tune of "Tea for Two" by Vincent Youmans)

Picture you upon my knee,
Just you for me, and me for me!
And then you'll see
How happy I will be, dear!
Though you beseech me
You never will reach me—
For I am autistic
As any real mystic!
And only relate to
Myself with a great to-do, dear!
If you dare to try to care
You'll see my caring soon will wear,
For I can't pair and make our sharing fair!
If you want a family,
We'll both agree you'll baby me—
Then you'll see how happy I will be!

Beautiful Hangup

(to the tune of "Beautiful Dreamer" by Stephen Foster)

Beautiful hangup, why should we part
When we have shared our whole lives from the start?
We are so used to taking one course,
Oh, what a crime it would be to divorce!
Beautiful hangup, don't go away!
Who will befriend me if you do not stay?

Though you still make me look like a jerk,
Living without you would take so much work!—
Living without you would take so much work!

GLORY, GLORY HALLELUJAH!
(to the tune of "Battle Hymn of the Republic")

Mine eyes have seen the glory of
   relationships that glow
And then falter by the wayside as
   love passions come—and go!
I have heard of great romances where
   there is no slightest lull—
But I am skeptical!
Glory, glory hallelujah!
People love ya till they screw ya!
If you'd cushion how they do ya,
Then don't expect they won't!
Glory, glory hallelujah!
People cheer ya—then pooh-pooh ya!
If you'd soften how they screw ya!
Then don't expect they won't!

I WISH I WERE NOT CRAZY
(to the tune of "Dixie" by Dan Emmett)

Oh, I wish I were really put together—
Smooth and fine as patent leather!
Oh, how great to be rated innately sedate!
But I'm afraid that I was fated
To be rather aberrated—
Oh, how sad to be mad as my Mom and my Dad!
Oh, I wish I were not crazy! Hooray, hooray!
I wish my mind were less inclined
To be the kind that's hazy!
I could, you see, agree to really be less crazy.
But I, alas, am just too goddamned lazy!

If you will use some of these rational humorous antianxiety songs, along with other humorous methods, you can make real progress against needless anxiety. The shoulds, oughts, and the musts with which you create your anxious feelings are overserious and completely unhumorous. When you interrupt these demands with humor, you are able to see that there are no reasons why you absolutely must perform well, must be completely free of discomfort, and must not ever feel anxious. Humor is open-minded and releasing. Musts and demands are close-minded and inhibiting. Keep as antimusturbatory as you can be and you will have minimal anxiety and be able to control your anxiety before it controls you.

20

Using Exposure and
Behavioral Desensitization

Rational Emotive Behavior Therapy, as I have been showing in this book, consists of the cognitive, the emotive, and the behavioral. In this chapter, I will describe some of the main behavioral methods REBT teaches to help you control your anxiety before it controls you.

As noted in the beginning of this book, I got myself over my extreme fears of public speaking and of approaching potential partners for dates by a combination of philosophical analysis and behavioral therapy. The idea that nothing, in truth, was very anxiety-provoking, especially a harmless pursuit such as public speaking, I derived mainly from philosophers. By the time I was nineteen, I had read a little cognitive therapy, particularly that of Alfred Adler's individual psychology, but that didn't impress me as much as the down-to-earth philosophy of the ancient Greeks and Romans, particularly Epicurus, Epictetus, and Marcus Aurelius. They all very clearly said that I created most of my own anxiety and phobias and that by straight thinking, I could minimize them. I thought that was a brilliant insight into the human condition and resolved to use it.

However, I also read about John B. Watson's experiments with little children who feared harmless mice or rabbits. He got them over their fears by giving them in vivo desensitization, exposing them to the feared animals until they became familiar with them, saw that they were harmless, and then actually started petting them. So I used exposure on myself to overcome my horror of failing at public speaking and my terror at being rejected by possible female partners. The combination of Disputing my Irrational Beliefs about failure and rejection and deliberately making myself uncomfortable by actually failing and getting rejected worked beautifully. Within a few months of self-help procedures, and no psychotherapy whatever, I was nonanxious and nonphobic.

Naturally, when I became a psychotherapist in 1943, I used these techniques with many of my clients and helped them considerably with their own anxieties. However, I was at that time partly enamored of psychoanalysis—not so much the Freudian kind but the more liberal analysis of Erich Fromm, Harry Stack Sullivan, Franz Alexander and Thomas French, and Karen Horney; and in 1947, I actually began my analytic training with Richard Hulbeck. So for several years I wore two hats—one as a non-Freudian analyst and another as a cognitive behavior therapist. I called myself an analyst, but I actually practiced both forms of psychotherapy (just as many other analysts of that day called themselves psychoanalysts but actually did much nonanalytic work) until 1953. Then, realizing that psychoanalysis was often harming people more than helping them, I abandoned that label in 1953, called myself simply a psychotherapist, and started to create Rational Emotive Behavior Therapy. By January 1955, I was already practicing what I then called Rational Therapy (RT), and I included in it a number of cognitive, emotive, and behavioral methods, particularly in vivo desensitization or exposure.

By 1955, I had already written five books on sex and love and more than forty professional and popular articles on relationships and marriage. A large percentage of my clients had sexual and love anxieties, so I used exposure with them. I persuaded them to make dates they were afraid of making, to keep trying to have sex relations with partners with whom they had failed, and to remain in marriages and relationships that were most difficult. While they changed their catastrophizing and awfulizing thinking, I wanted them to bite the bullet, to try and often fail, and to see in practice that doing so was not horrendous and that their worth as individuals didn't in the least shrink—except when they thought that it did.

My notable success with my clients who had serious sex and love problems helped me see that I was on the right track and that homework assignments consisting of exposure to failure and rejection for the most part worked. Clients who had a series of sex failures, and who had practically withdrawn from all sexual activity, went back into the fray and often failed a few times more, but then started to succeed and enjoy themselves immensely. Clients who almost committed suicide when they were rejected in love, and who were gun-shy about entering new love or marital relationships, started dating and relating—and soon a number of them were maintaining good love relationships.

I continued to urge more and more of them to assert themselves, take risks, and try out sex and love relationships that they had been anxious and phobic about for years. I wrote up the favorable results of my cognitive behavioral techniques of psychotherapy in a number of books and articles, and, through my seeing many clients for therapy as well as reaching them through my writings, I freed more people up for unanxious sex-love relating than probably any other psychotherapist. Kinsey and Masters and Johnson helped considerably in these respects with their scientific writings; but my paperback best-selling books, such as *The Art and Science of Love* and *Sex Without Guilt*, reached millions of people who would hardly ever open a scientific treatise. To this day, many people stop me at my public talks and workshops to gratefully inform me that they started overcoming their sex and relationship anxieties in the 1960s after they read some of my paperback best-sellers.

You, too, can tackle your sex, love, and other anxieties by using some of the behavioral methods that I started using extensively over fifty years ago and that I especially developed when I started to use REBT in January 1955.

The main one of these methods is still in vivo desensitization or exposure. When I first started to use it as a result of my experiments on myself at the age of nineteen, exposure was rarely used in psychotherapy, even in early behavior therapy. It was thought to be too active, too intrusive, and likely to be resisted by clients. More passive and indirect deconditioning methods were popular, especially behavior therapist Joseph Wolpe's imaginal desensitization or reciprocal inhibition. Wolpe figured that if you were irrationally afraid of something, such as a harmless garter snake, or even a picture of a snake, the thing for you to do was to imagine the snake as being a mile away and then use Jacobsen's progressive relaxation technique to relax. Then imagine the snake a half mile away and again relax. Then a quarter of a mile away, and again relax. And so on, until you became desensitized to the snake and no longer were afraid of thinking about it or actually confronting it. Many experiments in the 1960s showed that this technique of reciprocal inhibition often worked, though the experimenters came up with different theories of why it worked.

When you practice REBT, you can use Wolpe's imaginal desensitization to reduce your irrational fear of garter snakes or of many other "frightening" things. But in the final analysis, you'll probably have to go to a zoo and look the snake in the eye, or else you'll hardly be sure that you are no longer afraid of it. So imaginal desensitization usually has to be tested out by facing the feared object in vivo, and proving that you are no longer anxious about it. Also, as many experiments with behavior therapy have shown since the 1970s, some of people's worst irrational fears—such as their fear that unless they perform a certain obsessive–compulsive ritual they will be plagued forever with anxiety—do not seem to be extinguished by imaginal desensitization. Instead, some people require in vivo exposure and then the fears really do diminish or disappear.

A CASE OF SUBWAY RIDING ANXIETY AND
PANIC ABOUT PANIC

When you use REBT, I recommend that you use live exposure to minimize your irrational fears. Take the case of Mal, for example. He was a computer analyst who lived in Brooklyn and had to travel to Manhattan where he had held a job for fifteen years. It was a good job, he was happy and he had earned many salary increases. But the only feasible way to get to work was a one-hour subway ride, and he had enormous anxiety about taking such rides and practically never used the subway. He had an easily dislocatable shoulder, which made it very dangerous for him to drive to work, so he tried meeting up with other car owners who lived in Brooklyn (or even farther out in Long Island) and commuting to work with them. Because this was difficult to arrange, he often had to take a series of buses or a taxi to work and back again. This mode of transportation was expensive and, in the case of the buses, time-consuming. But his subway phobia remained, and the few times he took the subway, he suffered much anguish and dread.

Mal had no special reason for his terror of riding the subway. None of his friends or relatives had ever been hurt in a subway, and neither had he. One day, when he was on his way to college by subway, the train stopped for five minutes in between stations, and he went into a state of panic with a rapidly beating heart and much sweating. But nothing happened, and the train soon started up again. That was Mal's last subway ride for years. As with most panicked individuals, he was panicked about panicking again, and he insisted that he absolutely could not stand it if the subway train stopped and he went into a panic state. So he didn't stay with the panic and see that it was inconvenient but not terrible. He copped out and took cars, taxis, and buses.

Using REBT, I tackled the Irrational Belief behind Mal's secondary symptom, his panic about panicking. He had the usual low-frustration tolerance (LFT) that people often have about experiencing panic. He told himself, "I absolutely must not panic! It's the most unpleasant feeling I've ever had. I *can't stand* the heart palpitations, the gasping for breath, the paralysis in my limbs, and the other terrible feelings that it produces! I feel that I'm going to die, and I often feel that it would be much better if I did. Then I would be completely out of my agony. If I'm going to suffer like this and always feel in danger of having this terrible experience for the rest of my life, what's the use of living at all? If it weren't for the misery I would bring on my parents and my brothers, I would seriously consider ending it all and getting out of my own misery." Mal, in other words, was not merely telling himself that he greatly disliked his severe panic states, he was saying that he couldn't tolerate them, couldn't be happy *at all* if they continued. That is why, at great inconvenience to himself, he refused to ride the subways.

Secondly, although Mal at first denied how ashamed he would feel if he went into a panic state in the subway and the rest of the passengers saw how anxious he was and looked down on him for his state of paralysis, I persisted in questioning him about this and discovered a significant aspect of it. He really didn't seem to mind other people seeing him trembling and paralyzed when he was in a state of panic, but he was exceptionally afraid that he might then lose control of his bodily functions and urinate in his pants. That would *really* be shameful! He couldn't bear the horror that would be produced in his onlookers if his trousers became very visibly wet and smelly. That would be the worst possible thing that could happen, and something that had to be avoided at all costs. He would forever be disgraced if such a disaster occurred.

So Mal, to be sure, had both LFT and self-downing about experiencing extreme panic in the subway. Using REBT, we worked on his Irrational Beliefs and, theoretically at least, he was able to see that he *could* stand the severe feelings and the helplessness that went with his panic attacks and that he could also stand it if he urinated in his pants and his onlookers were completely turned off by his doing so and thought of him as a rotten smelly person. He even came to the conclusion, when he thought about his Irrational Beliefs about becoming panicked, that the people in the subway train who might be disgusted by his urinating in his pants were perfect strangers whom he would probably never see again and that they would soon forget about this disgusting incident. Some of them, he reasoned, would not even be turned off by his urination but would view it as an almost normal result of being paralyzed with panic and would be kind and solicitous if such a situation ever actually occurred.

So far, so good. Mal Disputed the Irrational Beliefs behind his panic, and his absolutistic demands that under no circumstances must he be panicked and show others that he was, and he partially got over his horror of experiencing panic in the subway. At least, he could think about this event happening and not become terribly anxious when he envisioned it. As for his actually taking rides in the subway, however, no go. He just wouldn't risk it.

Mal's transportation problems, meanwhile, became worse. His firm moved from Manhattan to Jersey City, and he found it almost impossible to ride by car to and from his work with fellow workers. Going by bus was more complicated and took longer than ever. Going by taxi or limousine was greatly expensive. The best alternative by far was his taking a subway from Brooklyn to Manhattan and then taking the Port Authority Path train, which was really another form of subway, to Jersey City. But then he would be more than ever in danger of feeling panic.

Mal desperately tried to get another computer analyst job in Brooklyn, even at much less salary, but to no avail. He even thought of changing his profession and working at almost any kind of job. But he would have had to sacrifice the fifteen years he had spent with his present company and his vested interest in his pension rights. There seemed to be no feasible options, and he became more and more anxious and depressed.

Finally, having run out of choices, he considered working on his subway phobia. After several months of endlessly talking about his Irrational Beliefs and Disputing them in his head, he actually approached me about the possibility of taking some real action to conquer his phobia. If I could suggest some reasonably easy action, he would uncomfortably do it and hopefully make some inroads against his subway avoidance.

Fortunately, I had a reasonably easy plan I had used with several other subway phobics and which I now proposed to Mal. He would go to the subway station closest to his home and take the train one short station to the next stop. Then, he would get off again, wait for the next train to come along five or ten minutes later, and take that train one stop. He would keep doing this, one stop at a time, until he got used to doing so and his phobia lessened. Moreover, since the subway at his point in the line was elevated above the ground, he would not feel trapped underground.

Mal theoretically agreed to this plan, but he kept finding excuses to put it off. He was still afraid that he would panic and then panic about his panic, and the thought of doing so horrified him. But one Sunday, when the trains were less crowded than on weekdays, he forced himself to get on at his local stop and go for one station on the second train that came along. The first train he had let go by. He was fearful about taking the train that he did take but kept telling himself, "One stop. One stop. One lousy stop!" When he reached the next station, he got off with a sigh of relief. Nothing terrible had happened. No panic, although he had considerable anxiety.

The following Sunday, Mal again took the subway train one stop, and the following Sunday two stops. By the end of two months, he was able to take the train for several stops, getting off at each stop and waiting awhile for the next train to come along. Then he tried taking the train two stops in a row, then three, and then more. Within several months, Mal was able to take the train for many stops on Sundays, when it was not crowded; and then he risked doing the same thing on weekdays, when it was crowded. Nothing terrible happened—no panic. He still was anxious and uncomfortable at times, but as he went on and on with his subway riding, he began to see that panic was hardly an issue. A few times, when the train was underground and stopped for five or ten minutes in-between stations for no known reason, he got a little more anxious than usual. But still no panic. One time, when it stopped for about 15 minutes, he even hoped that a state of panic would develop so that he could see whether he could handle it and not be panicked about having panic. Actually, however, once he started riding in subways no panic developed. After nine months of subway riding, Mal was quite sure that he would not panic and especially that he could handle it if panic ever did occur. He took the subway every day, as well as the Path train from Manhattan to Jersey City, and he was very happy about his ability to do so.

Among other things, he found that he could easily read a book or a newspaper in the subway and Path trains, while he had difficulty doing so in a car or a bus. So the hour and a quarter he spent going to work and back from work became a good rather than a bad experience.

You, too, can conquer anxiety that limits your daily activities. Explore, as Mal did with REBT's help, the Irrational Beliefs that make you anxious and prevent you from doing something either beneficial or enjoyable. Then force yourself to be uncomfortable about doing it but still force yourself to do it. Chances are, you won't die of your discomfort, and chances are you will soon overcome it.

A CASE OF ANXIETY ABOUT
SUBMITTING TERM PAPERS

Frances had a phobia against turning in complete term papers in her college history course, and she always cajoled and bribed her boyfriend, Sam, to finish each paper for her. She would do all the research and actually complete a first draft, but she would never quite finish it. She would convince Sam that he just had to polish it up and complete it for her or else she could not turn it in at all. Most of the time, Sam had very little to do before he thought the paper was in good enough shape to submit. But Frances never submitted it without his few final touches.

Because Frances severely castigated herself for not finishing off any of her term papers, I helped her first give herself unconditional self-acceptance (USA) when she relied on Sam to complete her work. Her behavior, I showed her, was weak, foolish, and inept, and it reinforced her horror of doing a paper completely on her own. But she was not a weak, foolish, and inept person; she simply behaved that way in regard to her term paper phobia.

Frances still refused to hand in a single paper unless Sam put some finishing touches to it. So I saw Sam and Frances for a session together and explained to him that he was really not enabling her by giving in to her demand that he help her with her papers. I got him to agree that during the next month, when three term papers were due, he would not touch them. She would just have to submit them without his help or else not submit them at all.

Frances was exceptionally anxious at the prospect of submitting three papers entirely on her own, and frantically she tried to get some of her other friends to substitute for Sam in putting them in final order. Fortunately, she found no one available to help her. So she sweated it out and kept telling herself that nothing terrible would happen if she submitted papers on her own. She forced herself, very uncomfortably, to finish the three that were due and hand them in. The first one she completed with great anxiety and much moaning and groaning. The second one she finished with less anxiety and less moaning and groaning. And the third one she finished with very little anxiety and no moaning and groaning. Thereafter, she was able to do all her term papers enthusiastically, without any help from Sam or anyone else, and to revel in her ability to do them by herself.

The case of Frances shows that exposure to frightening situations can sometimes be done quickly rather than gradually. Obviously, therefore, in your own case, you have the choice of either or both methods. By all means, see the Irrational Beliefs that are leading you to become very anxious and to phobically avoid certain difficult situations. Work at Disputing these IBs vigorously and persistently. If you still retain your phobia, make yourself do the act which you're so afraid of doing, no matter how uncomfortable you are. Do it and do it and do it. If you die of doing it, as I always tell my clients, have no fear—we will be sure to provide you with a great funeral, with lovely flowers, and a marvelous setting. But you won't die. Instead, very often you'll quickly or gradually get over your anxiety and your phobia and be very happy that you no longer allow yourself to indulge in them.

21

Tolerating and Staying in Anxiety-Provoking Situations

The trouble with most anxiety-provoking situations is that you can somehow manage to escape them. Thus, if you are panicked about speaking in public, you can usually avoid speaking. If you are terrified about approaching attractive people for dates you can avoid people you consider attractive. Whenever you avoid alarming situations, however, you almost always increase your anxiety about them. For you most often tell yourself, "If I spoke in public, I would be bound to do quite poorly, would be laughed at, and would feel like an idiot." Or, "If I approached this attractive person and asked her for a date, she would find me wanting, would definitely reject me, and then I would feel utterly worthless."

So avoidance of doing something you are greatly afraid to do brings temporary release but almost always increases your irrational anxiety. So does changing what REBT calls the A (Adversity) in its ABCs. For even if you do so, you may easily bring your Irrational Bs and a new disturbed C (Consequence) to the new As.

A CASE OF ANXIETY ABOUT CRITICISM AT WORK

Consider the case of Tanya. She was terribly afraid of criticism, especially at her job as a pattern maker. Whenever she had a critical boss or supervisor—or thought that she had one—she quickly found an excuse to quit her job and find a new one. In looking for another job, she did more interviewing than her interviewer—for she wanted to determine, in advance, how critical her boss or supervisor was likely to be.

Naturally, under these conditions, Tanya got no experience adjusting to a critical supervisor, and she became more and more anxious about being censured. She just took her supersensitivity to criticism to each new position; and because she was so chary of being put down, she often found put-downs where none really existed. Also, she reacted so badly to even constructive suggestions that her supervisors frequently felt afraid to hurt her feelings, held themselves unduly in check, and sometimes got rid of her because she was restricting them so much.

Tanya came to see me for psychotherapy because she was running out of places to find work, even in New York's large garment industry. She had run away from so many jobs and had been let go by so many others that she had very few options left. She was a good pattern maker, enjoyed her work, and made a decent income when she was working. But she seemed to be reaching the end of her occupational rope.

As you may have guessed already, I started Tanya off with the ABCs of her pathological job changing and her compulsive seeking for noncritical supervisors. First, she had a normal or rational dislike of criticism, as stated in her philosophy, "I don't like being criticized and told what to do, especially when I've been a good pattern maker for so many years. I wish my supervisors would simply let me do my work. If they have any objections or suggestions for change, I wish they would make them in a polite, civilized manner. I won't mind listening to their suggestions on how I can improve my work. But I *do* mind suggestions made in a harsh, nasty way that indicates I'm just no good as a pattern maker and had better go back to the work I used to do on the sewing machines." If Tanya had only stayed with this attitude, she would have felt sorry and frustrated whenever she was criticized but would have gotten into no job difficulties.

Simultaneously, however, and in a much stronger fashion, Tanya held the Irrational Beliefs, "I *absolutely must not* be criticized or censured. It means that my supervisors lack confidence in my ability and think I'm an inferior pattern maker and an inferior person. It's shameful to be put down like that, especially when some of them are much younger than I and know less about pattern making. I can't bear their looking down on me in this manner, and I can't let them take advantage of me and get away with it. I'll be a rotten weakling if I don't put an end to their unfair complaining immediately. I'll show them that I'm not going to let them shame me like this! I'll damned well quit!" These Irrational Beliefs, for which she had little factual evidence, hurt and enraged Tanya.

When Tanya clearly saw her IBs and actively Disputed them, she began to be somewhat less vulnerable to the supposed assaults of her supervisors, and she lasted two or three times as long on her jobs than previously. But sooner or later, someone over her would be in a bad mood and partly take it out on her, and she would return to her IBs with a vengeance and either quit the job or insist that she be transferred to another overseer.

I felt that I'd better be quite firm with Tanya, and I got her to agree with the rule that she would not quit any of her jobs, no matter how harshly she was criticized, until she first dealt with her hurt and her rage. Once she had calmed down by using REBT Disputing of her Irrational Beliefs and therefore felt healthily frustrated and sorry about people's "unfair" criticism but didn't feel hurt, self-downing, and angry about it, she could then quit her job—if she still wanted to do so. Otherwise, she agreed to stay and suffer until she got on top of her hurt and anger.

Tanya soon had a good test of this technique. She was bawled out by her supervisor, who had once been a pattern maker herself, for taking too much time on a job and therefore forcing the firm to get an extra pattern maker they didn't think it necessary for them to hire. Her supervisor scolded her for her slowness and said that in twenty years, she had not seen anybody as slow as Tanya. If Tanya didn't pick up her pace, they would not only fire her but let her potential future employers know how slow she was.

Tanya was crushed by this criticism, became very anxious and depressed, and actually slowed down even more. She would have definitely quit, but she remembered the rule we had set up and began Disputing her Irrational Beliefs.

She especially Disputed her Belief that Maria, her supervisor, was unfair because she was scolding Tanya on the basis of pattern making standards of twenty years ago that were different from those of today. Maria was not taking into account that today's pattern making was much more complicated than in the past and therefore took more time. Tanya Disputed Maria's unfairness and quickly came up with the self-statement, "Let's suppose that everyone would agree with me that she is very unfair. Who the hell says that she has to be fair? How, in fact, can she be fair when she obviously has a tendency, which I've known all along, to be unfair? So, dammit, she's unfair! Let her be. I don't have to be unfair to myself, just as she is, by taking her unfairness so seriously and putting myself down with it. I can *fairly* deal with her unfairness. Let her be as unfair as she likes. I'm going to see this situation clearly and still not beat myself with her unfairness."

Doing this Disputing, Tanya, for one of the rare times in her life, dealt nicely with Maria's moodiness and refused to be cowed by it. Tanya fully intended to calm herself down and look for another job, because she really didn't like having to be subject to Maria's unfair criticism. But she deliberately stayed on the job even after she had given up her hurt and her rage, just to see how long she could continue to do so and not get upset all over again.

For the next several weeks, Tanya stayed and put up with even greater criticism from Maria, who was upset because, for the first time, she saw that she was not upsetting Tanya. Therefore, she tried harder to do so, but to no avail.

Because Tanya Disputed her Irrational Beliefs and also stayed on the job when Maria continued to lean on her, she very clearly saw that she was able to control her own anxiety and rage before they controlled her. Her staying on under very difficult conditions dramatized her ability to control her feelings, no matter what Maria's provocation was. She finally was fired by Maria, who simply couldn't stand Tanya's newfound self-composure, but she took her firing, too, with remarkably equanimity. Thereafter, she was much less vulnerable to her supervisors' criticism and she rarely left her job in a state of despair and rage.

Following Tanya's model, you can make yourself stay in some very difficult situations—with your supposedly unfair and bitching bosses, mates, in-laws, friends, and other people. Work on your own talent to easily upset yourself about the unfortunate ways that you think they are acting; stay with them instead of leaving them until you are no longer feeling upset. Then decide whether, in fact, staying has more advantages than disadvantages before you make your decision whether to leave. The more you control your overreactions to their poor actions, the more you will train yourself to control your anxiety—before it controls you.

22

Using Reinforcement Methods to Control Your Anxiety

The techniques of rewarding people when they perform well and of penalizing them when they perform poorly have been used by parents, teachers, philosophers, religious leaders, and other shapers of human behavior for many centuries, and they have often been effective. Ivan Pavlov was one of the first scientists to use them in the conditioning of animals, and, following his lead, a number of other scientists began to use them to encourage good conduct and to discourage unwanted actions.

In the 1920s and 1930s, B. F. Skinner demonstrated in a number of psychological experiments that operant conditioning is a most important factor in encouraging children and adults to act in their own best interests. By this he meant that if they are reinforced or rewarded with something they like after accomplishing certain tasks, they will much more likely perform these tasks than if they are not rewarded. Their contingencies of reinforcement largely set the stage for their doing certain tasks, such as solving problems or doing their homework. The more they are reinforced or rewarded, the more they will tend to repeat their activities, and the less they are reinforced, the less they will repeat them. This, Skinner strongly implied, is the nature of animals and humans; and it can be used to get them to do good or helpful things and to get them to stop doing bad or unhelpful pursuits.

Behavior therapy, following Pavlov, Skinner, and many other

behavioral scientists, uses the principles of reinforcement to help clients overcome disturbed feelings and actions and to replace these with healthy emotions and deeds. Hundreds of controlled experiments have shown that reinforcement works. Therefore, REBT often uses it along with its many other thinking, feeling, and behavioral methods to help people control their anxiety.

A CASE OF ANXIETY ABOUT SHOWING COMPETENCY

Theodore, a forty-year-old attorney, had suffered from several kinds of performance anxiety all his life. He did very well when taking tests, going for job interviews, defending his clients in court, and playing several sports. But he often suffered from severe anxiety when doing these things—not out of fear that he would fail miserably but that he would succeed moderately instead of outstandingly well and would lose status in the eyes of his onlookers. So, although he was distinctly above average in his performances, as soon as a test date was set, he began to worry about being mediocre in it, "disgracefully" mediocre. He worried more as the time for the actual performance approached, and after it was over, even if he had done quite well, he worried that his friends and associates would not think he had done well enough and would see him as being an average performer—which to him meant that they would despise him. None of his close friends ever did seem to denigrate him for his "mediocre" performances, but he thought that they were merely being polite and really thought little of him.

Theodore, partly because of his legal training, understood the ABCs of REBT quite well soon after I discussed them with him. He especially became adept at figuring out his Irrational Beliefs whenever he was anxious. This was fairly easy for him to do because practically all his IBs were variations on a few simple themes that ran through his whole life and plagued him continually. Basically, whenever an important performance approached—even if it was scheduled to take place months away—he strongly told himself, and very much believed, "I must prove all over again, by this performance, that I am a competent and worthwhile person! Some people think they are good if they are kind to others or rigidly follow moral rules. But I know that that is stupid, because anyone can do that and thus merit universal goodness. How foolish! To be worthwhile as a person obviously means having the ability to survive and to perform efficiently. Darwin was right, for all of us it is the survival of the fittest. And to be fit means to be efficient at solving important life problems—again, obviously to be competent. Therefore, in order to be a good and worthy individual I have to be able to survive various tests of competence. To fail them means to be a real schnook, a hopeless soul who isn't able to compete well and come out on top. So, although I certainly don't have to do well at everything—obviously, that would be impossible—I do have to pass every important test of proficiency and usually best others at each test. Let's not quibble about this. I *must* do well in important areas or else I will fail to show how able to succeed I am and will not survive or will live very miserably. Human worth, clearly, equals competence at crucial tasks. To think otherwise would be to asininely fool myself—as most of the human race does. Not me. I'll accept the challenge of being one of the fittest to survive and I'll perform well at important tasks at all costs. I've got to. I must."

As noted, Theodore had many variations on this theme of demanding outstanding test performance, and consequently he was almost pandemically anxious. He realized some of this during our very first REBT session and was exceptionally clear about it after a few sessions and after filling out the REBT Self-Help form several times in between sessions. Realizing it, however, did not at first make him act in a less-anxious manner. As new tests of his ability arose, especially in regard to his courtroom appearances, he still was distinctly overconcerned rather than merely concerned about his doing well.

Supposedly to reduce his anxiety, but actually to preserve it, Theodore copped out of taking law cases where he would have to do more than negotiate a settlement with the opposing attorneys and instead would have to appear in court and conduct a trial before a judge and jury. His mistakes, if he made any, would then be very visible, and they would be more "awful" than if he merely made them in the course of negotiations with an opposing lawyer or two. If he thought that there was a good chance of a case actually coming to trial, he refused to take it and turned it over to one of the other partners of his law firm.

As part of his getting over his performance anxiety, I urged Theodore to deliberately take on all cases that might involve court appearances. In doing so, I showed him, he would then have to confront his severe anxiety instead of avoiding it. In being forced to confront it, he would become conscious of his specific Irrational Beliefs, would be encouraged to deal with them, and would make much greater progress with overcoming his anxiety than if he avoided them. In other words, I strongly suggested in vivo desensitization procedures to help him confront his anxiety about concrete courtroom appearances.

Theodore was even more anxious when he heard my plan of attack on his anxiety and agreed to it very reluctantly. But because he then managed to avoid practically all cases that involved courtroom appearances, the plan wasn't given a chance to work. Whereupon I used B. F. Skinner's procedure of operant conditioning with him. We determined that he really was good at negotiating cases outside of court and that he greatly enjoyed doing so. Where other lawyers in his firm would negotiate a case and perhaps arrange to get a ten thousand dollar settlement, Theodore would get the opposing side to agree to settle for two or three times that amount. Then, knowing that he had done a terrific job for the client, he would feel moved to try to settle more and more cases out of court. His firm knew he was good at doing this and deliberately threw many cases his way, where an out of court settlement could probably be reached.

To insure Theodore's taking on more court cases involving an actual trial, we made a one-to-one rule for him to follow for the next few months. Every time he participated in a case that allowed him to settle out of court, he was to take on the next case where there was a high degree of probability that he would have to go to court to settle it. If he did this, he would have a fair number of in-court cases to work on and to be anxious about where he could use REBT to Dispute his anxiety. If he took on these anxiety-provoking cases, he would then, and only then, have the ease and satisfaction of taking on the out-of-court settlement of his next case.

Theodore agreed to do this, though with real qualms at first. He forced himself to take on as many in-court cases as out-of-court settlements. At first, he was anxious, and sometimes panicked, but as he kept doing so, his anxiety decreased, and he became more adept at handling in-court cases which he had previously avoided doing. When he was anxious about an in-court case, he worked harder at using several REBT methods to control his anxiety, and soon he became more relaxed and adept at doing that, too. So the operant conditioning procedure was quite effective and enabled Theodore to take on exposure to anxiety-provoking in-court cases when, without rewarding himself for doing so by allowing himself to take on out-of-court settlements as well, he would have avoided the in-court cases and worked little at overcoming his anxiety about them.

Similarly, whenever you are very anxious about any test-taking procedure, any job interview, any participation in a sporting event, any public-speaking performance, or any other kind of activity that requires competency, you can usually devise a way to stop avoiding this activity and thereby temporarily get over your anxiety. For if you keep avoiding it, you will normally preserve your anxiety and allow it to build. So devise, instead, a method of exposing yourself to possible panic and then force yourself to go through with this actual exposure a good many times while Disputing your basic Irrational Beliefs that are leading to your anxiety. If you have difficulty exposing yourself to this kind of situation, you can use the principles of contingency management or operant conditioning to get yourself to do so. Allow yourself to do some easy, enjoyable task you have no trouble doing after you complete the difficult, anxiety-provoking procedure that you are doing your best to avoid.

Don't cop out. Don't give up. Keep at it until you routinely, perhaps without any reinforcement or reward, do the fearful task that you fear doing and work on your irrational fear of doing it. In the short run, you may have difficulty and even increase your anxiety. But in the long run, you will truly release yourself and create minimum overconcern.

23

Using Penalties to Control
Your Anxiety

According to B. F. Skinner, people will do difficult things if you reward or reinforce them, but you cannot get them to do the same things through threats and penalties. This is because people rebel against penalties, consider them unjust, and sometimes deliberately react against them. Thus, if you tell children or adolescents that they must not go into a certain room or closet or else you will punish them severely, they will sometimes deliberately react against your proscriptions and go out of their way to enter that room or closet. They take it as a real challenge to do so and will ignore or make light of the penalty you have set for doing so.

Well, Skinner may have been partly right, but he was also partly wrong. If you are addicted to self-defeating behavior, such as smoking cigarettes, the use of reinforcing techniques may not work to enable you to overcome this addiction. You get so much pleasure from indulging in your addiction that no amount of rewards will deter you from doing so. You may, for example, love watching a certain television show. But if you only reward yourself with watching that show when you refrain from smoking, you may still definitely smoke. The pleasure of seeing the show for the addicted smoker is far less intense than the pleasure of smoking. So TV just won't work as an effective reward.

On the other hand, penalizing yourself stiffly every time you give in to your addiction may help you to give it up. Thus, if you put the lit end of the cigarette in your mouth every puff you take or if you light each cigarette with a fifty dollar bill, you probably won't smoke for very long! Or if you get emphysema from smoking and know there is a good chance that you are on the way to developing lung cancer, you may quickly stop smoking.

For this reason, REBT sometimes encourages you to use stiff penalties to help you overcome some of your severe anxieties or other disturbances. It would be nice if reinforcements for giving them up worked just as well. But if you've tried reinforcements and failed, you may wisely resort to penalties.

Theodore, for example, whose case of overcoming his in-court appearances was greatly improved by using the reinforcement of making his in-court appearances contingent on his out-of-court settlements, did remarkably well with the use of reinforcements. But in one particular case, they didn't work. He was scheduled to try a case in court against a ruthless attorney who did everything possible to give his opposing attorneys a hard time and who usually won his trial cases by hook or by crook. Theodore had opposed this lawyer a few times before and had always lost the case; therefore, Theodore didn't want to try another case against him. He was all set to cop out and give the case to one of his law partners to try—and to hate himself for doing so. His usual reinforcement system—only allowing himself to arrange to settle a case out of court—wasn't working. So, after discussing the matter in his therapy session with me, he decided that if he didn't arrange to try the court case, he would penalize himself by sending a thousand dollar contribution to a rabid hate group that he opposed. He even wrote a letter to this hate group, put a thousand dollars in cash with it, and addressed the envelope to their headquarters. If he copped out on the difficult court case with his dreaded opponent, he would send it off.

The penalizing procedure worked. Theodore never sent the letter, and he did take on the court case, although he actually lost it because of the unfair tactics of the opposing lawyer. Still he didn't feel anxious or depressed about it. The potential penalty he set for himself would have hurt so much if he had not taken the case that he went through with it, though hating to do so.

You can use this penalizing method too, though you may only use it occasionally and in an extreme case. When you are very anxious about doing something, but are quite sure that doing it is the right way to go and that it will ultimately result in your decreasing your anxiety, first look at the Irrational Beliefs that stop you from doing this thing. See if you are telling yourself, for example, "If I do this—such as confront my mate with the fact that he has lied about an important matter—I will get very anxious about doing so, and I just can't stand that degree of anxiety." Actively and vigorously Dispute that Irrational Belief. Then, force yourself to do the confrontation you are terribly anxious about doing. If you have real trouble forcing yourself to do it, consider reinforcing yourself with something pleasant only *after* you do it. Or, if that will not work, give yourself a stiff penalty and be sure to enact it if you do not go through with the anxiety-provoking confrontation. Temporarily, you will probably feel more anxiety than you usually do. But in the long run, you'll probably bring about much less anxiety. Try forcing yourself and see.

24

Using the Method of Fixed Role-playing to Control Your Anxiety

George Kelly was a pioneering cognitive-behavior therapist, but he never seemed to try to help people Dispute their Irrational Beliefs in order to control their anxiety. Instead, he encouraged them to act against these Beliefs and particularly to use his method of fixed role-playing.

A CASE OF ANXIETY ABOUT TRYING FOR A BETTER JOB

Suppose, for example, you are afraid to go for a good job because you're certain you will be given a hard time in the interview. You are educated, experienced, and capable enough to hold a distinctly better job than the one you now have, but you know that you will have to go through several interviews and you know from past experience that you just don't interview well. So you stay at your present low-level job or you only apply for other jobs that are not challenging and where the interviewers won't give you too hard a time. You know, of course, about your anxiety and weakness in this respect, and you put yourself down for being such a coward and for never trying for the kind of jobs that would stretch your capabilities.

As usual, you use the ABCs of REBT and analyze your

Irrational Beliefs: "I'm very weak at interviewing and I *absolutely must* do much better. Other people are not as anxious as I am, and therefore they can get almost any kind of job they want. My anxiety is a terrible handicap, and I'll never be able to have a good career as long as I'm anxious. It's such a weakness that it makes me a totally incompetent person. If I didn't have it, I'd be okay, so I hate myself for having it. It makes me a real basket case! What must those interviewers think of me when I shake and tremble in front of them and give them the wrong answers to their questions? A total idiot! And they're right. Of all the handicaps I have in the world it has to be this rotten one! People in business will despise me; my friends will look down on me, too, knowing that I'll only be able to hold a rotten job like the one I have and never be able to make any real advancement. My own family sees how weak I am, since even with my education and experience I'm completely stuck vocationally. I'm really hopeless, and people can easily see that I am and that I'll never get anywhere in life!"

Using REBT, you dispute these Irrational Beliefs, and you come up with reasonable objections to them. You see that your anxiety is a handicap but that it is not the worst thing in the world. You see that you are demanding that you be calm and unanxious at job interviews and that this demandingness is actually making you anxious. You see that anxiety is a negative, especially in job interviews, but that it merely makes you somewhat incompetent, not a totally incompetent person. You see that your interviewers probably don't despise you for being anxious and that some of them may not even notice how frightened you are, and you see that those who do notice may not exactly want you as an employee but that doesn't mean they think you are a basket case as a person. You see that it is wrong to hate yourself for being anxious; you should hate your anxiety, not yourself, and do your best to correct it. For if, you see, you hate yourself completely, that will make you even more anxious and will "prove" to you that you can do nothing but fail in job interviews. You see that your friends won't think much of your low-level job but that they will hardly boycott you because of your holding it. You see that your family doesn't like your holding a poor job but they still love you and accept you with it. You see that you have some real difficulties but that even if you never conquer your anxiety about job interviews, you will not be a hopeless person who will get absolutely nowhere in life.

Disputing your Irrational Beliefs helps you considerably and you feel much better and determined to work on your anxiety. So you try Kelly's fixed role-playing technique. You sit down and write out a sketch of yourself that is in many respects quite the opposite of the attitudes and feelings that you actually have regarding your anxiety and its handicaps. It is quite an optimistic sketch, and it may go somewhat as follows:

> I am not greatly anxious about job interviews and therefore I keep looking for a better job than the one I now have. I know what I know and have good job experiences and I am sure that I can show this to the interviewers. When I don't answer their questions very well, I stop and think and make another stab at it. If I get really anxious for a while, I take my anxiety in stride and go on. Everyone gets somewhat anxious at times in job interviews and I guess I'm no exception to the rule. So there's no use putting myself down for my anxiety and I work at not doing so. If the interviewers don't like me, I realize that they don't despise me personally but just think I'm not the best person for their job. If I fail at getting some jobs, I realize that my friends and my family will accept me as a person in spite of these failures and will not totally put me down. I know that most people fail at job interviews because the interviewers may speak with twenty applicants for each job that they actually have. So I'll keep trying in spite of my failures, and I'm pretty sure that one of these days I'll find the kind of job I really want and be able to keep it and progress with it.

Write out this kind of optimistic and helpful sketch and go over it several times. Get it solidly into your head. See yourself as definitely less anxious and able to get through a job interview even when you are temporarily struck with anxiety. See that you are able to handle difficult questions and situations and come back with good responses. Then for a period of time—say, a week, a month, or a few months—act as if the sketch you wrote for yourself is actually true. Follow it as best you can, as you would follow the script of a play in which you had a part. Revise it from time to time when you think that it is desirable, and keep playing it up to the hilt. You'll tend to see that after playing it awhile, you actually take on, in practice, some of the aspects of the role you have written for yourself in this fixed role-playing sketch.

Sarah was very anxious about getting a job as a senior accountant because she had failed the CPA exam twice. Most of the accounting jobs she interviewed for required that the applicant had passed the CPA exam or had passed at least three parts of it and had a good chance of passing the remaining parts. Sarah was hardly in this category and knew that she would be turned down for most of the jobs she wanted. She disputed her Irrational Beliefs that her interviewers thought she was stupid because she had twice failed all parts of the exam, and she felt somewhat less anxious. She then wrote herself a fixed role-playing sketch in which she was calm and serene, and she handled questions about her failing the CPA exam very well. She practiced playing out this sketched role for three job interviews. She failed to get one of the jobs, came within a hair of getting the second one, and actually did get the third one, the best of the three, when she kept persisting at following out the fixed role-play sketch she had made for herself.

So, again, when you are anxious about any kind of presentation, and your anxiety is seriously interfering with your doing a good job at this presentation, find your Irrational Beliefs that lead to your anxiety, question and challenge them until you see how inaccurate they are, and then consider trying a fixed role-play sketch tailored to this kind of presentation. It won't always work, of course. But you may become a great actor!

25

What About Biology and the Use of Medications?

Some cognitive behavior therapies, as well as other types of therapy, are opposed to the medical model of psychotherapy in all but a few unusual cases. These therapies believe that just about all anxiety and other emotional problems are entirely learned or conditioned. Not REBT! Although it stresses constructivism and says that people largely construct their disturbances and can therefore—albeit with hard work—reconstruct their cognitions, emotions, and actions, it also contends that they are biologically prone to do so. Yes, they learn many of their dysfunctional thoughts, feelings, and actions—but don't forget that they are born to be suggestible, teachable, and conditionable!

REBT, in fact, takes the position that probably all humans construct healthy reactions to the problems of living, and particularly the dangers that they encounter from birth to old age, otherwise they would not survive. But humans also construct unhealthy or self-defeating reactions, such as overreacting to difficulties and underreacting to problems. They are born and reared to help themselves *and* to make poor choices that hinder themselves. They are often neurotic or self-defeating and sometimes they are prone to serious disturbances, such as severe personality disorders and psychosis. Fortunately, however, they are constructively self-helping for the most part, otherwise they would hardly survive. When they sabotage their own and their social group's well-being, they have considerable ability to observe their dysfunctional thoughts, feelings, and actions and to significantly improve them. They do this naturally, and they can also learn to be constructive—among other ways by reading and following the teachings in this book.

Anxiety, in particular, is created by many biological and social factors and can be controlled in various physical and mental ways. Recent studies of the brain, central nervous system, and the biochemical functions have discovered many physiological aspects of anxiety: thus, when you perceive something as a danger or as a difficulty, your brain quickly goes into action. Your amygdala sends signals back to your prefrontal cortex, which in turn sends signals back to your amygdala that you are worrying. Then, a good deal of your body becomes involved in various biochemical networks.

The many courses that your body may take, both to arouse you and to quiet you down in order to deal with your perceived problems, involve serotonin production, swelling of your caudate nucleus, excessive activity in your cingulate cortex, your endocrine system (such as adrenalin upsurges), your neurotransmitters, your autonomic nervous system, your respiratory rate, and numerous other physiological reactions. More biochemical aspects of normal caution and of extreme anxiety are being found every day, and it would be foolish to ignore them. As Edward M. Hallowell has noted, "Worriers seem to inherit a neurological vulnerability that life events can then trigger."

To make matters still more complicated, your body strongly influences your mind and its feelings of anxiety—and vice versa! Intense feelings can traumatize your brain and even your immune system and may lead to temporary and sometimes permanent physical problems, and these in turn can worsen your emotional reactions. The possibilities of dysfunction may be circular and almost endless.

Now let's not run this into the ground and conclude that anxiety may easily cause cancer and that thinking sound thoughts can quickly cure potentially fatal diseases. If you take the mind–body connection *too* seriously, as several recent best-selling books urge you to do, you will only increase your anxiety!

Granted that your anxiety, and especially your feelings of panic, may well have physical as well as psychological causes, what can you do about this? Several important things.

First, assume that you are at least partly upsetting yourself with Irrational Beliefs, even when your anxiety has a strong physiological element. By seeing and Disputing these IBs, you may therefore change them and reduce your anxious feelings. So, by all means, look for the three main *musts* and *demands* that you may have and give them up—but retain the healthy preferences that go with them. At the same time, look for the other core Irrational Beliefs that may accompany your musts—such as awfulizing, I-can't-stand-it-itis, and damning yourself and others globally for the failings that you think they presumably have.

Then, strongly and persistently Dispute your IBs using several of the thinking, feeling, and behavioral methods described in this book. Work diligently at employing these methods for several weeks or months. Don't conclude prematurely that because they are not yet working, they can't work. Persist!

If you have little success in working along these lines, consider the possibility of biochemical involvement. Check out your close blood relatives to see if any of them have suffered from severe anxiety (or other emotional problems). Find out what they did to recover and what medication, if any, was helpful. Anxiety sensitivity frequently has a genetic basis, so investigate this for a more accurate diagnosis of your own possible biochemical anomalies.

If you think that there may well be a physical factor in your anxiety, see your regular physician or internist and tell her or him about your symptoms and their history. If no regular medical reason is found, see a psychiatrist, particularly one who specializes in psychopharmacology and treats many individuals with psychotropic medication.

Be ready to experiment with antianxiety, antidepressive, or other medication that your psychopharmacologist prescribes. It may, in suitable doses, work for you or against you. Every individual is different, and some of the many available psychotropic medications may, temporarily or on a long-term basis, be of considerable help. With medical collaboration, experiment!

Don't rely only on medication, even if it seems to be working. It may help you, but you can also help yourself. Some studies have shown that even when medication works well in the short-run, cognitive behavior therapy is more effective in preventing a return of anxiety or depression. Some medication may be very helpful, but if you have an irrational fear of trying it, by all means Dispute the Irrational Beliefs involved in your having that kind of phobia. REBT, together with properly prescribed medication, may be the best treatment for you. Again, experiment with the help of a psychiatrist.

Warning! Don't try medication on your own! Tranquilizers, especially, can be addicting and can cause sleep problems and lack of effective functioning. Get good medical consultation before you try them. Medicating yourself with alcohol or other drugs can also be extremely dangerous!

When self-help methods and/or medication do not significantly reduce your anxiety, by all means try a licensed mental health practitioner for psychotherapy. To seek proper help when your anxiety is severe makes very good sense. Naturally, I am prejudiced, but I still say run, don't walk, to the best available psychologist, social worker, counselor, or psychiatrist whom you can find and who preferably practices REBT or some other form of cognitive behavior therapy.

26

A Remarkably Efficient Way to Control Your Anxiety Before It Controls You

As I was finishing the writing of this book, Kevin Everett FitzMaurice sent me a copy of his new book, *Attitude Is All You Need!* He is an unusual counselor who has written several outstanding books which are mainly based on the principles of general semantics as described in the writings of Alfred Korzybski and that combine them with some Asian philosophies and the principles of Rational Emotive Behavior Therapy (REBT) and Cognitive Behavior Therapy (CBT). He is an independent thinker and I would advise you to read some of his books, particularly *Attitude Is All You Need!* It will help you control your anxiety and overcome other emotional problems. Kevin is particularly thorough in explaining unconditional self-acceptance (USA) and how you can think, feel, and act your way into achieving it.

In his new book, Kevin particularly considers the human problem of anxiety or stress, shows you different attitudes that will help you experience minimum to maximum stress, and gives you the choice of which attitude you will take and what consequent degree of stress you will most probably have. Let me present his different attitudes and then see how I would modify them somewhat to aid your using REBT in getting to minimum levels of anxiety.

According to Kevin, when you deal with stressors in your environment and with the conflict or indecision that they provoke in your thoughts, feelings, and actions, you have the choice of five main coping attitudes.

Accepting   Accepting is the attitude of no choice, no desire, no distinction, no comparison, no measurement. When you have an attitude of accepting, you are at peace with "what is." You accept people the way they are; you embrace places and things as they are.

Searching   Searching is the attitude of looking for a choice. Searching is exploring, beginning planning, beginning proactivity, beginning problem-solving, brainstorming, looking for options, looking for possibilities. You study ways for you to behave more effectively. You check for ways to make places/things better.

Preferring   Preferring is the attitude of wishing, wanting, choosing one choice over another. When you have an attitude of preferring, you know what you want or would like, but you also know what you will take or live with. You wish you would behave differently. You want places and things to be different. You hope your life becomes better.

Shoulding   Shoulding is the attitude of knowing what is right, having a clear decision, making a clear choice, believing you know what is best. Shoulding is making a single choice, unlike preferring, which is only desiring one choice over less acceptable choices. You think people should behave differently. You think places and things should be changed.

Musting   Musting is the attitude of not accepting excuses, not permitting variation, not accepting the inferior, not tolerating defects. When you have an attitude of musting, there is only one way and one option and you are devoted to its realization. You think that people *must* be changed. Life *must* be respected more than it is.

Kevin's levels of attitudes, if you use it the way he recommends, will enable you to reduce your bad stress or anxiety, which is largely the inability to make progress or to complete your goals, and to increase your good stress, or the ability to complete your goals or to make progress in the completion of them. If you really acquire the *Accepting* attitude, he contends, you will make no choices and have no stress; with *Searching* you will have minimal stress; with *Preferring* you will have mild stress; with *Shoulding* you will have average stress; and with *Musting* you will have complete stress. In terms of demandingness, he also points out that *Accepting* gives you no demandingness, *Searching*, minimal demandingness; *Preferring*, mild demandingness; *Shoulding*, average demandingness; and *Musting* gives you complete demandingness.

Kevin makes some excellent points here. However, I take issue with his various definitions of *Accepting, Searching, Preferring, Shoulding,* and *Musting* because although they overlap with the concepts we use in REBT, I feel they are not precise enough. Therefore, I have changed them and adapted them somewhat and have come up with the following categories of attitudes, which I think are more precise and probably more useful for your tackling your anxiety and making it minimal, while at the same time maximizing your desires, choices, and goals to get more of what you want and less of what you don't want. My revised list of attitudes is as follows:

Desirelessness
Absence of choices
Lack of Goals and Purposes
Total Acceptance

You desire nothing. You have no preferences, goals, or purposes. You find that one choice or thing is as good as another. You don't care.

Desiring Better Conditions but Totally Accepting What Is (Resignation)   You wish people and things were different, but you fully accept them as they are. You want more than you have, but totally accept that you cannot or will not get it. You wish your life were better, but welcome it and enjoy it if it is not.

Desiring and Searching for Better Choices, Preferences, and Goals   You explore several choices, desires, and preferences and seek for ways to make them better and more enjoyable. You explore life and look for ways to make it better. You think that life could be better and see if you can find better choices, preferences, and goals.

Moderately Preferring   You moderately prefer people and things to be different and better but you can enjoy what you have and possibly improve on it. You moderately work to make your life better, but you also enjoy many things about it.

Strongly Preferring   You strongly prefer certain people and things, think that they are best for you, but are open to other possibilities. You strongly prefer certain people and things and try to seek them out or achieve them but are reasonably happy and enjoy life if you can't get them. You strongly prefer people to behave differently and things to work out better and dislike it if they don't. But you can still lead a good life if people and things don't change for the better.

Preferably Shoulding   You know what is right or best for you, make a clear decision or choice, but you will accept less than the best if you have to do so. You think people preferably should behave differently and that places and things preferably should be changed. But you accept people and things when they are less than best and you cannot change them. You feel sorry, disappointed, and frustrated when you, people, or things are less than preferable—but you do not make yourself seriously anxious, depressed, or angry about them.

Absolute Shoulding and Musting   You demand that you must do better than you are doing. You think you are an inadequate or worthless person when you don't do as well as you must. You insist that other people must behave better than they do. You think they are rotten or worthless people when they don't do as well as they must. You command that things and events be better than they are. You believe life is horrible and useless when they are not. When your musts and demands are not satisfied, you feel anxious, depressed, angry, and self-pitying.

If you compare my list of coping attitudes to Kevin Everett FitzMaurice's list, you will see that mine is more complicated, and presumably more precise, in several ways. First, his list puts desirelessness under *Accepting*. But I say that we had better clearly distinguish having no desire, and therefore no choice, from having desires, goals, and purposes but still accepting that you can live and be reasonably happy when they are not fulfilled. Quite a difference!

Actually, we may observe that humans (and animals) are practically never without desire and purpose—except when they are dead, or completely unconscious. To live means to desire and to have purpose, for without these conditions you would not last very long! So human desirelessness is exceptionally rare. But Kevin includes under *Accepting*—no choice and no desire. In REBT theory and practice, *Accepting* means having desire and goals and accepting, though not liking their lack of fulfillment. So I have clearly put that form of Accepting in my additions to Kevin's list of coping attitudes. This is where my list begins to differ significantly from Kevin's.

Second, under the heading of *Preferring*, I have added *Moderately* and *Strongly Preferring* to Kevin's list of coping attitudes. That is because human desires and choices have distinct degrees or gradations. You can moderately want to excel at a sport, at your job, or at socializing; you can strongly want to excel at these pursuits; or you can be convinced that your enjoyment in life practically depends on whether or not you excel. How you cope with failing to do well at these pursuits is closely related to both your desire to excel and the *strength* of this desire. Your stress or anxiety at performing these tasks tends to vary with the *intensity* or *power* of your wish to perform well. So I have included the strength of your desiring in my list of coping attitudes.

Third, Kevin's attitude of *Shoulding* is, I think, badly named, because in the English language *should* and *must* are often used synonymously and interchangeably. His *Shoulding* and *Musting* can therefore easily be confused. Yet in some ways, "I should do this" is quite different from "I must do this," because it frequently means, "I preferably should be friendly to people if I want them to accept me," which is a sensible, conditional *should*. However, "I must be friendly to people" may mean "At all costs and under all conditions I absolutely must be friendly to people or else I am an unworthy, bad person!" which is an unconditional and highly questionable *must*. Consequently, I have changed Kevin's attitude of shoulding to one of preferably shoulding.

Fourth, I have changed Kevin's coping attitude of *Musting* to *Absolute Shoulding and Musting*. Again, this is to make things clearer. Musting, he notes, has some good points because "Musting is working to make what is right come into being. Musting is the passion or the compulsion to do the work, to get the job done." Yes, when it is conditional musting, as in, "If I want a college degree, I must pay my tuition and must pass my courses." But if musting is absolute and unconditional, it usually won't work. Thus: "Whether or not I pay my tuition and pass my courses, I *absolutely must* get a college degree. Because I want it very much, they *absolutely* must give it to me!" So, again, I have tried to make Kevin's coping attitudes more precise and presumably more useful.

In looking over Kevin Everett FitzMaurice's description of attitudes which you can take to cope with stress and anxiety, and my expanded version of these coping attitudes, I naturally like my versions but find his more concise and easy to remember. Let me therefore put the two versions together and come up with five coping attitudes that you can choose in dealing with your personal anxiety.

Accepting   Accepting undesirable conditions when you definitely don't like them but cannot change them. Refusing to upset yourself about what you cannot change.

Searching   Desiring and searching for better choices, preferences, and goals.

Preferring   Wishing, wanting, choosing what you like but also knowing what you will take or live with.

Preferable Shoulding   Knowing what is best for you and others and trying to bring it about, but not insisting that what is best has to exist.

Absolute Shoulding and Musting   Knowing what is best for you and others and absolutely demanding that you and they do this and that conditions must be the way that you think is best.

According to Kevin, you have a definite choice of these coping attitudes, and all of them have advantages and disadvantages. I partially agree, because even Musting gives you drive, energy, and motivation and can be used conditionally. Thus, if you want to get good, better, or the best fulfillment of your goals, you can select one choice and can convince yourself, "*If* I want to achieve this, *then* I must do such and such to achieve it." Usually, that will work very well.

For the most part, however, REBT holds that the first four coping attitudes—Accepting, Searching, Preferring, and Preferable Shoulding—will all help you cope with anxiety. Truly Accepting what you desire to change but cannot (as yet) change will get you little anxiety, because Adversities will still exist and you will still be concerned, vigilant, and cautious about them.

Searching for better choices and goals will lead to a little anxiety, for you may not find them. But you can be enjoyably absorbed in the searching.

Preferring some choices over other choices will make you mildly anxious, because you may pick the "wrong" or "ineffective" choices.

Preferable Should, or knowing what are the best choices and trying to bring them about, will create moderate anxiety, because your knowledge may prove to be "wrong" or your choices may be "right" but unachievable.

If REBT is on the right track, the anxiety you produce with these four ways of coping with Adversities will be mild or moderate, you will well be able to live with it, and you will not be severely overstressed or panicked. You will therefore tend to get more of what you want and less of what you don't want in life.

Watch out, however, for the coping—or noncoping—attitude of Absolute Shoulding and Musting! I won't say that this is the only source of your serious anxiety, for humans are complex and may become anxious because of biochemical imbalances, because of drugs, because of sudden and severe traumatic events, as well as for other reasons. I will contend, however, that most of the time you suffer from severe and sustained anxiety, nervousness, and panic, you are consciously or unconsciously musturbating.

Thus, if you think about it—and I would advise you to really think about it—you will have great trouble making yourself anxious if you rigorously stay with your preferences. For even when you strongly prefer something, and when you ardently contend that you preferably *should* have it, you are implying a fairly firm *but*. Thus: "I strongly *want* to succeed, and I think that I *preferably should*. But I don't have to and need not be utterly miserable if I don't." "I greatly *wish* you would act properly and fairly, and I think that you *preferably should*. But I can live a good life if you don't." "I fervently *hope* that the conditions under which I live are good, and I think that they *preferably should* be. But if they're not, I can still find many things to enjoy."

Simple enough? Yes, but as I keep stressing in this book, not easy! The natural tendency is to turn your strong desires and preferences into arrogant musts and demands. You are born to do so and are trained to do so by your competitive culture. But you don't *have* to. You can choose *not* to. You can creatively think for yourself and control your anxiety before it controls you. You have the power to empower yourself. Use it!

27

104 Rational Maxims to Control My Anxious Thinking

Time to summarize the main points that I have been making in this book. Your anxious feelings and behaviors go with specific kinds of anxiety-provoking thinking. But, again, your anxious emotions and actions importantly influence, and are an integral part of, your thinking. You think, act, and feel together. That's the way, as a human, you behave.

To summarize what you can do to control your anxiety and panic is tricky because it involves maxims you can get yourself to strongly believe—but they include changing your thoughts, your feelings, and your actions—all three. And they overlap and are somewhat repetitive. But, fortunately, although they are somewhat different ways of saying the same thing, they also reinforce each other. Use the maxims and you soon will see.

In this chapter, I will emphasize Rational Beliefs you can hold to change your anxiety-provoking thinking; in the next chapter, I shall stress those that will mainly change your disturbed emotions; and in the final, summary chapter I will highlight those that will mainly change your dysfunctional actions. However, they include all three causes and effects. Your thoughts (maxims) control your thinking, feeling, and behaving, and your feelings and behaviors reciprocally influence your thoughts. Odd, but true. Work with the maxims in these three chapters and see for yourself.

First, what maxims can you strongly and persistently invoke to modify the kinds of thinking that often lead to your uncontrollable anxiety? Try these.

MINIMIZING MY ABSOLUTISTIC MUSTS, SHOULDS, OUGHTS, AND DEMANDS AND THE IRRATIONAL BELIEFS THAT GO WITH THEM

1. I will watch my unconditional, absolutistic musts and change them into strong preferences, such as "I would very much like to do well and be approved by others, but I don't *have to* do so and my worth as a person doesn't depend on doing anything!" "It is *not absolutely necessary* to get what I want."

2. I will watch my overgeneralizations and make them more concrete: "If I fail at something important, I won't *always* fail and may frequently succeed."

3. I will watch my awfulizing. "It's bad to lose out on something I really want, but it's not *awful* or *horrible*. There's a good chance I'll get it later, but if I never do, it is just very depriving. The earth will keep spinning! Life will go on!"

4. I will watch my personalizing. "Maybe I lost out on a relationship because of stupid things I did. But there may be several other reasons why it didn't work out. If it really was my fault, what can I learn from this to gain the relationship I want next time?"

5. I will watch my emotional reasoning. "Because I feel like a loser, am I really a loser? No, I hate losing and this time I failed to win. But my deep feeling makes me only a person with feelings, not a hopeless loser."

6. I will watch my going from one extreme to another. "Winning this campaign doesn't make me a glorious, noble person. But losing it doesn't mean that it doesn't matter *at all*. It does matter, and it would have been much better had I won. But losing doesn't destroy me and make me a nothing." I will watch my concluding that I *am* my behavior. "Failing miserably at my goal doesn't make *me* a failure. I am a *person* who failed this time and who may fail many times before I distinctly succeed."

7. Failing is very valuable if I don't take it too seriously and want—not need—to ultimately succeed.

8. Did other people who eventually succeeded in my field quit after a few bad tries? Where would they now be if they had not persisted in spite of initial failures?

9. I will often generalize, categorize, and help myself think, think about my thinking, and think about my thinking about my thinking. But I will try not to overgeneralize and to get what W. Quine called hardening of the categories. Thus, I will avoid saying that I *am* what I do, will stop labeling people as some of their traits, and will avoid thinking of my thoughts as things that are entities in their own right.

10. I will try to avoid saying that because I've failed I will *always* fail or that I am *a failure*. Or that because I often failed I will *never* succeed. Or that because I have done bad things that I am a *bad person*.

11. I will try to realize that things are not either this or that, good or bad, black or white, but are frequently this *and* that, good *and* bad, both black *and* white and shades of gray. I, too, have good and bad traits, black, white, and gray traits, and I have good, bad, and indifferent characteristics.

12. I had better realize that overgeneralization or overcategorizing is logically incorrect, is unrealistic, and gets me and others in emotional difficulties. I *am not* what I think, feel, and do; I have much too many different thoughts, feelings, and actions to put them under a single good or bad category. I *am* not lovable if a few people love me, nor am I unlovable if several people do not love me. The world *is not* a good place or a bad place, but has many good *and* bad conditions. People and things, as Alfred Korzybski said, cannot be accurately seen as black or white, good or bad. They also have traits and conditions, and my labeling them in one general way makes me see them in an inaccurate light. Especially if I overgeneralize about people's and my own unfavorable traits, I do a grave injustice to me and to them.

13. Let me try to be open-minded, skeptical, and experimental. Final answers to my and others' problems are to be highly suspect!

I can roll with the tide of new and changing evidence. But even this "evidence" may partly arise from my and others' views, desires, and prejudices. Absolute and final truths probably never exist!

DEALING WITH CATASTROPHIZING THOUGHTS ABOUT THE FUTURE

1. When I keep making myself anxious by telling myself *what if* bad things happen, *what if* people treat me unfairly, *what if* I act foolishly and bring about bad results, and similar *what ifs*, I can always tell myself, as Arnold Lazarus recommends, *so what if* these things occur or I make them occur? I can still change my anxious and panicked feelings to concern, regret, and frustration. When I do so, I can see that most of these "terrible" things will never occur, but if some of them do, I can handle them, cope with them, improve them, or fully accept them and live a *less happy* life but not an *utterly miserable one.*

2. Similarly, when I catastrophize about things happening, I can imagine them at their very worst and see that indeed that would be very bad, but realize ways I could deal with them and still have some degree of human happiness. Thinking that I *can't* cope with Adversity if and when it occurs will only make me *less* able to cope with it.

3. When I think of "terrible" *what ifs*, I can remember the wise saying of Mark Twain, "My life has been filled with terrible misfortunes—most of which never happened."

4. I can also call to mind a number of people to whom serious Adversity did occur—such as leprosy, cancer, blindness, deafness, quadriplegia and so on—and who still lead productive and happy lives. Adversity conquers many people because they let it conquer them. But not all!

5. When I plague myself with *what ifs*, I can again show myself that I can handle the worst possibilities, but then I can realistically see what the probability is of these dire things happening. It is usually very small.

6. Also, what is the probability of serious Adversities—such as

business failures and rejection by people I really like—lasting forever or being endlessly repeated? Slight, if I do not devastate myself about them if and when they actually occur.

7. Practically nothing lasts forever, even severe anxiety and panic. Providing I do not horrify myself about them, this too shall pass.

8. Many things are bad, because I don't want them to occur. Even catastrophes occur—such as wars, earthquakes, famine, mass killings, and torture. But quite rarely! I had better not *make* hassles and troubles into catastrophes. There is a Persian saying: "I was horrified at the loss of my shoes until I saw a person with no legs."

9. Whenever I am really anxious and overconcerned about things going or not going the way I want them to go, I shall assume that I have some Irrational Beliefs and that they include an absolute must, should, ought, or other demand or guarantee and that there is a chance that this demand may not actually be fulfilled. I shall find my must and change it to a preference or a wish.

10. I will enjoy the present as much as I can and also prepare for enjoying the future. I can control, to a large degree, my *reactions* to what happens in the future, but I can control only to a limited degree what the future actually will bring. The more I insist on controlling it, the more I will probably help screw it up.

11. When I worry about *what if this happens*, I will try to figure out some practical things I can do if by any chance it does happen.

12. When I make a mistake or the situation turns out badly for me, I will remember that there almost always is a next time.

13. When I say "I can't do it" in the present or the future, I may realistically see that it is hard but exaggerate the impossibility of doing it. "I can't do it" will often *make* it next to impossible for me to do. "I can learn how to do it" is much better!

14. The road to hell is paved with dogmatic and absolutistic, not probabilistic, expectations. To rigidly expect "good" behaviors of myself or others is to set myself up for "horrors."

15. Keep my desires and goals in mind. Don't insist that they must or must not be fulfilled. Let me work unfrantically to achieve them.

REBT INSIGHTS THAT WILL SIGNIFICANTLY HELP ME

1. Adversities frequently exist in my life and in the world, and I frequently have little control over them. Usually, however, when I become seriously disturbed about them, I choose to upset myself by my attitudes about them.

2. The past Adversities of my life may well have strongly contributed to my disturbances. But so did I! When I am now, years later, very upset about them, I am still making my powerful dysfunctional conclusions about the past. Still!

3. I can virtually always change my disturbing Irrational Beliefs about the past and the present—not merely by gaining insight into them but by considerable work and practice to think, feel, and act against them. Yes, considerable work and practice!

4. Recognizing what people and events did to help disturb me is healthy if I also recognize what I *believed about* their contributions to my disturbance. *That* is what I'd better largely see and work to change.

APPLYING A COST-BENEFIT ANALYSIS TO WHAT I DO

1. I will do my best to see that feelings of concern, caution, and vigilance will often prevent me from harming myself and will help produce results that I want, while feelings of overconcern, anxiety, and panic will often help me to harm myself and get results that I dislike. Anxiety and panic, therefore, may bring me some benefits, but they usually are not worth the costs they also bring.

2. When I am anxious about my anxiety or panicked about my panic, that, too, usually is too costly and does me more harm than good.

3. My making myself anxious or panicked about the possibility of undesirable things happening to me, or about my making them happen, will not change those things and make them better. Usually, those negative emotions will interfere with my coping and help make things worse.

4. I can stop my anxiety or panic about poor conditions by improving these conditions. But I often cannot change such conditions, and my anxiety and panic will often make them worse. So I'd better first work on changing my anxiety or panic by giving up my demands that poor conditions *absolutely must not* occur and that if they do occur my discomfort about them is something that I *absolutely cannot bear*. As Reinhold Niebuhr said, I'd better have the courage to change what I can change, the serenity to accept what I cannot change, and the wisdom to know the difference.

5. I'd better be somewhat concerned about my future and try to prepare for it, but if I am very overconcerned, anxious, or panicked about it, I will not be able to enjoy the present or think pleasantly about the things and relationships I enjoyed in the past.

6. I had better acknowledge that although my anxiety makes me suffer and brings poor results, it also may have payoffs and advantages that prevent me from surrendering it. For example, it may stop me from taking risks and failing. I can honestly search for these payoffs to see if they exist and if they are worth the pains of my anxiety.

7. Some possible payoffs that I may get from my anxiety are these: (a) People may give me special attention because I am anxious; (b) anxiety to some extent protects me from danger and trouble; (c) it makes me feel alert and may be exciting and interesting; (d) it's a natural feeling and I may think that it makes me really "be myself"; (e) I may be able to pity myself and feel good because of my self-pity; and (f) I may like to see myself as a victim who is sorely put upon by the cruel world and the people in it.

OVERCOMING MY DIRE NEED FOR CERTAINTY AND PERFECTIONISM

1. The one thing I can be fairly certain about is that there is no certainty. But there is a high degree of probability that if I try hard, even in this uncertain world, I can get more of what I really want and less of what I don't want than if I whine about certainty's nonexistence.

2. Uncertainty and ambiguity are sometimes a drag. But they can also be a challenge and an adventure.

3. I am not sure what I will achieve outstandingly. But I am pretty sure that if I use my creativity to keep trying, and ask for no guarantees, I will enjoy my efforts.

4. The one guarantee I now have is my ultimate death. But it is even possible, though not too likely, that someday science will give me and other people new bodily parts to keep me alive forever. Well, that will be interesting if it ever occurs.

5. If I want certainty, or at least a high degree of probability, that things will go well for me, fine. If I need a guarantee that they will go well, I will most probably be anxious.

6. If I think there is only one correct answer to a problem or a situation, I will not allow for alternate answers or solutions. If I rigidly insist on the one solution, I will have no other options and can easily make myself anxious and depressed if I fail to find it. Therefore, I had better keep my options open and consider alternate solutions.

7. One thing I can be pretty certain about is that people can sometimes do perfect things—such as spell or do math perfectly for a period of time. But they and I are fallible and highly imperfect in most tasks much of the time. I can therefore try for some perfection but never absolutely need it.

HOW I CAN USE MODELING METHODS

1. I can find some models among people I know or can learn about who thought remarkably rationally under difficult situations.

2. I can find some models of people who conquered real Adversities and handicaps and led happy and productive lives.

3. I can model good and bad as well as helpful and unhelpful behaviors. I'd better make my modeling selective and watch that I don't become too suggestible or gullible. I can try out behaviors that I model to check on them and to discover how well they work for me.

USING PROBLEM-SOLVING METHODS

1. Life's great hassles and difficulties give me more fascinating problems to solve as well as greater challenges!

2. Life presents one problem after another. Avoiding and not facing them won't make them go away. Usually, it increases them.

3. Having a goal in mind and making efforts to achieve it makes problems easier to solve—and even enjoyable to attempt.

4. I may have less-difficult problems if I pick less-stressful goals. But I'll also probably have less-interesting and less-enjoyable rewards.

5. I don't *have* to achieve outstandingly and pick difficult and more-stressful goals. I can *choose* whether or not to pick them.

6. This means *selecting* what I most desire and focusing first on that. My selection can largely be out of desire to enjoy, or desire to avoid present and future pain. There is no absolute order in which things must be done. My desire largely *makes* the order.

7. I'd better not let my upset feelings interfere with my skill-training. I can acquire skills even when anxious and depressed, and working at acquiring them will often distract me from my anxiety and depression.

8. Doing problem-solving and skill-training in my head will often help me do better in practice—and will tend to sharpen my problem-solving abilities.

9. Problem-solving and skill-training take time and patience. My low frustration tolerance is increased by putting them off or quitting prematurely. It makes doing seem harder and overwhelms me with things to do.

10. When trying to solve a problem, I will do some research, get sufficient information on it, try to discover how others solved it, ask for suitable help if it is available, and try to solve it because it is an interesting and valuable problem to solve rather than trying to solve it to "prove" what a great person I am.

11. My Beliefs about myself, other people, and world conditions are opinions and hypotheses, not necessarily facts and truths. I had better question, challenge, and test these out, particularly when

they seem to be Irrational Beliefs that lead to my anxiety. I'd better not see these Beliefs as written in stone!

12. I am not the focal point of all events. People and things may be related to me but are not necessarily run by me. People will often do what they do and things will be how they are arranged regardless of my wishes and choices. I may not like this, but I had better accept it.

13. What I'd better do to get through this situation is think about alternative solutions. Experiment with them. Check them out. Revise them. Think about them some more. Keep going! But I don't *have* to come up with the right or true or perfect answer.

USING FAITH, HOPE, PURPOSIVENESS, AND CARING FOR ONESELF AND OTHERS

1. If I have faith and hope in my ability to cope with Adversity and often to make things better than they are, I will tend to be less anxious when things go wrong. By using caution rather than severe anxiety, I will also be more able to prevent some things from going wrong.

2. If I have faith in my own ability to control and change my anxiety, I will do the work required to change it. I will give up my unrealistic and grandiose demands, changing them to preferences, and I thus most likely will reduce or eliminate my anxiety.

3. If I have faith in other people helping me, or faith in the goodness of the universe, or faith in some higher power that is on my side that may help me temporarily relieve my anxiety. But these things are not to be counted on, so I had better have faith in my own power to reduce or eliminate my anxiety. If I rely on other people or powers and they don't come to my aid, I may become disillusioned and increase my anxiety.

4. I had better have strong purposes and goals in life and the passion to pursue them. Then I will have relationships and projects to work for as well as vital absorbing interests that will distract me from anxieties and bring me persistent enjoyment that will let me

live better even if I have anxiety. My vital interests will tend to override my anxieties and make my life worthwhile in spite of them. Knowing that I have strong goals and purposes will make me intent on trying to achieve them rather then worrying about life's difficulties.

5. I will try to discover things that I really want to do, and absorb myself in these things rather than try to please others by doing what I think they want. By being quite absorbed in these things and trying to solve the problems that are involved in them, I will try to flow with them, lose myself in them, and not be overinvolved with getting my way. If I do them for the enjoyment of them, I will not worry that much about proving that I can do well.

6. I will try to get a long-range, vital, absorbing interest in some project or cause, and because I truly care for it and want to be devoted to it, I will not worry too much about the things I easily worry about. I will truly be connected with the people or things involved in my vital, absorbing interest and which have a major purpose in my life.

7. Like most people, as John Bowlby has shown, I am born with a special tendency to be attachable to my parents, siblings, and other people and to love them individually and collectively. If I use this innate tendency, I can become strongly attached to one person, several people, or a group of people, and I sometimes do so on a longtime basis. I can use my vital interest in loving individuals or a group of people as a form of connectedness that will preoccupy a large part of my time, give me an intense purpose, and ward off piddling worries. But I'd better not insist that my love involvements have to be reciprocated. It is great if they are, but I can devote myself to them unilaterally and enjoyably.

8. I'd better not have a Pollyannaish philosophy and be absolutely certain that everything will happen for the best and life will be an ecstatic ball. Such an unrealistic outlook will relieve my anxiety temporarily, but will probably lead me to panic and depression when things turn out badly.

HOW I CAN REFRAME SOME ADVERSITIES

1. I'd better not view Adversities in a completely bad light. They usually have some advantages and good points as well. And they are often not *as* bad as they at first seem to be. I will check them out realistically, especially when I overreact to them.

2. When other people create problems for me, I will try to see their own frame of reference. They often have different ways of seeing things. And they could be right!

3. Let me try to look at my Adversities as others might see them, particularly those who are not too involved with them. Let me try to gain some distance from my Adversities and thus decatastrophize them.

4. I can often review the "bad" and particularly the "horrible" things that happen to me with another reasonably unbiased person. That may help me see my problems in a different light.

5. When I strongly object to doing things that would be preferable for me to do, I can act as if I liked them or even as if I were enthusiastic about doing them. That *as if* attitude may alleviate my self-defeating resistance to doing them.

6. I will do my best to view difficult people and situations as interesting challenges to be solved instead of "horrors" to be faced. I will then tend to have a much more fascinating, instead of terribilizing, life!

USING IMAGERY TO CONTROL MY ANXIETY

1. I can use positive imagery or positive visualization to see that I can do difficult things I would like to do and to rehearse doing them in my head. This kind of behavior rehearsal can enhance my chances of accomplishment.

2. Positive imagery will often give me a sense of self-efficacy or confidence that I can do difficult things and do them well.

3. I can use positive imagery or visualization to see myself coping with difficult situations and handling them with minimal anxiety.

4. I can practice negative imagery, as Maxie Maultsby Jr. has shown, and see myself failing at important tasks or being very frustrated and deprived. At first, I will feel unhealthy emotions such as anxiety, depression, and rage. Then, I can work to change these unhealthy feelings to healthy negative feelings, such as sorrow, regret, and frustration. I can do this mainly by changing my irrational musturbatory beliefs for rational preferential beliefs, and thereby training myself to easily and automatically have healthy negative feelings when things go wrong in my life. This kind of imagery is called rational emotive imagery.

USING DISTRACTION METHODS OF INTERRUPTING MY ANXIETY

1. Because the human mind has difficulty concentrating on more then one thing at a time, there are many ways that I can distract myself from anxious ruminations. Most of them provide only temporary distractions so that my worrisome thoughts—including my *musts*, demands, and other Irrational Beliefs—tend to quickly return. So, it would be better if I discovered these IBs, and vigorously and actively Disputed them, and stayed with my Rational Beliefs (RBs) about the actual or potential Adversities of my life. But by using suitable distraction, I can interrupt my IBs, and give myself a breather and help marshal my forces for active Disputing. As long as I don't *only* use them, or use them to avoid Disputing, they can be very helpful and prepare me for effective Disputing.

2. I can try to experiment with a number of distraction techniques such as thought stopping, meditation, Yoga, breathing, relaxation sports, reading, entertainment, and so on. I can try one or more of these that I am comfortable with and that take my mind off my worries.

3. If I focus on the bad and "awful" things that may happen to me (particularly on "What if this terrible thing occurs...!" and "Suppose this horrible thing happens...!"), I will tend to worry obsessively. I can always tell myself "So what if this actually

happens..." and show myself that at worst it would be highly inconvenient but hardly devastating: Unless I foolishly *define* it as devastating!

4. I can use positive distractions, things I like getting mentally and physically into, and use them not only to turn off my worries but actually to enjoy them for themselves.

5. I can distract myself by actually listening to my worrisome chatter, viewing it interestedly instead of taking it too seriously. With this mindfulness method, I can see that I do not have to let my thinking take hold of me and control me.

6. One of the best kinds of distractions is for me to get interested in a difficult and absorbing problem and to persist at it until I begin to flow with it, thoroughly enjoy it, and be so involved with it that I find it almost impossible to do my usual kind of worrying. My genuine concern—instead of overconcern—about solving the problems I am working on, and my trying to come up with constructive solutions to them, will often absorb me so much that for the time being I actually am not inclined to do much destructive worrying. If, however, I insist that I *must* solve the problem or project I am working on, and especially that I must do so remarkably well, I will make myself anxious and interfere with my constructive flow experience.

7. By throwing myself into a long-term, vital, absorbing interest—such as devotion to building a family, a business, or a career—I will be distracted from piddling worries and stay structured and interested for many months or even years. My regular worries will seem relatively trivial and I will often have little time to devote to them. If, however, I insist that I *absolutely must* succeed in my long-term interest or project, that other people *must* favor me for it and aid me in it, and that conditions *must* be set up to assure its satisfactory achievement, then I will make myself anxious and the anxiety may interfere with its fulfillment.

8. Assigning myself specific, structured tasks to do, and then actually doing them, without demanding perfection of myself, will distract me from my anxieties and also can be quite productive and enjoyable.

9. I can use pleasant thoughts, fantasies, daydreams, plans for the future, and other ideas and images to distract me from my worries as long as I don't insist they must lead to marvelous outcomes.

10. Making an effort, with thought and action, to master some skill, sport, activity, game, performance, art, or project will distract me from my worries as long as I don't insist that I must master it well and as long as I don't put my worth as a person at stake in an attempt to master it.

SOME ALTERNATIVE RATIONAL BELIEFS I CAN USE

1. I can create and use positive or coping self-statements to allay my anxiety, as long as they are realistic, logical, and practical and as long as they do not include rigid musts and demands. Thus, I can tell myself: "I strongly hope people will treat me well and situations will turn out to be the way I prefer, but they don't *have to* be this way. Too bad, but it's not the end of the world if I don't get my wishes fulfilled." "I *strongly prefer* to do well and be approved of by significant others, but if I'm not, I'm not. Tough, but it's not awful." I'd better fully believe these rational self-statements and not merely parrot them and think that I really do believe them. I'd better vigorously and forcefully convince myself of them, especially when I see that I have slipped back to making myself anxious.

2. I can realistically Dispute my Irrational Beliefs, and particularly my musts, by showing myself that they don't exist in social reality. If I *had to* do well, I couldn't possibly fail to do so. If you *must* treat me nicely, you would always do so. If conditions always *had to* be fine, they would be. Obviously, these musts do not exist!

3. I can Dispute my illogical *musts* by showing that it doesn't follow that because I insist that I succeed, I have to do so. It doesn't follow that because I say you must treat me fairly that you are obliged to do so. It doesn't follow that because I demand that conditions work out beautifully they must turn out that way.

4. I can pragmatically Dispute my Irrational Beliefs by showing myself that if I believe I absolutely must do well, that it is *horrible* whenever people treat me shabbily and that I *can't stand* unpleasant situations, I will then almost automatically be and remain anxious, enraged, and depressed.

5. I can see that my anxiety and other disturbed feelings are usually highly correlated with Adversities happening in my life. Thus, I don't feel anxiety when I succeed or am loved by significant people and I often feel anxious when I fail and am unloved. But correlation does not equal cause and effect. Adversities help me feel anxious, but I still have to tell myself Irrational Beliefs to produce my anxiety. Many factors may "cause" anxiety, but IBs are some of the main factors, and luckily ones that I can change.

6. I had better not confuse my conditional musts with my absolute musts. If I want to eat, I must get some food. If I want to lower my level of anxiety, I must acknowledge that I have it, try to find its main causes (such as my Irrational Beliefs), and do something to change or remove them. If I want something, I'll rarely get it by doing nothing or waiting for magic to give it to me. Conditional musts therefore are useful—and at many times necessary. Unconditional and absolutistic musts are different. I'd better not demand that I *absolutely must at all times* perform well. Nor that because I want you to treat me nicely, you *absolutely must at all times* do so. So I can keep many conditional musts and give up my unconditional absolute commands.

7. If I try to keep an idealized image of myself, as Karen Horney showed, and have to be great and flawless to maintain it, I will almost certainly wind up with a negative image of myself and consider myself pretty worthless.

8. To convince myself that my Rational Beliefs are accurate and effective and that I really am forcefully (that is, emotionally) convinced of them, I can argue against them and then bat down my arguments. Or, I can let another person who knows me Dispute my Rational Beliefs as I hold them up to him or her in order to see whether I can really sustain them.

9. I will strongly Dispute my perfectionistic goals and beliefs and give myself the permission and the courage to be imperfect—a notable phrase coined by Sophia Lazasfeld. I may have a strong preference to do perfectly well, especially in limited areas, but will resist making that into a demand.

10. I can almost always stand what I greatly don't like because (a) I will rarely die of it; (b) I can be happy, though not as happy, in spite of it; (c) I can often benefit from standing it; (d) I can learn from it; (e) I can increase my frustration tolerance by standing it; and (f) I will be extremely miserable and will not be happy *at all* if I forcefully and persistently insist that I can't stand it!

11. If I tell myself that I *can't stand* my anxiety, I shall be doubly miserable: first about my not getting what I think I absolutely *must* get and second about my misery itself. Anxiety is only very uncomfortable, not a horror—unless I *think* it is.

12. I can realize that given the same unfortunate failures, unfair treatment by others, and poor conditions of life, many other people would not overreact the way I do and would not suffer from anxiety and despair. Thus, some of my friends would not damn themselves for failing, would not enrage themselves about other people's unfairness, and would be sorry and disappointed but not horrified by poor situations. I, like others, therefore, have the *choice* of feelings and reactions to Adversities—if I think rationally about them.

13. If I have failings for which I am putting myself down as a person, I can realize that I am a decidedly fallible human with unavoidable failings and that other humans are similarly fallible and had better not be damned for their shortcomings. Who among us never errs or sins?

14. Positive thinking is usually much better than negative thinking as long as it is not unrealistic and Pollyannaish. But realistic negative thinking—such as "Be cautious and vigilant!" "Reconsider immediate gratifications that may be harmful in the long run!"—can be quite useful. A balance between positive or optimistic thinking and realistic or skeptical thinking tends to make for my optimal happiness.

28

62 Rational Maxims to Control My Anxious Feelings and My Bodily Reactions to Anxiety

I can work on my anxious feelings and my bodily reactions to anxiety in a number of ways, including these:

WORKING TO ACHIEVE UNCONDITIONAL SELF-ACCEPTANCE (USA)

1. I am a person in my own right and have individual and personal wants and dislikes. I am entitled to strive for what I want and to avoid what I dislike as long as I don't needlessly interfere with the individual and social rights of others. I justly subscribe to unconditionally other-acceptance (UOA) because I choose to live in a social community and to gain the benefits of social living. To get more of what I want and less of what I dislike, I will set up goals and purposes along the lines of my desires. I will rate my thoughts, feelings, and actions as "good" or "valuable" when they fulfill these goals and purposes and as "bad" or "less valuable" when they get me what I don't want or don't get me what I do want.

2. I will rigorously refrain from rating myself globally—that is, from giving myself a general rating or evaluation. I do "good" and "bad" things, but I refuse to see myself as a "good" or "bad" person. I *am not* what I *do*. I am a *person who* acts "well" and "badly."

3. I have both an innate and a learned tendency to inaccurately

give myself global ratings and evaluations and it is hard for me to resist doing so. When I slip into self-rating, I will try to arbitrarily rate myself as "good" just because I am alive, am human, and am unique, but *not* for other reasons. This is useful for me to do because thinking of myself as "good" will help me achieve my goals and purposes while thinking of myself as "bad" or "unworthy" will tend to sabotage my goals. So I will unconditionally accept myself as "good" rather than conditionally rate myself as "worthy" because my thoughts, feelings, and actions are—quite temporarily—fulfilling certain standards. My gaining unconditional self-acceptance (USA) by tying it up to my aliveness, my humanity, and my uniqueness is safe, because these will not change during my lifetime. I can therefore securely define myself as "good" even though I can't empirically confirm this definition. It will work! It will help me achieve my chosen goals and purposes. But it is only pragmatically, not absolutely, "true."

4. Instead of saying, "I don't like myself for having this behavior or trait," I will say, "I don't like having this behavior or trait. What can I do to improve it?"

5. I will compare my traits to my past traits and to other people's traits in order to work to improve them. But I will not compare my*self* to my past or to other people's *selves*.

6. I am a *unique* person, but not a *special* person in the sense of being better than other *people*. Some of my traits are better than their traits and some are worse then theirs. But, again, I *am not* what I think, feel, or do. Nor are other people their behaviors.

7. I *choose* to accept myself *with* my behaviors, both "good" and "bad," and to try to improve my "poor" behaviors. I *choose* to accept other people as people, but may try to help them (uncommandingly and undesperately) to change some of their ways.

WORKING TO ACHIEVE UNCONDITIONAL OTHER-ACCEPTANCE (UOA)

1. Just as I will rate my thoughts, feelings, and behaviors, but not give a global rating to myself, I will try to do the same for

others. I will not sacredize or damn them *as persons* but evaluate as "good" or "bad" what they do in relation to my own goals and purposes and to usual social standards.

2. If I do rate people—which I am prone to do—I will give them unconditional other-acceptance (UOA) and just rate them as "good" persons because they are human, are alive, and are unique individuals and not because their thoughts, feelings, or actions make them "good." Better yet, I will preferably rate what they do and not who they globally are.

3. When I succeed in my attempts at giving people unconditional self-acceptance, I will often dislike or hate what they do but do my best not to hate them, the doers, and not to be angry at them as persons. I may try to correct them but not to damn or punish them—accept the sinner but not what I consider the sin.

TAKING RESPONSIBILITY AS A MEMBER OF MY SOCIAL GROUP

1. I am not responsible for being born—and born with limitations and failings. I am responsible for doing the best I can do with my failings and with my talents. But even though I am responsible for many of my thoughts, feelings, and actions, there is no necessity for me to behave responsibly, only a high degree of desirability. I am not a worm or a "no-goodnik" for choosing to act irresponsibly, even though I am responsible for my irresponsibility and therefore am acting badly.

2. I am a social animal, with many ties to my family, group, and community. If I want companionship and help from others, I in all fairness had better not harm them and had better act fairly and responsibly to them. I and they will live better if we are mutually responsible to one another. In some respects, I can choose to favor myself over others, but if I only consider myself, and if I needlessly harm them, I am behaving immorally and irresponsibly, helping to harm them individually and collectively, and probably harming myself. I don't *have to be* moral absolutely but will tend to be much

better off if I am. If I want good social results, I therefore must act morally and responsibly to others. This I will choose as a conditional rather than an absolute *must*.

3. Although other people can needlessly harm me and deprive me, I am still largely responsible for my own feelings. If and when they act unfairly, I can choose to feel healthily sorry and frustrated or I can choose to feel anxious, depressed, and enraged. My feelings only partly depend on how they treat me, but also importantly depend on my attitudes toward their treatment. So I largely am responsible for—and can control—my emotions. Even when I am biologically prone to react to people and things in an unhealthy emotional manner, I have considerable ability, with thought, hard work, and practice, to reprogram myself to react in healthier ways.

4. Even when I have biological and socially conditioned tendencies to overreact in destructive emotional and behavioral ways, I am still responsible for not trying hard to correct them mentally and medically. If I have a physical ailment, such as diabetes or a heart condition, I can still get treatment for it, cope with it, and quite possibly improve my condition, and I am irresponsible to myself and perhaps to others when I do not deal with it adequately. Similarly, I can, responsibly or irresponsibly, deal with my emotional problems even when I did little to bring them on. But if I deal with them irresponsibly, I am merely a *person who* acts badly, not a *bad person*.

5. I can irresponsibly bring on or exacerbate physical and emotional ills—by drinking, drugging, smoking, and overeating. If so, let me acknowledge my irresponsibility but not put myself down for it. Then, I am much more likely to correct it.

6. When my emotional disturbances are overwhelming, and especially when they seem to have a biochemical or physical aspect, I may attempt to improve them with suitable medication, diet, physical methods, and sometimes in-patient treatment and not consider myself a weakling for doing so. But I will not rely exclusively or obsessively on physical treatment and will also work at psychological methods of thinking, feeling, and acting dif-

ferently and more effectively. Perhaps then I will be able to deal more permanently with my emotional disturbances.

7. Because my mind and body significantly interact and affect each other, I shall responsibly watch my physical health, diet, sleep habits, possible substance abuse, strenuous overstressing of my body, and other aspects of hygiene to see that my nonabused body is less likely to contribute to mental disorder than if I fail to respect it and keep it in good shape. To be emotionally healthy also involves my physical responsibility.

8. I am still responsible for my dysfunctional habits even when I am anxious. Thus, I can say that my anxiety is so great that it drives me to smoking or drinking. But no, it may be great and may be very *uncomfortable*, but I am still telling myself something like, "It is *so* uncomfortable that I *can't stand* it. Therefore, I must smoke or drink." It may well be my can't-stand-it-itis *about* my anxiety that is "making me" smoke or drink.

9. My social responsibilities include responsibility to make myself enjoy and actualize myself in my relationships with other individuals and groups. By birth and by social conditioning, my "own" personality results from my biological propensities *and* my social upbringing and contacts. I am born and reared with important capacities to relate, to love, to be connected, and to be emotionally and enjoyably involved with individuals and groups. My vital absorbing interests can be in ideas and projects, but they can also be in deep relationships and social causes. I can fulfill myself uniquely and intensively by loving and caring for people and groups that I find special.

ENHANCING MY SOCIAL SKILLS AND PLEASURES

1. I don't have to be sociable, to care for others, and to help them, but I can get a great deal of pleasure from doing so and add to my enjoyment in life and to my interests. Getting along better with others will also help prevent some of the Adversities that I easily could get anxious about.

2. I have little ability to profoundly change other people, but I have real ability, if I use it, to accept people the way they are and thereby to love and enjoy them in spite of what I consider their failings.

3. Depending on myself and not *needing* others to help me "prove" my worth by liking me, will help me be much less anxious—for arrant dependency is one of the main sources of anxiety since I have no guarantee that others will support me and cater to my dependency. My being unneedy frees me to really see things as others see them, consider their goals and values, and love them more. For I am no longer overconcerned with their caring for me, me, me. Unneediness makes me more attuned to sociability. I can love people for themselves, not mainly because they rate me highly.

4. If I think win/win instead of winning by besting others, I don't *have to* win. I can enjoy others winning instead of feeling enviously horrified that they are "better" than I am. I am not in frantic competition with them. If I actually lose, I won't take it too seriously.

5. If I make self-sufficiency a dire necessity, I really become *dependent* on how to completely and perfectly achieve it.

6. To sacredize other people means to be needy and lose myself. To sacredize myself means to make myself unable to deeply appreciate and relate to other people. Either path will make me anxious. For I and other people lead ungodlike, inconstant lives.

7. Loving and helping people won't make me a good person, but it is one of the most enjoyable things I can do. It will deflect me from being overinvolved with myself as the center of the universe.

8. Loving myself and others are not necessarily conflicting goals but can add a double vital interest and pleasure to my life.

9. If I try to see things from other people's frame of reference, in the light of their goals and values, I will not upset myself that much about how they behave. I will understand them better and enjoy them more.

10. I will often compare my assets and traits to other people's to

learn how to do better, if I can. But I will not compare my *self* to their *selves* with global ratings. They will often have better—and worse—assets and traits than I have.

11. Let me seek to understand others—and thereby increase my chances of being understood by them.

USING SUPPORT AND REASSURANCE

1. To some extent, I can rely on other people—such as relatives and friends—to support me and help me face some of my problems, and I can gratefully accept their help and reassurance and make the most of it. This may help me reduce my anxiety.

2. If I treat others in a friendly and helpful manner, I can probably gain more support from them when I am faced with difficulties.

3. Accepting help from others does not make me a weakling and does not mean that I can't also take care of myself.

4. It is wrong to rely too much on others and too little on myself. It is against my best interests, and I had better rely more on myself.

5. Maybe there is some Higher Power I can ask to help me when I have serious problems, but for good results, it is best to rely on myself.

6. To refuse help from those who are willing to give it, in order to prove how noble and greatly self-sufficient I am, can lead to narcissism and grandiosity.

7. Having some support and the reassurance that my family, friends, or others will help me when I am anxious will often reduce my anxiety and panic. But because such support and reassurance may not exist or may not continue, I'd better not rely on it solely. I also had better gain self-confidence and self-support.

8. If I think that I absolutely must have support and reassurance and it is not available, I will tend to make myself anxious or panicked. Therefore, I had better prefer—but not need—such bolstering when I encounter difficulties.

9. I can arrange for support and reassurance from individuals and groups by cultivating friends and relatives and supporting

them. I can also find support in therapy, therapy groups, self-help groups, and support groups with people who have similar problems to mine.

10. I do not have to take the advice, support, or reassurance that I am offered, but I can listen to it, consider it, and take that part of it that I think may be particularly helpful to me.

11. The best reassurance I can give myself is that however badly things turn out and however unfairly I am treated by others, my life is not horrible. I can stand it and still find some kind of enjoyment; I can cope with it and probably make it better than it is.

FOCUSING ON THE PLEASURES AND GOOD ASPECTS OF LIFE

1. Yes, I have failings, limitations, and frustrations, and sometimes more than my share. But look at the good side of my life—the pleasures, the successes, my friends, my talents, my interests. Certainly, some unfortunate things inhabit my life. But what will over-focusing on them do me? Only help me worry!

2. This world, goodness knows, can be a difficult place. But what about the wonders of its art, music, literature, science, sports, animals, natural resources, and scientific and medical breakthroughs? If I must focus on the negatives, how can I change and improve them? How about some concentration on the positives!

3. Sure, I can predict a gloomy future and rail against the unprepossessing present. But how about imagining the good things that can happen and that I can make happen? How do I work at that?

4. Bad things exist, and I wish they didn't. But endeavoring to improve them, for myself and for others, can be both constructive and enjoyable so long as I think creatively about doing so and work at reconstructing my little part of the world.

WORKING TO CREATE HEALTHY EMOTIONS

1. If I strongly desire something or if I strongly dislike something, it is important to remind myself that I do not run the

universe. I'd better not make my strong likes and dislikes into demands. If I do so, I will most probably often be disturbed.

2. I can have strong feelings of like and dislike, but if I make them into preferences rather than commands, I will only feel healthily sorry and disappointed when they are not fulfilled instead of feeling unhealthy and anxious, depressed, or angry. So, I can choose to have strong healthy feelings instead of unhealthy feelings if I think rationally and don't demand that I *absolutely must* get what I really want.

3. I can legitimately have almost any desires, even if they seem harmful and foolish to other people, as long as I acknowledge the possible harmful consequences of their fulfillment and am willing to take the consequences. I had better be moral and not harm others, but I can choose to harm myself if I acknowledge this harm and am willing to accept it. If I wish to avoid harmful consequences, I can keep my pleasures as preferences instead of commands and usually see that my desires do not *have to be* fulfilled and that I can forgo them when they seem to lead to harmful results.

4. People who act badly poorly can't *make me* feel bad. They often *contribute* importantly to my feelings because, if I see their actions as bad, I normally don't like them and therefore have healthy negative feelings of sorrow, regret, or frustration. But I could be indifferent to people who act badly, and I could even enjoy them. In regard to very bad events that are strongly against my interest, I will normally feel frustrated and sorry about them. But I can choose—or not choose— to also feel anxious and depressed about them. I'd better, therefore, stop saying, "He upset me," or "It made me anxious." I can more accurately say, "I chose to upset myself about what he did" or "I chose to upset myself about it." Then I can make more healthy choices!

5. My moderate and weak desires will rarely get me into trouble, because I easily acknowledge that I don't have to fulfill them. But I often make some of my strong desires into demands and musts, which then often lead me to disturbed feelings if they are not fulfilled. Caution! I'd better not jump from strongly desiring something to absolutely needing it!

USING A SENSE OF HUMOR

1. I'd better take many things seriously—such as my relationships and my work—but not *too* seriously. Let me try to lighten up at times and see many things with a sense of humor.

2. It is really funny that I often think I can change others, over whom I have little control, but that I cannot change myself, over whom I have much more control. And I frequently think that people absolutely must not act the way they have always acted. However, because they ostensibly *could* act differently—maybe!— they absolutely *should*. Where oh where is my sense of humor?

3. If I keep resolving to change my ways and I often don't, why *must* I insist that others change, just because they resolve to do so? Why must they even have the firm intention to change when I myself frequently don't follow my own intentions?

4. "I *should* change for the better!" means: (a) It would be highly preferable if I did; (b) I therefore *have to* change. Not the same idea! The second viewpoint will likely make me anxious and interfere with the first. And foolishly, I think that it *helps me* to change!

ACKNOWLEDGING MY BIOLOGICAL AND PHYSICAL PROPENSITIES AND LIMITATIONS

1. I have some control over my bodily and psychosomatic reactions if I am quite disciplined about my diet, exercise, sleep habits, alcohol and drug intake, and other habits, but I still have limited control and will often suffer from physical pains and restrictions. Too damned bad! I'd better be disciplined but put up as best I can with my remaining limitations.

2. I can enjoy my body more if I abuse it less. I can be quite concerned and vigilant about controlling it without being anxious and panicked over possible diseases, illnesses, and disabilities, over which I may have little or no control. Severe anxiety and obsessiveness about my body will tend to make it less hardy and functional.

3. Mental, emotional, and physical disturbances often have biochemical and genetic factors over which I and other people have little control. Mental and physical handicaps are unfortunate but

not disgraceful. I and other people are not to be rated as weak or shameful persons for having these handicaps. It also is not in the least weak or shameful to use proper medications or remedial work to try to improve my biochemical handicaps. Help from physicians, psychiatrists, and other reputable practitioners may be very helpful and I can sensibly try it.

4. I am easily prone to enjoy alcohol and many physical substances, such as marijuana, cocaine, LSD, and heroin. They relax me and give me very pleasurable highs, but they are addictive and may harm me in the long run. Various medications may also relieve my pain and give me highs, but, these are also potentially dangerous. I had better learn a great deal about them and use them only under medical advice and even be careful about that. The short-term pleasures of such usage are often not worth the long-term disadvantages and disabilities.

5. Tranquilizers, antidepressants, and other psychotropic medications may be quite useful when medically prescribed—especially by a psychopharmacologist or psychiatrist. But self-medication with these substances is dangerous!

6. Some physical states, such as low blood sugar and exhaustion, can temporarily lead to mental and physical dysfunction, so I'd better be aware of my susceptibility to them.

7. If I have a strong family history of mental illness, I had better be aware that I, too, could be prone to it, and I should preferably check for signs of it.

8. My body may well influence my emotions, but my strong and persistent feelings may affect my body and even create havoc with my immune system. Rationality very much includes physical *and* mental fitness as well as strong, *healthy*, positive and negative feelings.

---

29

65 Rational Maxims To Help Me Act Against My Discomfort Anxiety and My Irrational Fears

Much of my anxiety is ego-anxiety which stems from the Irrational Beliefs that I *absolutely must* accomplish important projects and *must* be approved of by other people or else I am an incompetent and worthless person. But I also tend to have discomfort anxiety or low-frustration tolerance (LFT) along with the Irrational Beliefs that difficulties and trouble are *awful* and *horrible* and that I *can't stand* them and be happy *at all*. These often include my views that my feelings of anxiety are *terrible* and that I can't stem their discomfort.

Minimizing my low-frustration tolerance usually requires distinct and persistent actions as well as anti-LFT thoughts and feelings to counteract the avoidances, compulsions, phobias, procrastinations, and other dysfunctional behaviors that go with discomfort anxieties. Here are some important rational maxims I can use to think, feel, and especially act against my low-frustration tolerance.

ACQUIRING HIGH-FRUSTRATION TOLERANCE

1. I will rate or evaluate the things that happen to me and to others as "good" when they fulfill my goals and purposes and when

they are socially acceptable and as "bad" when they sabotage my goals and purposes and those of my community. I will not give them absolute, rigid, and total evaluations but consider their "good" and "bad" aspects.

2. I will rate some conditions and situations as "very bad" or "exceptionally bad" when there is evidence that they block my and other people's well-being, but I will refrain from seeing them as "awful," "terrible," or "horrible." These terms inaccurately imply that conditions are as bad as they can be—which they practically never are. They also imply that things are *so* bad that they *absolutely must not* exist.

3. When I define conditions as "awful," I make myself anxious or panicked and interfere with my possibly improving them. I stew, rather than do.

4. I also tend to say, "I *can't stand* very bad conditions" or "I *can't bear* them." False! I *can* stand them, as long as I am alive, and they rarely will kill me. "I can't stand them" implies that I can't be happy *at all* while they exist, and that is rarely so unless I *think* that it is. Then I won't *allow myself* to be happy at all!

5. I will definitely try to change the undesirable things in my life that I can reasonably change. But when I can't change people or things, or it requires more time and effort to do so than is worth my taking, I will then accept what I can't change. I will not whine and rave that it *absolutely must not* exist, but instead I will try to get as much as I can from it, as it most probably has some advantages as well as disadvantages. At least by accepting it, I can raise my low-frustration tolerance!

6. To overcome difficult tasks and phobias, I will do my best to enjoy the challenge of accepting difficult self-assignments and tasks from others.

7. I will look for the possible fun and enjoyment that I can often find in doing difficult things that are wise for me to do.

8. Yes, life is often unfair. So I'd better promptly and energetically cope with its unfairness and injustices that I am not able to change.

9. Avoiding onerous tasks will prolong and increase them.

Avoidance creates more discomfort anxiety and prevents my overcoming that which I already have.

10. I don't *have to* change or control harsh reality. Thinking that I *must* do so when I can't will often enormously increase my low-frustration tolerance.

USING HOMEWORK ASSIGNMENTS

1. I recognize that I have created a good many dysfunctional thinking, feeling, and activity habits, particularly in regard to making and keeping myself needlessly anxious, and that I have worked hard and persistently—if often unconsciously and automatically—to maintain them. Because it will take considerable work and practice to undo and change them, I will do my homework, preferably every day, to facilitate change. Tough assignment! But it will be tougher if I don't!

2. I don't need a teacher or monitor to assign and review my remedial homework. I will give it and monitor it *myself*. For *my* good.

3. I will give myself reminders—such as notes and bulletins—to keep doing my homework and reviewing it regularly. I will carry out minimum assignments daily or weekly.

4. I will tell my friends and relatives about my homework assignments and encourage them to keep checking up on me.

5. I will sometimes collaborate with my friends and relatives to do some homework with me in order to help both of us.

6. If I fail to do my homework regularly, I will look at my Irrational Beliefs that block me from doing it, particularly, "It *must* be easy!" "It's *too* hard to do!" "I *can't stand* doing it!"

7. I will make contracts with myself to do my homework, write down specific assignments, and reward myself only when I do them and deprive myself when I fail to do them.

8. I will write down the disadvantages of doing my homework and the advantages of doing it and review these daily or regularly if I fail to do it.

9. I will do behavior rehearsal in my head to prepare myself to

do some of the homework. Or, I will role-play my doing it with a friend or relative.

10. I will make a list of some of my useful Rational Beliefs, such as the Maxims in this chapter and the previous two chapters, and review them regularly to remind myself of them. This will be good cognitive homework.

11. I will deliberately arrange to fail at some projects in order to encourage myself to do them uncomfortably and to show myself that failure is not awful and can be a useful learning process.

12. I will especially plan homework assignments that put me at risk for failure, rejection, and frustration so that I can demonstrate to myself in practice that my Irrational Beliefs about the horror of not getting what I want are exaggerated and mistaken.

13. I will convince myself that virtually all the "catastrophes" and the "horrors" that I experience or might experience are only very *inconvenient*. Period.

USING EXPOSURE OR IN VIVO DESENSITIZATION

1. I can avoid facing my anxieties and stay away from people and things that I am phobic about, and by doing so I may reduce my tension. Temporarily! But the more I do this, the more anxious I will often become. Real fears, like fear of falling off a high ladder, are sensible to avoid. But anxieties about safe places (such as elevators) or safe people (such as friends) increase when I refuse to participate in the experiences that would show me that there is really no danger. So, I will do my best to often confront and expose myself to people and things that I irrationally fear. I will risk present discomfort to rid myself of prolonged discomfort until I feel comfortable with—and frequently enjoy doing—things that previously panicked me.

2. I can gradually expose myself to anxiety-provoking situations and thereby get comfortable with them. Or I can give myself the challenge of quickly and steadily exposing myself, which often brings better and more dramatic results.

3. The more risk-taking I do to combat my irrational anxieties

and phobias, the better off I will usually be. Freedom from my self-imposed "horrors" is one of the best freedoms I can have. And in the long run, it is the least expensive!

4. I can practice desensitizing myself by imagining fearful things happening and using relaxation methods to help me decondition myself to feared situations and face them in reality. But, I finally will have to bite the bullet and face these situations to show myself that my imaginal desensitization is actually effective. Desensitizing myself by live exposure, if I can force myself to uncomfortably do so, often works quicker and better.

5. I can make a hierarchy of things I irrationally fear and first desensitize myself to my lesser and then to my greater fears. But, I can also plunge into risking my greater fears—even doing so quickly rather than gradually—and thus overcome them fast and thoroughly.

6. Let me face the fact that my worst irrational fears are often fear of disapproval or of public shame and embarrassment. One of the best ways for me to desensitize myself to these fears is to do REBT shame-attacking exercises in which I deliberately do some harmless foolish, ridiculous, and "shameful" things in public and risk being put down by others. If I do a good many shame-attacks while convincing myself that I would like to be approved by others but don't *need* their approbation, I will healthfully work on my shame. I will feel sorry and disappointed that some people disapprove of my "shameful" behavior, but I will not put my worth on the line and denigrate myself as a person.

ACTING TO EXPRESS MYSELF AND ASSERT MYSELF

1. I will try to be myself and do what I want to do—and let others be themselves and do what they want to do.

2. I will try to express myself and assert myself when I am with other people—and let them express and assert themselves. When I don't want to do what people want me to do, I will refuse to do so—and will give them permission to refuse to do what they don't want to do when they are with me.

3. When I disagree with people, I will try to express my disagreement with them—but will not necessarily do so when they have power over me or I will get in trouble by expressing myself.

4. I will especially speak up when I consider something important, but I don't have to get others to agree with me or do what I want. I merely would prefer them to know how I feel about things.

5. To be assertive and get what I want from people, and also to refuse to do what I don't want to do, I had better not *absolutely need* others' approval. I am a social creature who usually wants the love and approval of others and can greatly enjoy and benefit from it. But, it is also important to be myself and not unassertively sell my soul for the porridge of approval. I can enjoy being with others who largely let me be and express myself and still like me. Let me find more people like that!

ACTING, ACTING, ACTING AGAINST MY ANXIETIES

1. Taking action to solve my problems and to show that I can bear their unsolvable aspects is the best proof that I can deal with them and live with difficulties that I can't change.

2. The more actions I take in regard to my problems, the less time and energy I will have to obsessively worry about them.

3. Action will help me structure my life and thereby help me be less overconcerned about it.

4. If I risk failing at things, I will at least discover how well or how poorly I can do them and thus shortcut my constant worrying about failing.

5. 'Tis better to have tried and failed than never to have tried at all. Action leads to experience; inaction, to boredom.

6. If I make an effort to experience and enjoy the moment, I will worry less about the what-ifs of the future.

7. Worry about the future will do little good. Acting in regard to it may well make it better.

8. Action itself can interrupt worrying, energize me, and often lead me to think better about solving my problems. Exercising,

running, sports, and other kinds of activity may all help in this respect.

9. If I force myself to act more rationally, I may think more sensibly. Giving up procrastinating or overeating may encourage me to think more rationally about my life and my health.

10. My actions influence my thinking and my feeling, just as my thoughts and feelings influence my actions. Therefore, if I get in the habit of acting in my best interests, I may more easily think and feel in my best interests.

11. If I act to take risks, that is more dangerous than merely thinking about taking them. But I will learn more and ascertain the real dangers they involve instead of the fantasized "horrors" in my mind. I can demonstrate to myself that my Irrational Beliefs are false by acting against them.

12. I can mainly learn what is good and bad for me by experimenting. Experimenting means acting.

13. Goal setting is fine, but I can find out whether the goal is achievable or whether achieving it will be satisfying only by acting on it.

14. Acting against my Irrational Beliefs is one of the best ways to disconfirm them.

15. If I promise myself to take action and refuse to take it, revealing my intent to others will often make it easier for me to take it.

16. My concern about something will help motivate me to take action. My overconcern or severe anxiety about it will tend to block my action or bollix it up.

17. Action often generates inspiration; inaction generates more inaction.

18. I won't let panic intimidate me. I'll act in spite of it. My panic about my panic is what really paralyzes me.

19. I can often stop my overly critical backseat driver by forcefully telling it to shut up.

20. If I act with confidence, I'll do what I think I can't do and do it much better.

21. My main mistake in making a mistake is refusing to make it.

22. I will act as if some of my main core Rational Beliefs are true to solidly show myself that they are. For example, I will deliberately try to do some things at which I may fail—or I may deliberately fail to do well—to show myself that I am never a failure or a no-goodnik, even though other people may think that I am. For a while, I will deliberately stay in unpleasant situations—such as a poor job or a boring course—to show that I can overcome my discomfort anxiety and my low-frustration tolerance.

23. I will take on manageable problems and not unrealistically kill myself trying to solve unmanageable ones. I will experimentally try to do a number of important things but not take on too many projects and let myself be overwhelmed by trying to succeed at them. If I begin to be overwhelmed, I will try to withdraw from some projects without any feelings of shame.

24. If I go to great lengths to protect myself from anxiety, I will often intensify and prolong it. Thus, if I am anxious about doing certain things, such as speaking in public, I may refuse to do them—and temporarily feel okay but keep my anxiety going forever. If I am anxious about facing my anxiety and fear talking about it—yes, even to a therapist—I will probably be telling myself that I cannot tolerate it. I then will stop myself from trying to face it, get acclimated to it, and work on minimizing it. My original anxiety and my anxiety about my anxiety will probably intensify. To protect myself from immediate pain is very human and normal, but it may do me considerably more harm than good.

25. Exactly how I got my bad habits is fascinating knowledge. But what am I going to *do* about changing them is the real issue.

26. It is hard to overcome my inertia and to get myself moving, but that doesn't mean it's *too* hard. It will be harder later, and I will have wasted valuable time being inactive.

27. After I am dead, I will be inactive for a long time. *Now* is the time to get going!

28. To discover what I really like and do not like, I have to experiment. Experimentation means action!

29. Taking risks may be dangerous. Not taking them may be

more dangerous, as life will "safely" pass me by and I will not even know what I'll miss.

30. When I am anxious during any public presentation and afraid that the audience will see how anxious I am, I can still get by and give successful performances. I can try to incorporate my mistakes into the show, as if they are part of the show or as if I deliberately created them. I can laugh at my "mistakes" and get my audience to laugh at them, too.

31. When I make a mistake, I will admit it without downing myself. Then I can learn from it and reduce my tendency to make it again. I can also learn to remove or change some of the stressful situations that contributed to my mistake if I accept myself with my errors instead of whining about them.

Selected References

The items preceded by an asterisk (*) in the following list of references are self-help books, largely on Rational Emotive Behavior Therapy (REBT) and Cognitive Behavior Therapy (CBT). Many of these materials are obtainable from the Albert Ellis Institute, 45 East 65 Street, New York, NY 10021-6593. The Institute's free catalog and other materials for distribution may be ordered on weekdays by phone (212-535-0822) or by Fax (212-249-3582). The Institute will continue to make available these and other materials, and it will offer talks, workshops, and training sessions as well as other presentations in the area of human growth and healthy living and list these in its regular free catalog. Some of the references listed here, especially a number of self-help materials, are not referred to in the text.

Adler, A. *What Life Should Mean to You.* New York: Greenberg, 1926.
———. *Understanding Human Nature.* Garden City, New York: Greenberg, 1927.
*Alberti, R., and Emmons, R. *Your Perfect Right.* 7th rev. ed. San Luis Obispo, California: Impact, 1995.
*Ansbacher, H. L., and Ansbacher, R. *The Individual Psychology of Alfred Adler.* New York: Basic Books, 1956.
Antonovsky, A. *Unraveling the Mystery of Health: How People Manage Stress and Stay Well.* San Francisco: Jossey-Bass, 1987.
Antony, M. M., Craske, M. G., & Barlow, D. H. *Mastery of Your Specific Phobia.* Albany, New York: Graywind, 1995.
*Baldon, A., and Ellis, A. *RET Problem-Solving Workbook.* New York: Institute for Rational-Emotive Therapy, 1993.
Bandura, A. *Self-Efficacy: The Exercise of Control.* New York: Freeman, 1997.
Barlow, D. H. *Anxiety and its Disorders: The Nature and Treatment of Anxiety and Panic.* New York: Guilford, 1989.

*Barlow, D. H., and Craske, M. G. *Mastery of Your Anxiety and Panic*. Albany, New York: Graywind Publications, 1994.

Beck, A. T. *Cognitive Therapy and the Emotional Disorders*. New York: International Universities Press, 1976.

———, and Emery, G. *Anxiety Disorders and Phobias*. New York: Basic Books, 1985.

Beck, J. S. *Cognitive Therapy: Basics and Beyond*. New York: Guilford, 1995.

*Beckfield, D. F. *Master Your Panic—and Take Back Your Life!* San Luis Obispo, California: Impact Publishers, 1998.

*Benson, H. *The Relaxation Response*. New York: Morrow, 1975.

Bernard, M. E., ed.. *Using Rational-Emotive Therapy Effectively: A Practitioner's Guide*. New York: Plenum, 1991.

*———. *Staying Rational in an Irrational World*. New York: Carol Publishing Group, 1993.

———. "Special Issue: Self-Acceptance and Beyond: How to Feel Good Without Rating Yourself." *Journal of Rational-Emotive and Cognitive-Behavior Therapy*, 15(1), 1997 (pp. 3–92).

Bernard, M. E., and DiGiuseppe, R., eds. *Inside RET: A Critical Appraisal of the Theory and Therapy of Albert Ellis*. San Diego, California: Academic Press, 1989.

Bernard, M. E., and Wolfe, J. L., eds. *The RET Resource Book for Practitioners*. New York: Institute for Rational-Emotive Therapy, 1993.

*Berne, E. *What Do You Say After You Say Hello?* New York: Grove, 1972.

Bowlby, J. *Attachment and Loss: III: Loss: Sadness and Depression*. New York: Basic Books, 1980.

*Broder, M. S. *The Art of Staying Together*. New York: Avon, 1994.

*Broder, M. (Speaker) *Overcoming Your Anxiety in the Shortest Period of Time*. Cassette recording. New York: Institute for Rational-Emotive Therapy. 1995.

Buber, M. *I and Thou*. New York: Scribner, 1984.

*Burns, D. D. *Feeling Good: The New Mood Therapy*. New York: Morrow, 1980.

*———. *Ten Days to Self-Esteem*. New York: Morrow.

Clark, D. A., Steer, R. A., and Beck, A. T. "Common and Specific Dimensions of Self-Reported Anxiety and Depression: Implications for the Cognitive and Tripartite Models."*Journal of Abnormal Psychology*, 103, 1994 (pp. 645–654).

*Clark, L. *SOS: Help for Emotions*. Bowling Green, Kentucky: Parents Press, 1998.

*Coué, E. *My Method*. New York: Doubleday, Page, 1923.

*Covey, S. R. *The Seven Habits of Highly Effective People*. New York: Simon and Schuster, 1992.

*Crawford, T., and Ellis, A. "A Dictionary of Rational-Emotive Feelings and Behaviors." *Journal of Rational-Emotive and Cognitive-Behavior Therapy*, 7(1), 1989 (pp. 3–27).

*Csikszentmihalyz, M. *Finding Flow: The Psychology of Engagement With Everyday Life*. New York: Basic Books, 1997.

Dewey, J. *Quest for Certainty*. New York: Putnam, 1929.

DiGiuseppe, R. "Comprehensive Cognitive Disputing in RET." In M. E. Bernard, ed., *Using Rational-Emotive Therapy Effectively* (pp. 173–196). New York: Plenum, 1991.

Drelkurs, R. "Holistic Medicine." *Individual Psychology*, 53, 1997 (pp. 127–237).

Dryden, W. *Brief Rational-Emotive Behavior Therapy*. London: Wiley, 1995a.

_____, ed. *Rational-Emotive Behavior Therapy: A Reader*. London: Sage, 1995b.

_____. *Developing Self-Acceptance*. Chichester, England: Wiley, 1998.

Dryden, W., and DiGiuseppe, R. *A Primer on Rational-Emotive Therapy*. Champaign, Illinois: Research Press, 1990.

*Dryden, W., and Ellis, A. *A Dialogue with Albert Ellis: Against Dogma*. Philadelphia: Open University Press, 1991.

*Dryden, W., and Gordon, J. *Think Your Way to Happiness*. London: Sheldon Press, 1991.

Dryden, W., and Hill, L. K., eds.. *Innovations in Rational-Emotive Therapy*. Newbury Park, California: Sage, 1993.

*Dryden, W., and Neenan, M. *Dictionary of Rational Emotive Behavior Therapy*. London: Whurr Publishers, 1995.

Dryden, W., and Yankura, J. *Daring to Be Myself: A Case Study in Rational-Emotive Therapy*. Buckingham, England, Philadelphia: Open University Press, 1992.

Dubois, P. *The Psychic Treatment of Nervous Disorders*. New York: Funk and Wagnalls, 1907.

D'Zurilla, T. J. *Problem-Solving Therapy: A Social Competence Approach to Clinical Intervention*. New York: Springer, 1986.

*Edelstein, M., and Steele, D. R. *Three Minute Therapy: Change Your Life* (pp. vii–ix). Lakewood, Colorado: Glenbridge, 1997.

*Ellis, A. *How to Live With a Neurotic: At Home and at Work*. New York: Crown, 1957. Rev. ed., Hollywood, California: Wilshire Books, 1975.

_____. "Rational Psychotherapy." *Journal of General Psychology*, 59, 1958a (pp. 35–49).

*_____. *Sex Without Guilt*. New York: Lyle Stuart, 1958b. Rev. ed., New York: Lyle Stuart, 1965.

*_____. *Executive Leadership: The Rational-Emotive Approach*. New York: Institute for Rational-Emotive Therapy, 1972a.

*_____. *How to Master Your Fear of Flying*. New York: Institute for Rational-Emotive Therapy, 1972b.

_____. *Psychotherapy and the Value of a Human Being*. New York: Institute for Rational-Emotive Therapy, 1972c. Reprinted in A. Ellis and W. Dryden, *The Essential Albert Ellis*. New York: Springer, 1990.

*_____. (Speaker) *How to Stubbornly Refuse to Be Ashamed of Anything*. Audio cassette. New York: Institute for Rational-Emotive Therapy, 1973a.

_____. *Humanistic Psychotherapy: The Rational-Emotive Approach*. New York: McGraw-Hill, 1973b.

*_____. (Speaker) *Twenty-one Ways to Stop Worrying*. Audio cassette. New York: Institute for Rational-Emotive Therapy, 1973c.

*_____. (Speaker). *Rational Living in an Irrational World*. Audio cassette. New York: Institute for Rational-Emotive Therapy, 1974.

*_____. (Speaker). *RET and Assertiveness Training*. Audio cassette. New York: Institute for Rational-Emotive Therapy, 1975.

_____. "The Biological Basis of Human Irrationality." *Journal of Individual Psychology*, 32, 1976a (pp. 145–168). Reprinted: New York: Institute for Rational-Emotive Therapy, 1976.

*_____. (Speaker). *Conquering Low Frustration Tolerance*. Audio cassette: New York: Institute for Rational-Emotive Therapy, 1976c.

*_____. *Sex and the Liberated Man*. Secaucus, New Jersey: Lyle Stuart, 1976b.

*_____. (Speaker). *Conquering the Dire Need for Love*. Audo cassette. New York: Institute for Rational-Emotive Therapy, 1977a.

*_____. (Speaker). *A Garland of Rational Humorous Songs*. (Audio cassette and songbook). New York: Institute for Rational-Emotive Therapy, 1977b.

_____. "Discomfort Anxiety: A New Cognitive Behavioral Construct. Part 1." *Rational Living*, 14(2), 1979a (pp. 3–8).

*_____. "A Note on the Treatment of Agoraphobia with Cognitive Modification Versus Prolonged Exposure." *Behavior Research and Therapy*, 17, 1979b (pp. 162–164).

_____. "Discomfort Anxiety: A New Cognitive Behavioral Construct. Part 2." *Rational Living*, 15(1), 1980a (pp. 25–30).

_____. "The Place of Meditation in Cognitive Behavior Therapy and Rational-Emotive Therapy." In D. H. Shapiro and R. Walsh eds., *Meditation* (pp. 671–673). New York: Aldine, 1984.

*_____. *Intellectual Fascism*. New York: Institute for Rational-Emotive Therapy, 1985a. , Rev. 1991.

_____. *Overcoming Resistance: Rational-Emotive Therapy With Difficult Clients*. New York: Springer, 1985b.

_____. "Anxiety About Anxiety: The Use of Hypnosis with Rational-Emotive Therapy." In E. T. Dowd and J. M. Healy, eds., *Case Studies in Hypnotherapy* (pp. 3–11). New York: Guilford, 1986a. Reprinted in A. Ellis and W. Dryden, *The Practice of Rational-Emotive Therapy*. New York: Springer, 1987.

_____. "The Evolution of Rational-Emotive Therapy (RET) and Cognitive-Behavior Therapy (CBT)." In J.K. Zeig, *The Evolution of Psychotherapy* (pp. 107–132). New York: Brunner/Mazel, 1987a.

_____. "The Impossibility of Achieving Consistently Good Mental Health." *American Psychologist*, 42, 1987b (pp. 364–375).

_____. "A Sadly Neglected Cognitive Element in Depression." *Cognitive Therapy and Research*, 11, 1987c (pp. 121–146).

_____. "The Use of Rational Humorous Songs in Psychotherapy." In W. F. Fry, Jr. and W. A. Salameh, eds., *Handbook of Humor and Psychotherapy* (pp. 265–287). Sarasota, Florida: Professional Resource Exchange, 1987d.

*_____. *How to Stubbornly Refuse to Make Yourself Miserable About Anything—Yes, Anything!* Secaucus, New Jersey: Lyle Stuart, 1988.

_____. "Is Rational-Emotive Therapy (RET) 'Rationalist' or 'constructivist'?" In A. Ellis and W. Dryden, *The Essential Albert Ellis* (pp. 114–141). New York: Springer, 1990a.

_____. "My Life in Clinical Psychology." In C. E. Walker, ed., *History of Clinical Psychology in Autobiography*, vol. 1 (pp. 1–37). Homewood, Illinois: Dorsey, 1990b.

_____. "Achieving Self-Actualization." *Journal of Social Behavior and Personality*, 6(5), 1991a (pp. 1–18). Reprinted: New York: Institute for Rational-Emotive Therapy.

_____. "The Revised ABCs of Rational-Emotive Therapy." In J. Zeig, ed., *The Evolution of Psychotherapy: The Second Conference* (pp. 79–99). New York: Brunner/Mazel, 1991b. Expanded version: *Journal of Rational-Emotive and Cognitive-Behavior Therapy*, 9, (pp. 139–172).

_____. "Using RET Effectively: Reflections and Interview." In M.E. Bernard, ed., *Using Rational-Emotive Therapy Effectively* (pp. 1–33). New York: Plenum, 1991c.

_____. "Brief Therapy: The Rational-Emotive Method." In S. H. Budman, M. F. Hoyt, and S. Friedman, eds., *The First Session in Brief Therapy* (pp. 36–58). New York: Guilford, 1992a.

*_____. Foreword to Paul Hauck, *Overcoming the Rating Game* (pp. 1–4). Louisville, Kentucky: Westminster/John Knox, 1992b.

_____. "The Advantages and Disadvantages of Self-Help Therapy Materials." *Professional Psychology: Research and Practice*, 24, 1993a (pp. 335–339).

_____. "Changing Rational-Emotive Therapy (RET) to Rational Emotive Behavior Therapy (REBT)." *Behavior Therapist*, 16, 1993b (pp. 257–258).

_____. "Fundamentals of Rational-Emotive Therapy for the 1990s." In W. Dryden and L. K. Hill, eds., *Innovations in Rational-Emotive Therapy* (pp. 1–32). Newbury Park, California: Sage Publications, 1993c.

_____. "General Semantics and Rational Emotive Behavior Therapy." *Bulletin of General Semantics, No. 5–F*, 1993d (pp. 12–28). Also in P. D. Johnston, D. D. Bourland Jr., and J. Klein, eds., *More E-Prime* (pp. 213–240). Concord, California: International Society for General Semantics, 1993d.

_____. "Reflections on Rational-Emotive Therapy." *Journal of Consulting and Clinical Psychology*, 61, 1993e (pp. 199–201).

*_____. "Vigorous RET Disputing." In M. E. Bernard and J. L. Wolfe, eds., *The RET Resource Book for Practitioners* (pp. ii–7). New York: Institute for Rational-Emotive Therapy, 1993f.

*_____. *Rational Emotive Imagery*. Rev. New York: Institute for Rational-Emotive Therapy, 1994a.

_____. *Reason and Emotion in Psychotherapy*. Rev. Secaucus, New Jersey: Birch Lane Press, 1994b.

_____. "Rational Emotive Behavior Therapy." In R. Corsini and D. Wedding, eds., *Current Psychotherapies*, 5th ed. (pp. 162–196). Itasea, Illinois: Peacock, 1995a.

_____. *Better, Deeper, and More Enduring Brief Therapy*. New York: Brunner/Mazel, 1996a.

_____. "How I Learned to Help Clients Feel Better and Get Better." *Psychotherapy*, 33, 1996b (pp. 149–151).

_____. "How I Manage to Be a Rational Emotive Behavior Therapist." *Journal of Rational-Emotive and Cognitive-Behavior Therapy*, 14, 1996c (pp. 211–213).

*_____. *How to Maintain and Enhance Your Rational Emotive Behavior Therapy Gains*. Rev. New York: Institute for Rational-Emotive Therapy, 1996d.

*_____. *REBT Diminishes Much of the Human Ego*. Rev. New York: Institute for Rational-Emotive Therapy, 1996e.

_____. "The Treatment of Morbid Jealousy: A Rational Emotive Behavioral Approach." *Journal of Cognitive Therapy*, 10, 1996f (pp. 23–33).

_____. "The Evolution of Albert Ellis and Rational Emotive Behavior Therapy." In. J. K. Zeig, ed., *The Evolution of Psychotherapy: The Third Conference* (pp. 69–82). New York: Brunner/Mazel, 1997a.

_____. "Must Musturbation and Demandingness Lead to Emotional Disorders?" *Psychotherapy*, 34, 1997b (pp. 95–98).

_____. "Postmodern Ethics for Active-Directive Counseling and Psychotherapy." *Journal of Mental Health Counseling*, 18, 1997c (pp. 211–225).

_____. "REBT With Obsessive-Compulsive Disorder." In J. Yankura and W. Dryden, *Using REBT With Common Psychological Problems: A Therapist's Casebook* (pp. 197–239). New York: Springer Publishing Company, 1997d.

*Ellis, A., and Becker, I. *A Guide to Personal Happiness*. North Hollywood, California: Wilshire Books, 1982.

Ellis, A., and Bernard, M.E., eds.. *Clinical Applications of Rational-Emotive Therapy*. New York: Plenum, 1985.

Ellis, A., and Dryden, W. *The Essential Albert Ellis*. New York: Springer, 1990.

*_____. *A Dialogue With Albert Ellis: Against Dogma*. Philadelphia: Open University Press, 1991.

_____. *The Practice of Rational Emotive Behavior Therapy*. Rev. New York: Springer, 1997.

Ellis, A., Gordon, J., Neenan, M., and Palmer, S. *Stress Counseling: A Rational Emotive Behavior Approach*. New York: Springer, 1997.

Ellis, A., and Grieger, R. *Handbook of Rational-Emotive Therapy*, 2 vols. New York: Springer, 1986.

*Ellis, A., and Harper, R. A. *A Guide to Rational Living*, 3rd Rev. Ed. North Hollywood, California: Melvin Powers, 1998.

*Ellis, A., and Knaus, W. *Overcoming Procrastination*. New York: New American Library, 1977.

*Ellis, A., and Lange, A. *How to Keep People from Pushing Your Buttons*. New York: Carol Publishing Group, 1994.

*Ellis, A., and Tafrate, R. C. *How to Control Your Anger—Before It Controls You*. Secaucus, New Jersey: Birch Lane Press, 1997a.

*_____. *How to Control Your Anger—Before It Controls You*. Audio cassettes, read by Stephen O'Hara. San Bruno, California: Audio Literature, 1997b.

*Ellis, A., and Velten, E. *Optimal Aging: How to Get Over Growing Older*. Chicago: Open Court Publishing, 1988.

*_____. *When A A Doesn't Work for You: Rational Steps for Quitting Alcohol*. New York: Barricade Books, 1992.

*Emery, G. *Own Your Own Life*. New York: New American Library, 1982.

Epictetus. *The Works of Epictetus*. Boston: Little Brown, 1899.

*FitzMaurice, K. E. *Attitude Is All You Need*. Omaha, Nebraska: Palm Tree Publishers, 1997.

*Foa, E. B., and Wilson, R. *Stop Obsessing: How to Overcome Your Obsessions and Compulsions*. New York: Bantam, 1991.

Frank, J. D., and Frank, J. B. *Persuasion and Healing*, 3rd ed. Baltimore, Maryland: Johns Hopkins University Press, 1991.

*Frankl, V. *Man's Search for Meaning*. New York: Pocket Books, 1959.

*Freeman, A., and DeWolf, R. *Woulda, Coulda, Shoulda*. New York: Morrow, 1989.

*————. *The Ten Dumbest Mistakes Smart People Make and How to Avoid Them*. New York: Harper Perennial, 1993.

Glasser, W. *Reality Therapy*. New York: Harper and Row, 1965.

Goldfried, M. R., and Davison, G. *Clinical Behavior Therapy*, 3rd ed. New York: Wiley, 1994.

Greenwald, H. *Direct Decision Therapy*. San Diego, California: Edits, 1997.

*Grieger, R. M., and Woods, P. J. *The Rational-Emotive Therapy Companion*. Roanoke, Virginia: Scholars Press, 1993.

Guterman, J. T. "A Social Constructivist Position for Mental Health Counseling." *Journal of Mental Health Counseling*, 16, 1994, (pp. 226–244).

Hajzler, D., and Bernard, M. E. "A Review of Rational-Emotive Outcome Studies." *School Psychology Quarterly*, 6(1), 1991 (pp. 27–49).

Haley, J. *Problem Solving Therapy*. San Francisco: Jossey-Bass, 1990.

*Hallowell, E. M. *Worry: Controlling It and Using It Wisely*. New York: Pantheon, 1997.

*Hauck, P. A. *Overcoming Worry and Fear*. Philadelphia: Westminster Press, 1975.

*————. *Overcoming the Rating Game: Beyond Self-Love—Beyond Self-Esteem*. Louisville, Kentucky: Westminster/John Knox, 1991.

Heidegger, M. *Being and Time*. New York: Harper and Row, 1962.

Hollon, S. D., and Beck, A. T. Cognitive and Cognitive-Behavior Therapies." In A. E. Bergin and S. L. Garfield, eds., *Handbook of Psychotherapy and Behavior Change* (pp. 428–466). New York: Wiley, 1994.

*Jacobson, E. *You Must Relax*. New York: McGraw-Hill, 1938.

Kanfer, F. H., and Schefft, B. K. *Guiding the Process of Therapeutic Change*. New York: Pergamon, 1988.

Kassinove, H., ed. *Anger Disorders: Definition, Diagnosis, and Treatment*. Washington, D.C.: Taylor and Francis, 1995.

Kelly, G. *The Psychology of Personal Constructs*, 2 vols. New York: Norton, 1955.

Knaus, W. *Rational-Emotive Education*. New York: Institute for Rational-Emotive Therapy, 1974.

Korzybski, A. *Science and Sanity*. San Francisco: International Society of General Semantics, 1933.

*Lange, A., and Jakubowski, P. *Responsible Assertive Behavior*. Champaign, Illinois: Research Press, 1976.

Lazarus, A. A. (1989). *The Practice of Multimodal Therapy*. Baltimore, Maryland: Johns Hopkins.

*Lazarus, A. A., Lazarus, C., and Fay, A. *Don't Believe It for a Minute: Forty Toxic Ideas That Are Driving You Crazy*. San Luis Obispo, California: Impact Publishers, 1993.

Lazarus, R. S. *Emotion and Adaptation*. New York: Oxford, 1994.

Lazarus, R. S., and Folkman, S. *Stress, Appraisal, and Coping*. New York: Springer, 1984.

*Losocncy, L. *Today! Grab it: 7 Vital Nutrients to Build the New You*. Boca Raton, Florida: St. Lucie Press, 1998.

*Low, A. A. *Mental Health Through Will Training*. Boston: Christopher, 1952.

Lyons, L. C., and Woods, P. J. "The Efficacy of Rational-Emotive Therapy: A Quantitative Review of the Outcome Research." *Clinical Psychology Review*, 11, 1991 (pp. 357–369).

Mahoney, M. J. *Human Change Processes*. New York: Basic Books, 1991.

———. *Cognitive and Constructive Psychotherapies: Theory, Research and Practice*. New York: Springer, 1995.

Mahrer, A., Ellis, A., Nichols, M., Norcross, J., and Strupp, H. (Speakers). *What Are Some Breakthrough Problems in the Field of Psychotherapy?* Audio cassettes. Washington, D.C.: American Psychological Association, 1996.

*Marcus Aurelius. *Meditations*. Boston: Little, Brown, 1890.

Masters, W. H., Johnson, V. E., and Kolodny, R. C. *Human Sexuality*. Boston: Houghton Mifflin, 1982.

*Maultsby, M. C. Jr. *Rational Behavior Therapy*. Englewood Cliffs, New Jersey: Prentice-Hall., 1984.

*———. *Coping Better... Anytime, Anywhere*. New York: Prentice-Hall, 1986.

McGovern, T. E., and Silverman, M. S. "A Review of Outcome Studies of Rational-Emotive Therapy from 1977 to 1982." *Journal of Rational-Emotive Therapy*, 2(1), 1984 (pp. 7–18).

*McKay, M., and Fanning, P. *Self-Esteem*, 2nd ed. Oakland, California: New Harbinger, 1993.

Meichenbaum, D. *Cognitive-Behavior Modification*. New York: Plenum, 1977.

Meichenbaum, D., and Cameron, R. "Stress Inoculation Training." In D. Meichenbaum and M. E. Jaremko, eds., *Stress Reduction and Prevention* (pp. 115–154). New York: Plenum, 1983.

Meichenbaum, D., and Jaremko, M. E., eds. *Stress Reduction and Prevention*. New York: Plenum, 1983.

*Mills, D. *Overcoming Self-Esteem*. New York: Institute for Rational-Emotive Therapy, 1993.

Palmer, S., and Dryden, W. *Stress Management and Counselling*. New York: Cassell, 1996.

*Peale, N. V. *The Power of Positive Thinking*. New York: Fawcett, 1952.

*Peck, M. S. *Further Along the Road Less Traveled*. New York: Simon and Schuster, 1993.

Phadke, K. M. "Some Innovations in RET Theory and Practice." *Rational Living*, 17(2), 1982 (pp. 25–30).

*Pietsch, W. V. *The Serenity Prayer*. San Francisco: Harper San Francisco, 1993.

Raimy, V. *Misunderstandings of the Self*. San Francisco: Jossey-Bass, 1975.

Reiss, S., and McNally, R. J. "Expectancy Model of Fear." In S. Reiss and R. R. Bootzin, eds., *Theoretical Issues in Behavior Therapy*. New York: Academic Press, 1985.

*Robin, M. W., and Balter, S. *Performance Anxiety*. Holbrook, Massachusetts: Adams, 1995.

Rogers, C. R. *On Becoming a Person*. Boston: Houghton-Mifflin, 1961.

*Russell, B. *The Conquest of Happiness*. New York: New American Library, 1950.

Schwartz, Robert. "The Idea of Balance and Integrative Psychotherapy." *Journal of Psychotherapy Integration*, 3, 1993 (pp. 159–181).

*Seligman, M. E. P. *Learned Optimism*. New York: Knopf, 1991.

Silverman, M. S., McCarthy, M., and McGovern, T. "A Review of Outcome Studies of Rational-Emotive Therapy from 1982–1989." *Journal of Rational-Emotive and Cognitive-Behavior Therapy*, 10(3), 1992 (pp. 111–186).

*Simon, J. L. *Good Mood*. LaSalle, Illinois: Open Court, 1993.

Skinner, B. F. *Beyond Freedom and Dignity*. New York: Knopf, 1971.

Spivak, G., Platt, J., and Shure, M. *The Problem-Solving Approach to Adjustment*. San Francisco: Jossey-Bass, 1976.

Taylor, S. E. *Positive Illusions: Creative Self-Deception and the Healthy Mind*. New York: Basic Books, 1990.

*Tillich, P. *The Courage to Be*. New York: Oxford, 1953.

Vernon, A. *Thinking, Feeling, Behaving: An Emotional Education Curriculum for Children*. Champaign, Illinois: Research Press, 1989.

Walen, S., DiGiuseppe, R., and Dryden, W. *A Practitioner's Guide to Rational-Emotive Therapy*. New York: Oxford University Press, 1992.

Warren, R., and Zgourides, G. D. *Anxiety Disorders: A Rational-Emotive Perspective*. Des Moines, Iowa: Longwood Division Allyn and Bacon, 1992.

*Watson, D., and Tharp, R. *Self-Directed Behavior*, 6th ed. Pacific Grove, California: Brooks/Cole, 1993.

Wiener, D. *Albert Ellis: Passionate Skeptic*. New York: Praeger, 1988.

*Wolfe, J. L. *Assertiveness Training for Women*. Audio cassette. New York: BMA Audio Cassettes, 1977.

*_____. *What to Do When He Has a Headache*. New York: Hyperion, 1992.

*_____. *Overcoming Low Frustration Tolerance*. Video cassette. New York: Institute for Rational Emotive Therapy, 1993.

Wolpe, J. *The Practice of Behavior Therapy*, 4th ed. Needham Heights, Massachusetts: Allyn and Bacon, 1990.

Xenakis, J. L. *Epictetus: Philosopher–Therapist*. The Hague, Netherlands: Martinus Nijhoff, 1969.

Yankura, J., and Dryden, W. *Doing RET: Albert Ellis in Action*. New York: Springer, 1990.

_____. *Albert Ellis*. Thousand Oaks, California: Sage, 1994.

_____. *Special Applications of REBT*. New York: Springer, 1997a.

_____. *Using REBT With Common Psychological Disorders*. New York: Springer, 1997b.

*Young, H. S. *A Rational Counseling Primer*. New York: Institute for Rational-Emotive Therapy, 1974.

*Zilbergeld, B. *The New Male Sexuality*. New York: Bantam, 1992.

Index

237

About the Author

DR. ALBERT ELLIS is the author of more than sixty-five books, including *Sex Without Guilt, New Approaches to Psychotherapy Technique,* and *How to Control Your Anger Before It Controls You.*

Rated by his peers in the United States and Canada as one of the world's most influential psychologists, Ellis received, from 1957 to 1980, more citations in major counseling psychology journals than any other author. When Dr. Ellis abandoned psychoanalysis to create Rational Emotive Behavior Therapy (REBT) in 1955, he revolutionized American psychotherapy. Since then, he has paved the way for the development of acceptance of modern cognitive-behavior therapy. Dr. Ellis is president of the Albert Ellis Institute for Rational Emotive Behavior Therapy in New York City, where he makes his home.